ROUTLEDGE LIBRARY EDITIONS: RELIGION IN AMERICA

Volume 5

ISRAEL AND ZION IN AMERICAN JUDAISM

ISRAEL AND ZION IN AMERICAN JUDAISM
The Zionist Fulfillment

EDITED WITH INTRODUCTION BY
JACOB NEUSNER

LONDON AND NEW YORK

First published in 1993 by Garland Publishing, Inc.

This edition first published in 2021
by Routledge
2 Park Square, Milton Park, Abingdon, Oxon OX14 4RN

and by Routledge
52 Vanderbilt Avenue, New York, NY 10017

Routledge is an imprint of the Taylor & Francis Group, an informa business

© introduction copyright 1993 Jacob Neusner

All rights reserved. No part of this book may be reprinted or reproduced or utilised in any form or by any electronic, mechanical, or other means, now known or hereafter invented, including photocopying and recording, or in any information storage or retrieval system, without permission in writing from the publishers.

Trademark notice: Product or corporate names may be trademarks or registered trademarks, and are used only for identification and explanation without intent to infringe.

British Library Cataloguing in Publication Data
A catalogue record for this book is available from the British Library

ISBN: 978-0-367-49869-6 (Set)
ISBN: 978-1-00-308009-1 (Set) (ebk)
ISBN: 978-0-367-50753-4 (Volume 5) (hbk)
ISBN: 978-1-00-305114-5 (Volume 5) (ebk)

Publisher's Note
The publisher has gone to great lengths to ensure the quality of this reprint but points out that some imperfections in the original copies may be apparent.

Disclaimer
The publisher has made every effort to trace copyright holders and would welcome correspondence from those they have been unable to trace.

Israel and Zion in American Judaism: The Zionist Fulfillment

edited with introduction by
Jacob Neusner

Garland Publishing, Inc.
New York and London 1993

Introduction copyright © 1993 by Jacob Neusner
All rights reserved

Library of Congress Cataloging-in-Publication Data

Israel and Zion in American Judaism : the Zionist fulfillment / edited by Jacob Neusner.
    p.   cm. — (Judaism in Cold War America, 1945-1990 ; v. 3)
  ISBN 0-8153-0073-5
  1. Zionism—United States—History. 2. Jews—United States—Identity.
3. Jews—United States—Attitudes toward Israel. 4. Israel and the diaspora.
5. United States—Ethnic relations. I. Neusner, Jacob, 1932-   .
II. Series.
DS149.I75 1993
320.5'4'0956940973—dc20   92-34800
                                                                                       CIP

Printed on acid-free, 250-year-life paper
Manufactured in the United States of America

Contents

Volume Introduction vii

Zionism and Judaism
Yehudi Adam 1

Seeking Ease in Exile
Edward Alexander 9

Where is Zion?
Edward Alexander 13

Liberalism and Zionism
Edward Alexander 18

Zionism as Americanism
Jerold S. Auerbach 25

American Jews and Israel: Two Views II
Judah M. Eisenberg 30

An Agenda for Conservative Judaism in Israel
Hertzel Fishman 36

American Jews and Israel: Two Views I
Roland B. Gittelsohn 40

A Strategy for Non-Orthodox Judaism in Israel
Alfred Gottschalk 45

Judaism and the Land of Israel
Arthur Hertzberg 49

Israeli Imperatives and Jewish Agonies
Irving Louis Horowitz and Maurice Zeitlin 61

Zionism the Ideal and an Idea of Religion
Berel B. Lang 85

Judaism and the Zionist Problem
Jacob Neusner 93

A Stranger at Home: An American Jew Visits in Israel
Jacob Neusner 107

Zionism and "The Jewish Problem"
Jacob Neusner 112

Diaspora Judaism—An Abnormality? The Testimony of History
Jakob J. Petuchowski 125

Zionist Polemics in a Post-Zionist Age
Jakob J. Petuchowski 138

The Tasks of Israel and Galut
David Polish 147

Israel: The Ever-Dying People
Simon Rawidowicz 161

Can There be a Revival of Zionist Ideology?
Nathan Rotenstreich 173

Israel and American Youth
Ronald Sanders 177

Israel, Galut and Zionism: The Changed Scene
Efraim Shmueli 184

Whither Diaspora Judaism?
Phillip Sigal 197

Reform and Conservative Judaism in Israel: Aims and Platforms
Ephraim Tabory 208

Acknowledgements 219

Introduction

Before 1948, when people spoke of "Israel," they meant the Jewish people, the holy people, wherever they lived. There were the people, Israel; there also was "the land of Israel," which Jews revered and hoped would in time become the locus for the State of Israel. In 1948 the Jewish State came into being, and this brought about a crisis of self-definition in American Jewry—who now is "Israel"?

The "holy people" in archaic times certainly knew who they were, and confidently defined their relationship with Gentiles. Jews saw themselves as "Israel," the people to whom Torah had been revealed, now living in exile from their homeland. "Israel" was a nation within other nations. But eventually Israel would return to the holy land, with the coming of the Messiah. Gentiles were outsiders, strangers to be respected but feared, honored but avoided except when necessary. Modern times were different. From the nineteenth century onward, Western European Jews consciously entered the society of the nations among which they had lived for generations. They became German, French, and British citizens, ceased to form a separate community, and sought normal relationships both with Gentiles and with their culture. For the immigrants to America the nineteenth-century Western Europeans' experience repeated itself. At first the Jews formed separate, Yiddish-speaking enclaves in large cities, but as time passed, they and their children moved to less uniformly Jewish neighborhoods, entered less characteristically Jewish occupations, wholeheartedly adopted the language and culture of the America they had chosen. The assimilation of Jews into American culture continued apace in the second generation, and by the third it was virtually complete. Then the questions became, and now remain, What is a Jew? Who is Israel? What makes a person a Jew? Are the Jews a religious group? Are they a "people"? A nation? Jews have entered a lingering crisis of group identity: they are not certain who they are or what is asked of them because of what they claim to be. Individual Jews face a severe dilemma of personal identity as well—Why should I be a Jew? What does it mean, if anything, that I am born of Jewish parents?

One important measure of modernity is the loss of the old certainties about who one is. The question of who is a Jew, always chronic, became critical in the 1940s and 1950s. The sense of a "crisis of identity" is a condition of being a modern person. At one time, men and women were confident of their place in the life of the community and certain about the definition of that community in the history of mankind. To be a Jew not only imposed social and economic roles, but also conveyed a considerable supernatural story. Israel was the people of the Lord, the bearer of revelation, and engaged in a pilgrimage through history to the promised land at the end of time. To be a Jew was to know not only who one was, but also what that meant in the economy of universal history. To identify oneself as a Jew was a privilege and a responsibility. The world, however, posed problems to the Jew, particularly in the 1930s and 1940s. Judaism and "being Jewish" solved those problems as everyday reality was interpreted in terms of a grand and encompassing vision of human history and destiny. "We are Israel, children of Abraham, Isaac, and Jacob, loyal sons of the Torah of Moses at Sinai, faithfully awaiting the anointed of God." What difference did it make, then, that Gentiles treated Jews contemptuously, despised them, maligned their religion? In the end everyone would know the truth. Before the eyes of all the living would God redeem Israel and vindicate the patience and loyal faithfulness of its disagreeable experience in history, among men.

What characterizes the imagination of the classical Jew, practitioner of Judaism, is the centrality of Israel, the Jewish people, in human history, the certainty that being a Jew is the most important thing about oneself, and that Jewishness, meaning Judaism, is the dominant aspect of one's consciousness. The "holy people" of today has disintegrated from its classical form. First, Jews are no longer certain of what makes them a people. Second, they see themselves as anything but holy. They interpret in a negative way the things that make them Jewish and different from others, and above all, they introduce into their assessment of themselves the opinions of Gentiles. So the advent of modernity seems to have changed everything. A group once sure of itself and convinced of its value under the aspect of eternity is now unsure of who it is and has persuaded itself that the hostile judgments of outsiders must be true. The "children of Abraham, Isaac, and Jacob" have lost touch with the fathers. The people of the Lord seems to have forgotten why it has come into being. Everyday reality for ordinary Jews contains no hint of a great conception of human history. It has become a long succession of meaningless but uncongenial encounters. Sinai is a mountain. Tourists make the trip to climb it. The "Torah of Moses" is a scroll removed from its holy ark on the Sabbath, normally in the absence of the "loyal sons," who rarely see it, less often hear it, and cannot understand its language. The Messiah at the end of time is too far away to be discerned; anyhow, no one is looking in that direction.

It is easy enough to draw invidious contrasts between the virtues of the archaic world and the shortcomings of modernity. But since the old certainties

Introduction

and securities are mostly gone, one might observe that not only necessity, but choice moved Jews away from them. When Jews in Eastern Europe began to feel the birth pangs of modernity, all the more so when the emigrants came to America and plunged into the modern condition, they scarcely looked backward. Whatever virtues they knew in the old way of being did not restrain them. Something in the traditional life seemed to them to have failed, for in their thirst for whatever was new and contemporary they demonstrated that the old had not fulfilled their aspirations.

Why is the State of Israel so critical to the consciousness of all Judaisms in the USA? It is because that State bears the name that it does, for it was David Ben Gurion's profound understanding that led him to name the new state, formed in the Land of Israel by the people of Israel in 1948, the State of Israel. And that is why the relationship between Zionism and Judaism forms the centerpiece of contemporary Judaic theology as well as of Jewish thought today. In debating issues as now formulated, with the Israeli legislature passing laws on "who is a Jew," and with issues of definition of peoplehood, state, land, and exile forming the center of public discourse, Jews carry forward in a perfectly straight line the discussions that have characterized their shared existence from remote beginnings. For every Judaism defines not only "Judaism" but also "Israel," that is, the social entity that embodies this Judaism and forms the holy people envisioned within the given Judaic system. Accordingly, in calling this state simply "Israel," people deliver a profound statement upon who is Israel, what is [an] Israel (a state, not merely a community, a political entity, or a religious fellowship), and who is the true Israel, and similar, long-vexing dilemmas of religious thinkers in Judaism, past and present, as well as secular Jewish thinkers today. Still, among the many definitions of who is Israel and who is a Jew, is that of the Talmudic rabbis—all Israel, born of a Jewish mother, is Israel—which remains authentic to the liturgy of Judaism, on the one side, and its sacred scripture, on the other. And Ben Gurion's daring utilization of "Israel" in an exclusive and land-centered framework challenges that liturgy and scripture. For at prayer and study, "Israel" refers to the entire Jewish people, wherever they may live: "God who keeps Israel does not slumber or sleep" is everywhere and so watches over Israel everywhere, including Israel in the Land of Israel.

The issue of Zionism and Judaism and how they relate is not narrowly political, but central to the formation of Judaism in America. It is in our own country that matters provide subject for debate. Israelis do not debate "Judaism," which they deem to be Orthodoxy, and they also know that to be "Israel" means to be an Israeli. But here, where we are by nationality and loyalty Americans, by religion and ethnic identity Jews, and by common consensus, also part of one people, which has built its state and nationality somewhere else and not here, we have to reflect with some care on Zionism and Judaism. It is important to confront that peculiarity of today's language, because within it we uncover the deep issue confronting American Judaism as a religious expression and the American Jewish community as a distinctive social group.

That issue is whether or not Judaism and Jews will survive, endure, and flourish in the free society of the United States of America and in other free nations like it. When the large Jewish migration began from the several countries of Eastern Europe—white Russia, Poland, the Ukraine, Lithuania, Romania, Slovakia and Bohemia, Hungary, and Austria—many reflective people thought it was the end of the Jews. "In America you cannot be a Jew, or you should not, or you do not have to." However people framed matters, the expectation remained the same. After a generation or two, it would be all over for the Jews as a distinctive group—a nation-religion, an ethnic entity, however one classifies the group. The paradox is that there are, in large numbers, American Jews in the third, fourth, and fifth generations beyond the great migration.

There is another paradox. It is a dogma of contemporary Israeli thought that only in the State of Israel will the Jewish people endure as a nation, and Judaism in its authentic form will continue as a viable and vital religious tradition. The Golah, that is to say, the Jews in exile from the Land of Israel, cannot for long sustain either a distinctive social life or an authentic cultural and religious existence. For instance, there can be no scholarship. There can be no everyday life to express Jewish faith, on the one side, and cultural or social distinctiveness, on the other. So the judgment of European Jews who came to America and the opinion of Israeli thinkers three or four generations afterward remains the same: there can be no American Judaism, there can be no American Jews. Indeed, there should not be any.

But clearly there is Judaism in America, and there are Jews in America, now extending into the fifth, sixth, and seventh generations. So Jews have found ways of sustaining their ethnic identity and collective existence in a free society, and speaking of "Israel" as the holy people, children of Abraham, Isaac, and Jacob, no one can doubt that there is [an] Israel in America. That is to say, a valid Jewish way of life, an authentic and enduring Judaic religious expression, a continuing Jewish social entity ("community," or "people," or "ethnic group") do endure here. Exactly what it means to be "Israel" forms the center of discussion and defines what is at stake. From both Jews in the State of Israel and Jews in America the relationship of Zionism to Judaism demands sustained consideration.

Archaic religions usually focus on a holy place, where God and humanity come together, the focus for the sacred upon earth. In classical Judaism, Palestine ("the Land of Israel") was not merely the place where Jews lived, but the holy land. It could never legitimately be governed by pagans—thus, the continuing efforts of Jews to drive pagan rulers out of the land. There the Temple was built, the nexus of the God-man relationship in olden times. The mountains of the land were the highest in the earth. The land was the center of

Introduction

the world and of the universe. Jerusalem was most beautiful and most holy. No element of the classical myth at the turn of the twentieth century could have seemed more remote from the likely preferences of American Judaism when it grew to maturity. When the emigrants left Russia, they could have gone southward to Palestine, and a few of them did. But most went west, and of these, the largest number came to the United States. Even then Zionism was an important option in Eastern European Judaism, yet one can hardly regard the emigrants as Zionists. A few who were stayed in America for a while, then left for Palestine. The vast majority of emigrants came and settled down.

Now, eighty or ninety years later, the vast majority of third- and fourth-generation American Jews support the State of Israel. Whether they are called Zionists hardly matters. The sole commitment shared by nearly all, uniquely capable of producing common action, is that the State of Israel must live. Zionism accounts for the predominance of the welfare funds. To American Jews, "never again"—referring to the slaughter of nearly six million European Jews—means that the State of Israel must not be permitted to perish. But there is a second, less articulated fact about American Jewry. Alongside the nearly universal concern for the State of Israel is, by definition, the quite unanimous Jewish commitment to America, to remain Americans. Emigration to the State of Israel since 1948 has been negligible. Indeed, until the present time, five times more Israelis have settled in America than American Jews in Israel.

Clearly, Zionism, with its focus upon the State of Israel, solves problems for American Jews. How does it do so, and why, then, do American Jews in the vast majority find Zionism so critical to their sense of themselves as a "holy people?" Zionism provides a reconstruction of Jewish identity, for it reaffirms the nationhood of Israel in the face of the disintegration of the religious basis of a Jewish peoplehood. If in times past the Jews saw themselves as a people because they were the children of the promise, the children of Abraham, Isaac, and Jacob, called together at Sinai, instructed by God through prophets, led by rabbis guided by the "whole Torah," written and oral, of Sinai, then with the end of a singularly religious self-consciousness, the people lost their understanding of themselves. The fact is that people remained a community of fate, but, until the flourishing of Zionism and the facts of its continued existence, they were deprived of a heuristic foundation. Jews continued as a group, but could not persuasively say why or what this meant. Zionism provided the explanation: The Jews indeed remain a people, but the foundation of their peoplehood lies in the unity of their concern for Zion and their devotion to rebuilding the land and establishing Jewish sovereignty. The realities of continuing emotional and social commitment to Jewish "grouphood" or separateness thus made sense. Mere secular difference, once seen to be destiny—"who has not made us like the nations"—once again stood forth as destiny.

Herein lies the ambiguity of Zionism. It was supposedly a secular movement. Yet in reinterpreting the classic mythic structures of Judaism, it compromised its secularity and exposed its fundamental religiosity. For the primary conviction of Zionism constitutes an extraordinary reaffirmation of the primary element in the classical mythic structure: salvation. What has happened in Zionism is that the old has been in one instant destroyed and resurrected. The "holy people" are no more, the "nation-people" take their place. How much has changed in the religious tradition, when the allegedly secular successor has preserved not only the essential perspective of the tradition, but done so pretty much in the tradition's own symbols and language?

Nor should it be supposed that the Zionist solution to the Jewish crisis of identity is merely theological or ideological. We cannot ignore the practical result of Zionist success in conquering the Jewish community. For the middle and older generations, as everyone knows, the Zionist enterprise provided the primary vehicle for Jewish identify. The Reform solution to the identity problem—we are Americans by nationality, Jews by religion—was hardly congruent with the profound Jewish passion of the immigrant generations and their children. The former generations were not merely Jewish by religion. In fact, religion was the least important aspect of their Jewishness. They felt themselves to be Jewish in their bone and marrow and did not feel sufficiently marginal as Jews to affirm their Americanism or Judaism at all. Rather the first generation and the second (1890-1950) participated in a reality; they were in a situation so real and intimate as to make unnecessary such an uncomfortable, defensive affirmation. They did not doubt they were Americans. They did not need to explain what being Jewish had to do with it. Zionism for the second generation was congruent with these realities, and because of that fact, being Jewish and being Zionist were inextricably joined together.

But Zionism also constitutes a problem for Judaism. The mythic insufficiency of Zionism renders in its success a dilemma for both contemporary American Jews and Israeli Jews. Let us begin with the obvious. How can American Jews focus their spiritual lives solely on a land in which they do not live? It is one thing for that land to be in heaven at the end of time. It is quite another to dream of a faraway place where everything is good—but where one may go if one wants. The realized eschatology is insufficient for a rich and interesting fantasy life, and, moreover, in worldly terms it is hypocritical. It means American Jews live off the capital of Israeli culture. The "enlandisement" of American Judaism—the focusing of its imaginative, inner life upon the land and State of Israel—therefore imposes an ersatz spiritual dimension: "We live here as if we lived there—but do not choose to emigrate."

It furthermore diverts American Judaism from the concrete mythic issues it has yet to solve: Why should anyone be a Jew anywhere, in the USA or in Israel? That question is not answered by the recommendation to participate in

Introduction

the spiritual adventures of people in a different situation. Since the primary *mitzvot* (commandments) of American Judaism concern supplying funds, encouragement, and support for Israel, one wonders whether one must be a Jew at all in order to believe in and practice this form of Judaism. What is "being Jewish" now supposed to mean? The importance of the State of Israel to American Judaism lies in the challenge to the religious-ethnic definition of "being Jewish" that the State of Israel, with its political definition of the same matter, presents.

Zionism and Judaism

YEHUDI ADAM

THE JEWISH PEOPLE IS UNIQUE. IT IS unique because from its very beginnings as a nation at Mt. Sinai it has seen in its existence not a supreme end and value but a task and destiny whose fulfillment is the purpose of that existence. When asked what it is to be a Jew, any Jew of pre-modern times could answer: It is to be a member of the people that was called into being by God in order to serve Him, irrespective of what others thought and did. Judaism is awareness of a spiritual task and destiny to which the Jewish people has committed and dedicated itself. In other words, Judaism is the will of the Jewish people to be what it ought to be. There can be no living Judaism without that will.

To have a task is neither virtue nor merit. Nor does it imply a special quality. When the Bible or the Jewish prayerbook speaks of the "Chosen People" it is giving expression to something that is the very opposite of what most people assume when they hear those words. When we have a choice we usually select what is best. Therefore, the words "Chosen People" sound like the "best people." But when, in his daily prayer, a believing Jew thanks God for having him made a Jew, the idea that the Jews are people with higher qualities is far from his mind. Indeed, he would have no reason to be thankful if the Jews had been chosen because they were better than others. For, if so, they would have received only what is due to them. The Jews of the past felt thankful for being Jews but were not proud of it. Only modern Jews, who have lost the belief that the Jewish people were chosen by God for a specific task and destiny, say that we should be proud. Seeing no reason why there should be a Jewish people they are afraid of feeling inferior. That is why they say: we have no reason to feel inferior, because our people is a nation like other nations; let us be proud of it.

It is for a different reason that, for most of the world, whether Jewish or not, the Jews seem to be unique. They are the only ancient people that survived and kept their identity up to the modern age, and they have done so under the most adverse and unnatural living conditions, dispersed over the globe and exposed to all sorts of deprivation, persecution and humiliation. Indeed, that there is still a Jewish people must appear as a miracle to anyone who is not familiar with the Jewish belief in the task and destiny of the Jewish people. It will seem to be even more miraculous when one remembers that the Jews have almost always been tempted to escape from their harsh lot by conversion to the religion of the surrounding world.

YEHUDI ADAM *is the pen-name of a writer who is concerned with the spiritual substance of Jewish tradition in terms of modern thought.*

Although some Jews did succumb to the temptation, the majority refused to abandon their holy task and destiny. If we know and understand the belief that animated the Jews throughout the age of religion, the survival of the Jewish people will be, for us, not a miracle but the natural effect of their living Judaism. Dedication to the fulfillment of their task and destiny made the Jewish people immortal. It imbued them with the conviction that their existence was of absolute value regardless of what they had to suffer, and maintained in them the unshakeable will to live and to have children who would carry on the holy task in defiance of whatever might happen. How could a people thus inspired cease to exist? Against the danger of total extermination by enemies, the Jewish people was protected by dispersion. Hence, the survival of the Jewish people was not a Jewish problem in the past. But when the belief in the task and destiny of the Jewish people faded away in the modern age, symptoms of disintegration made their appearance and survival became the foremost problem.

The history of the Jewish people is as different from that of other nations as is the Jewish people itself. It is not a story of wars, of defeats and victories, of political, economic, and cultural achievements and developments. Its most important events are catastrophic disasters, to which the Jewish people responded by turning inward and finding new ways to achieve their spiritual task and destiny. Thus, when the First Temple was destroyed, when land and state were lost and the people led away into captivity, synagogues were founded for study and prayer. When the Second Temple was destroyed, the leaders of the Jewish people developed a comprehensive system of ritual living by means of which Jews could live a Jewish life everywhere. When the Jews were expelled from Spain, Jewish mysticism became a living force. When the false Messiah, Sabbatai Zvi, converted to Islam and the illusion that the messianic age had come was shattered, Hassidism created a new mode of living Judaism.

In the modern age, the Jewish people have had to face the great challenge of rising anti-Semitism, climaxing in Hitler's extermination policy. Again the Jewish people responded, but in a manner which differs greatly from the responses with which it had met disasters in former times. When, in the era of emancipation, the gates to the modern world were opened to the Jews, they embraced western culture and all of its achievements with alacrity and enthusiasm. The modern world, which offered to them equal rights and citizenship and whose thought and knowledge they admired immensely, seemed to them superior to Jewish tradition in all respects. They gave themselves wholeheartedly to it and wanted to be nothing but equal participants in its culture. Judaism as a living way of thinking ceased to exist for them. When anti-Semitism destroyed the illusion that modern civilization could give the Jews what they had hoped for from the messianic age, they experienced it as a challenge and responded to it, not as heirs to Jewish tradition, but as products of the modern world. Oblivious of the task and destiny of the

Jewish people, they thought only of ending the tribulations and sufferings of *galut*. Thus there arose political Zionism, a movement aiming not at the fulfillment of the task and destiny of the Jewish people but at making of it a nation like any other nation living in its own land.

Political Zionism is a movement which has two aspects. It can be looked at from the view of what it has done for the Jews, and it can be looked at from the view of the task and destiny for which the Jewish people has lived and suffered for thousands of years. Bearing in mind that "Jewish" may mean "of the Jews" and "of Judaism," we may say: political Zionism is a thoroughly un-Jewish Jewish movement. The ideology of political Zionism is a negation of all that Judaism has stood for since the Hebrew tribes became a nation at Mt. Sinai.

Zionists often rail at assimilation. When doing so they think of non-Jewish customs, especially some of religious character and origin. They do not notice that political Zionism is itself the very acme of assimilation, for it is assimilation of the Jewish people as a whole to the spirit of the present western world which finds its most extreme expression in the unrestricted self-centeredness of nations claiming sovereignty, i.e., the right to do what they like and to pursue their aims and interests subject to no higher norms and values. There could never have been a Jewish ideology like political Zionism if assimilation had not estranged the Jews from Judaism.

So little are Zionists aware of the spiritual task and destiny of the Jewish people that they identify Judaism with the memory of the lost promised land and with the longing for return to it. Thus, they equate Zionism and Judaism. True, the Jews have never forgotten Jerusalem. Tradition kept it present in their minds, and the tribulations of *galut* fed the longing for it. They never lost hope that the time would come when *galut* would end, and that they would dwell again in the land that they believed God had given them. But, in pre-modern times, the Jewish memory and longing for that ancestral homeland was never divorced from their awareness of the Jewish task and destiny; the land never took the place of Judaism, as it does in the ideology of political Zionism. In Jewish tradition, the hope for a return to Jerusalem was closely linked to the hope for the advent of the Messianic age. When, at the end of the celebration on the eve of Passover the Jews said, "Next year in Jerusalem," they gave voice to their belief in the coming of the Messiah who would lead them to the Holy Land with the approval of all mankind in a world of lasting peace, justice and good will. The Jews of the age of religion did not believe in a return of the Jewish people to the Holy Land in an unchanged world with the means of that world, which would inevitably involve the Jewish people in all the evils of that world and would expose it to largely uncontrollable dangers. They had learned from history that the fulfillment of the eternal Jewish hope cannot be forced.

It goes without saying that there is nothing in Judaism to object to a return to the Holy Land and to its rebuilding. But for anyone who is sufficiently familiar with the Jewish sources and with Jewish history to know that dedication to a spiritual task and destiny is the very essence of Judaism, which has made the Jewish people unique and immortal, it is a plain fact that Judaism and the ideology of political Zionism are mutually exclusive. Whoever affirms the political Zionist's aim to normalize the Jewish people repudiates Judaism, and whoever understands what Judaism is and stands up for it implicitly rejects political Zionism, whether he is aware of it or not. But, of course, that holds true only where there is a living Judaism and not where there is only something that is a mere shadow or wraith of what Judaism was in the past. If that is correct, then, since hardly any Jew today is aware of the incompatibility of Judaism and political Zionism, it follows that there is no living Judaism today, and that, indeed, is so. What we have today is not a living Judaism but merely a memory of a Judaism that was alive in a bygone age. True, we have the institutions of the past and keep them going because they have a certain value which has nothing to do with what Judaism really is. But anyone who protests that there is a living Judaism because there are rabbis and synagogues and because Jewish festivals are celebrated and mizvot are performed bespeaks only his lack of insight into what Judaism is.

There is no living Judaism, and there can be no living Judaism as long as a false idea about what is Judaism is generally accepted by the Jews of the modern age as though it were an evident truth: that false idea is that Judaism is a religion. The word Judaism, no less than the word religion, both of which are foreign to Jewish tradition, derives from a misunderstanding of the nature of Judaism. The word Judaism has been coined in order to have one word for "Jewish religion," as Christianity is one word for Christian religion. The cause of the misconception is that there is neither in the modern languages nor in Jewish tradition a word for what Judaism really is. Because of its uniqueness, the Jewish phenomenon cannot be placed into any of the classes of phenomena for which language possesses a word, without misunderstanding its nature. In pre-modern Jewish thought it was not necessary to classify Judaism. The believing Jew of the past had the Torah, which was a name for something unique. For him it was the word of God, not a human phenomenon comparable to other human phenomena with which it could be placed into one class. It was when Jews started to think in terms of non-Jewish modern thought that they came to see the Jewish phenomenon from outside, as did the non-Jews, and to understand it as a religion comparable to Christianity. There was a powerful incentive for the Jews to regard Judaism as a religion. They had been promised equality and citizenship on the assumption that they would be citizens of the modern state like others, differing only by their religion, which was considered a private affair. Moreover, Jewish tradition is, in some sense, a religious tradition. But what is overlooked was that religion in the sense in which Jewish tradition can be justly called a religious tradition is something very different from religion in the sense in which the word is commonly employed and understood.

Jewish tradition may be called religious because its whole thought and interpretation of the world is centered on the belief in a living, personal God. For the Jews of the age of religion, as for Jewish tradition, the totality of all that consisted of God and the world. God was thought of as a living being with a mind similar to the human mind but free of its limitations and imperfections. God was by no means only the creator of the world. Above all, He was the ruler of the world, in which nothing could happen that He did not want to happen. As a living being, the God of Jewish tradition could see, hear, think, judge, will, decide, act. He was believed to be concerned with every human creature and, especially, with the Jewish people, and all events which were not results of the order of the cosmos as it was then known were interpreted as responses of God to human conduct. Furthermore, God was not only the creator and ruler, He was also the revealer who had made known His will to the Jewish people in the Torah. Thus, everything was seen in relation to God.

Religion in the sense in which it is generally understood today is belief or faith (faith is trusting belief) in metaphysical, specifically religious matters, particularly on so-called ultimate questions. It is not a view of the world which is knowable through science, but of that which transcends it and is not accessible to human knowledge. It is experience of the transcendent and it is the feelings and emotions which accompany such experiences or arise from them. It is belief in something which cannot be known. The origin of the current idea of religion lies in Christianity, which is, in its essence, a message of a divine mystery. It proclaims and teaches what God has done for mankind through Jesus. A Christian is one who accepts that message, regardless of whether he is, or is not, a member of a Christian church. That is why, for Christianity, religion is belief, and why Christian thinking takes it for granted that every other religion is also belief, differing from Christianity in what it believes, and especially in what it does not believe, namely, in Jesus as the Savior. Therefore, Christianity and, with it, all modern thought, understands Judaism as a belief, and that notion has been accepted uncritically by assimilated Jewry.

But Judaism is not belief or faith. Its essential content does not consist in a divine mystery. Compare the Jewish Bible, called by Christians the Old Testament, with the New Testament. The latter is the story of the life and death of the divine Savior and of the beginnings of the Christian church. The Jewish Bible is the history of the Jewish people and the record of the divine law, whose fulfillment is the purpose for which the Jewish people has come into being and to which it has committed itself.

What, then, is Judaism if it is misconceived as religion in the accepted sense of the word? It is — nothing; at least nothing Jewish. Judaism is not a message to be believed, it proclaims no divine mysteries. Like anyone else, a Jew may have experiences which may be interpreted as personal revelation or as encounters with God. But Judaism does not consist of such experiences and is not a faith grounded in such experiences. The God who becomes present in such experiences is not the living God of Jewish tradition, as will be shown immediately. The Jew of the past took the existence of the living God as self-evident. However, Judaism did not consist in faith in God, but in the service that the Jewish people owed to Him so that the Jewish community could be seen as a kingdom of God.

Can we not go back to Jewish tradition and to its way of serving God? No. When we perform a miẓvah or attend a service we can only pretend that ours is the religion of our ancestors. For, although we may subscribe to the basic traditional tenets and practice all the miẓvot, our thought and life cannot be God-centered, and our religious life cannot but be an area separated from the rest of our life and thought. What changed when the Jews entered the modern world is not only their attitude toward religion, as most of our leaders seem to think. The God-centered worldview of the age of religion, in which Jewish tradition is embedded, has become obsolete, and with it have gone all of the important traditional teachings about God and His relation to man, to human life and to the Jewish people. The religious worldview, which saw everything in relation to God, was a product of imagination. It could not survive in an age which possesses the modern knowledge of the world. Modern man knows that all causes of events and phenomena lie in the world itself, which is an autonomous self-contained whole, and all events take place according to the immanent order of the world, which science describes as laws. There is no room for a living God who acts from decision to decision in response to human action and behavior and has revealed His will to the Jewish people in the commandments of the Torah. From respect or love for tradition, or for the sake of the Jewish people, modern Jews may subscribe to the tenets of tradition. But they cannot have the belief of their ancestors. Is there a modern Jew who believes, and can believe, that a human being or a people could enter into a covenant, a contractual relationship, with God? Is there a modern Jew who can believe that, in order to free the Israelites, God, or His angel (can a modern Jew believe that there are angels?) killed the firstborn of the Egyptians? Is there a modern Jew who can believe that God spoke out of a burning bush to Moses, or that God came down — from the non-existing heaven — on Mt. Sinai in a cloud with thunder and lightning and Himself wrote the Ten Commandments on the tablets of stone? The Jew of the past could accept the teachings of tradition without asking whether they were true because within the religious outlook the teachings of the Torah seemed plausible, and there was no knowledge which contradicted them. But no modern Jew can believe in the living God of our ancestors, and whoever thinks that he does believe in Him deceives himself.

Does that mean that Judaism is finished? Only if we cling to the axiomatic assumption that Judaism is a religion and cannot be anything else and that the religious Jewish tradition is the final, lasting form of

Judaism. Surely it is difficult to free oneself of that preconceived idea if he fails to realize that when one worldview is succeeded by another, the ideas and beliefs characteristic of the old worldview vanish with it but that the spirit which found expression through them can survive if it is articulated in beliefs and ideas which are in harmony with the living thought of the new age. We, today, see clearly that all thought is human thought, even if it claims to be of superhuman origin, the very possibility of the distinction between human thought and divine thought being a product of human thought. Since Jewish tradition, too, is human thought it is, on the one hand, conditioned by the thought and outlook of its age and, on the other hand, expressive of human impulses and aspirations which are not transient but enduring and capable of being articulated in any age.

In this essay only a few hints can be given of what Judaism is if it is spoken of in terms of the contemporary universe of thought. Judaism sprang from a vision of a world that is free from man-made evils. It is the undertaking of a people to realize that vision within its own sphere. From that vision there arose, in the age of religion, which interpreted reality through its belief in living personal deities, the belief in a spiritual, perfect God, who loves good and hates evil and wants man to choose good and reject evil. From the same source there sprang the belief in the task and destiny of the Jewish people to serve the perfect spiritual God. In the post-religious age, in which religion is no longer the medium through which the world is seen, the Jewish vision of a human world without man-made evils must lead to a conception of man and his life governed by the higher forces of the human mind, which are found nowhere in nature. We may call those higher forces of the human mind the spirit, and we can express the meaning and aim of Judaism by saying: the task and destiny of the Jewish people is to be a spirit-governed community.

The modern world in an essentially unspiritual world. It originated from a vision of man's power to conquer nature by knowledge. It has no vision of a humanity without man-made evils. Like ancient paganism, the modern world lives on the level of nature, which does not know the distinction between good and evil and in which there is a never-ending struggle for survival and for a larger share in the good things of the world. Zionism, being a product of the spirit of the modern world, not of the spirit of Judaism, has engulfed the Jewish people in that struggle. It has thereby exchanged the passive evils of *galut* for the active evils of political and military life. It is not aware of the meaning of Judaism and the spiritual demands implied in it. Designed by assimilated Jews, it knows nothing of the spiritual task and destiny of the Jewish people. Today, Zionism is identified with Judaism to such a degree that most Jews who are active in Jewish life consider it a duty of every Jew to be a Zionist. But the verdict of the future will be that the ideology of political Zionism was a deviation from the task and destiny of the Jewish people.

Seeking Ease in Exile

EDWARD ALEXANDER

DURING THE LAST ROSH HASHANAH SERVICE in the *shul* that I attend, the president of the congregation offered a few observations on the Torah reading for the second day of the holiday, the 22nd chapter of Genesis, in which Abraham is instructed by God to "Take now thy son, thine only son, whom thou lovest, Isaac, and get thee into the land of Moriah; and offer him there in sacrifice . . ." He told his congregation of American Jews that the story of the binding of Isaac was a reminder that Jews are still called upon to make sacrifices, but that they ought to find consolation in the fact that whereas Israeli Jews are called upon to sacrifice their sons, we American Jews are asked only to sacrifice, to contribute, our dollars. Later in the service we participated in a memorial prayer for (among others) "our brothers and sisters who have fallen in the defense of our holy land."

During both the sermon and the memorial prayer I could not but think of a young man who had spent many years of his childhood in my city (Seattle) and who had lost his life fighting as a paratrooper in the battle for control of Beirut Airport in the second week of June. I returned from *shul* and looked through a set of old photographs in which this young man, then but a little boy, appears at a Chanukah party alongside other Jewish boys from Seattle, Jewish boys now blithely pursuing their respective academic, business, and legal careers while poor Ronen Eidelman lies dead in the military cemetery in Haifa. It struck me then that every discussion of the problematic relation between Jewishness and American loyalty, and between Israeli and Diaspora Jewry must begin with this terrifying, overwhelming question of life and death. Who, after all, decreed that these Jewish boys should have such contrasting destinies? Can a people which believes itself bound together, by covenant to the living God and by history to each other, assume that an accident of birth is sufficient justification for complacency in distinguishing between the sacrifices expected of the Abrahams called to Moriah and the Abrahams called by the United Jewish Appeal, which asks not for your life but only for your money?

But at least the president of my congregation interpreted this distinction with modesty and the recognition that American Jews, however they may insist on their "oneness" with Israel, are not, and have no right to be,

---

EDWARD ALEXANDER *is professor of English at the University of Washington, Seattle.*

equal partners in their relationship with the Jews of Israel. Professor Auerbach, in his fine essay, makes a similar acknowledgement when he says that "my body is in the United States; my heart and soul are in Jerusalem." Here he is in the tradition of Yehuda Halevi rather than in the newly-invented one of our American Jewish ethical idealists, the intrepid signers of anti-Israel letters to the *New York Times*, the rabbis, who, in the studios of the major television networks, struggle for Israel's moral purity, and the assorted sociologists and political scientists for whom Israel is a Jewish zoo that they visit from time to time in order to validate their credentials as experts on the *genus* Israeli. In their imagination, as Hillel Halkin has shrewdly remarked, the Jewish people is indeed one, but its body is in the east and its soul in the west.

> To each according to his needs: while eighteen-year-olds here are defending their country's threatened borders . . . their Diaspora comrades can be picketing for Mexican farm workers or writing term papers on varieties of ethical theory. Truly a convenient division of labor!

Not long ago I heard a leading political reporter of *Ha'aretz* address a group of American professors and rabbis. He said that Israel lived with two threats to her existence: one came from the Arabs, the other from the Jews of America, who sat in the fleshpots dispensing dollars and advice to their poor, threatened cousins in Israel, who *were* poor and threatened precisely because there were only three million of them and not six million. At this point a rabbi-professor rose indignantly to tell the reporter that no Jew had the right to read any other Jew out of the people Israel, who are "one, united, equal." "We all," insisted the rabbi, "stood at Sinai together." "Did you stand there," responded the reporter, "in 1956 or 1973?"

The question of Jewish "dual loyalties" within American society does not seem to me a compelling one. Who, after all that has happened to world Jewry in the past forty years, has the right to ask it of us? Roman Catholics whose primary allegiance is to a Pole sitting in the Vatican? Protestants whose missionary interests once determined our China policy and whose National Council of Churches now funnels millions of dollars to anti-American terrorist groups all over the world? Besides, according to a poll of American Jews conducted in August 1982 by Steven M. Cohen of Queens College, 81% of the American Jews questioned flatly disagreed with the statement that "each American Jew should give serious thought to settling in Israel." Perhaps the people who should be asking us American Jews hard questions about our dual loyalties are not our fellow American citizens, but our fellow Jews in Israel. In the *Jerusalem Post International Edition* of Oct. 10-16 1982, two separate stories perfectly illustrated how incredible, impossible, and unthinkable to our "leaders" is the prospect of living in a free and independent Jewish state. Henry Siegman, executive director of the American Jewish Congress, after berating American Jews who, on principle, refrain from open criticism of Israel as "marranos" and "*galut* Jews," told them that if they think *hasbarah* for the State of Israel must be their overriding consideration in life, then *aliyah* is indeed the only answer, and they should act on that inescapable conclusion." That, in Mr. Siegman's view, would serve them right! If they cannot be, like him, perfectly at ease in exile, let them go suffer in Zion. Elsewhere in the same paper, Leon Hadar quotes an unidentified American Jewish "activist" who wants so much to get rid of the Likud government that he in desperate moments *almost* thinks of "making aliyah together with other American Jews who could add the 10 Knesset seats Labour needs for victory." One wonders what it was that kept such rhapsodic celebrants of "the Israel it used to be" (thus Milton Viorst in the *Washington Post* and on National Public Radio) from making aliyah during the twenty-nine years when Israel could be certified as socialist and liberal and "democratic" (i.e., before Oriental Jews changed their voting habits).

It is ironical that American-Jewish liberals are troubled by a sense of conflicting or "dual" loyalties at precisely the time when the presidency of this country is occupied by a man whom they have long hated with a passion that they nowadays reserve for Menachem Begin. This irony might have revealed to them (but it has not) that their current discomfort as supporters of Israel is a function of the new potency of the worldwide campaign long waged against Israel by the Arabs and their greedy, pusillanimous supporters, and not of any particular government either in Israel or in the United States. What I have elsewhere called the journalists' war against Israel began after the 1967 war; the UN Zionism-Racism resolution came in 1975; and organized American-Jewish attacks on Israel came immediately afterwards. These same, suddenly very "American" Jews have also conveniently forgotten that anti-Semitic fulminations by racist agitators like Jesse Jackson preceded not only the arrival of a Likud government but even Mr. Jackson's discovery that there was such a place as the Middle East. The Jews who now blame the Lebanese War or Israel's famous "intransigence" for their own discomforts in American society are the spiritual successors of countless Jews in many generations who have blamed anti-Semitic outbreaks not on the anti-Semites but on their victims. Thus, the Joint Program Plan of the National Jewish Community Relations Advisory Council of 1982-82 placed the blame for "anti-Semitism in the Black community" on "anti-black animus among Jews." Liberalism tends to assume that everybody is guilty of a crime except the person who happens to commit it; Jewish liberalism goes a step further to discover that it is precisely the victim who is guilty of (provoking) the anti-Semitic attack against him. American Jews who, in their panic (generally excessive) over instances of anti-Semitism, blame their difficulties on Menachem Begin, or on settlers in Judea, or on the Lebanese War, are very much like the emancipated German Jews mentioned in Dr. Gordis' third question, people who blamed the hostility aroused by their own assimilation upon their unassimilated (and notoriously unkempt) brethren from the east who had moved into Germany.

We Jews who linger in the American Diaspora bear a burden of guilt because, despite our financial contributions and political support, we remain essentially spiritual parasites whose Jewish identity feeds upon the State of Israel. Those American Jews who compound their guilt with the rationalization that they remain physically outside of, and ethically superior to, Israel because of their devotion to world betterment and pure justice remind me of the young man who asked Thomas Carlyle how he could reform society and was told by the Scottish sage: "Make an honest man of yourself and there will be one less rascal in the world."

Observations

Where Is Zion?

Edward Alexander

To anyone resident in Israel during the months since the Arab uprising (*intifada*) began in December 1987, or who has followed newspaper accounts of the effects it has had on Israel's "image" abroad, it will come as no surprise that among those effects has been a conspicuous drop in the numbers of American Jews visiting the country. Some Israeli hotels have reported cancellation rates by American Jewish groups approaching 100 percent. According to one press item, numerous Conservative rabbis, planning to attend an assembly in Israel in July, cancelled their visits because "many rabbis were planning to come with tour groups from their congregations to help cover expenses. But . . . many of these tours are not coming." The few prominent American Jewish intellectuals who have kept their commitments to participate in conferences and the like have been received in Israel with a gratitude in no way diminished by their own seemingly compulsive desire to bite the hand that (very lavishly) feeds them, by publicly "testifying" against Israeli policies.

Of course, the *intifada* in its various forms has kept most Israelis too busy to worry about the mysterious absence of their American cousins. But awareness of it grows apace. As one young acquaintance of mine, just back from three weeks of reserve duty (now increased to sixty days a year) in Nablus, asked me sharply: "What are your American Jews, who are always declaring 'We Are One,' doing while we

Edward Alexander *is professor of English at Tel Aviv University and at the University of Washington. His most recent book is* The Jewish Idea and Its Enemies *(Transaction Books).*

are dodging bricks and petrol bombs?"

Some of them, I answered, are dutifully reciting, for the benefit of the great American public, what the Israeli critic Gavriel Ben-Ephraim calls "the Anthony Lewis conjugation, in serialized weekly numbers: Israel will lose its soul; Israel is losing its soul; Israel has lost its soul." Others, including editors of magazines and heads of large Jewish organizations, are lining up in television studios and in print to explain why their sense of ethical idealism requires that they condemn all Israeli use of force against Arab rioters in the most forceful language they can marshal.

Still a third group—so I told the astonished young soldier—is deeply immersed in considering the special Jewish mission to Gentile America, a mission it defines as nothing less than *tikun olam*, repairing the universe. The concerns of the earthly Jerusalem, pressing though they may seem to its inhabitants, can hardly be expected to distract those who are building the heavenly Jerusalem in America.

Now, the idea of America as a new Zion was a prominent theme of the Puritans who built the country; even the enlightened Thomas Jefferson wanted "Israel" on the seal of the United States. But recently this idea has been infused with a specifically Jewish—and also anti-Zionist—energy, and it has found articulate spokesmen in more than one sector of the ideological spectrum of American Jewry.

Thus, in March 1987, a few days after Jonathan Pollard had been sentenced to life imprisonment for spying for Israel, the scholar Jacob Neusner, who usually identifies himself as a political conservative, published an article in the Washington *Post* designed to show the absurdity of American Jews' attaching themselves to Israel when they were already walking the streets of El Dorado: "If ever there was a Promised Land, Jewish Americans are living in it." As it happens, this is the same Neusner who in a 1981 book (*Stranger at Home*) had written that "American Jewry simply does not add up to much. Its inner life is empty, its public life decadent." Yet here he was, at a particularly delicate moment in relations between Israel and the United States, praising the cohesiveness, security, prosperity, philoprogenitiveness, and "authentically Jewish voice" of the American Jewish community.

A much more ambitious attempt to relocate Jerusalem in a greener, more pleasant, and more peaceful place than the state of Israel is that of the leftist Leonard Fein, the founder and first editor of *Moment* magazine and a veteran fomenter-from-within of American Jewish agitation against Israel's government, especially when that government has been dominated by the Likud coalition. "Where is Jerusalem?" is the crucial chapter in Fein's *Where Are We?*,* a book whose title conveys the sense of befuddlement of someone lost in a troubled universe, a sense that is not belied by the text. Although Fein's stated subject is "the inner life of America's Jews," he can only approach that subject by elaborately disentangling himself from the claims of Zionism or, as he puts it, by constructing a "theory of American Jewish life" that can match that of Zionism, a "coherent ideological view with which to counter the ideological argument for *aliyah*."

Why does Fein feel compelled to guide the American Jewish community into spiritual, psychological, and political competition with the Jewish state? The answer is

* Harper & Row, 329 pp., $19.95

13

implicit in the anecdote with which the book begins. It is a tale of 19th-century East European Zionists who believed in their moral superiority and in their ability to sustain that superiority in Jerusalem, where they would "prove that even with guns we will not become hunters." But since that time, according to Fein, and especially "in our generation, the Jews have come to power, in Israel and in America." So certain is Fein that Jews are now "an empowered people," an "empowered community," that he confidently declares, covering both American Jews and their Israeli cousins in a single possessive pronoun, "today it is no longer our physical safety that is the principal item on the Jewish agenda." Rather, the principal item is "whether, now that we have guns, we are on the way to becoming hunters." Fein formulates this supreme question in his introduction, and hands down the verdict eighty pages later: it is "now plain" that the Israelis, at least, "have come to hunt, have even perhaps become hunters." In between, he sets forth his own considered view of "Jews, God, and Judaisms [sic]."

FEIN presents himself as (by traditional standards) a "non-believing Jew" who takes what he likes from tradition; who does not admit the Jews to be a chosen people; who prefers anarchy to authority; who is eager to "reassure" the reader that his "references to God neither presume nor recommend belief"; and who rejects the characteristically Jewish idea of distinction that separates Jew from non-Jew, clean from unclean, man from woman.* Fein does allow that Judaism is "a religious way," but he repudiates the notion that there can be "a 'Jewish view' of this or that." His oceanic receptivity to all forms of Jewish experience, "from studying Talmud to marching with the lettuce workers," calls to mind Joseph Epstein's severe judgment that "In our age vulgarity does not consist in failing to recognize the fish knife or to know the wine list but in the inability to make distinctions."

Yet even Fein must draw the line somewhere. He too must show that he can say no to something, and he does. "I have," he writes, "set 'us' against the Orthodox . . . ." Because they have failed to see that "relativism" is the "necessary consequence" of the Enlightenment, the Orthodox force him to speak of "Judaisms, not a single Judaism." In Fein's "necessarily" relativistic Judaism, by contrast, "the question of whether or not there was a Revelation at Sinai seems to me considerably less important than the question of whether or not I was there."

But Fein's uncertainty over whether or not Sinai "happened" is in any case only a foil for his certainty that Sinai's place as a starting point for Jewish life has been wrongfully usurped by the double obsession of American Jewry with the Holocaust and with the state of Israel. It is guilt over their "shameful silence" during the Holocaust that in Fein's judgment fuels the attachment of American Jews to Israel, and it is their feelings of inadequacy in the face of the Zionist claim of Israel's centrality in Jewish life that ensure the uncritical nature of that attachment. Since, according to Fein, American Jews expect Israel to "sustain our sense of moral distinction," "we have not written of Israel's flaws in our journals or spoken of them from our pulpits." (Is this breathtaking assertion owing to simple amnesia, or to the self-deception that afflicts people incapable of dissenting from the conformity of dissent?)

Fein undertakes to cure his fellow American Jews of their sense of guilt, to remove this major impediment to their reascent to Sinai, by enlisting a distinction advanced by the Zionist thinker Ben Halpern: the distinction between merely geographical exile, or dispersion, and Exile as the symbol of a disordered condition of the universe. The Jews' physical exile and its theological meaning are by this means psychologized and universalized—"A Jew is also in Exile whether he lives in Boston or in Jerusalem"—into a condition that can never be set right by a simple return to Zion, but only by tikun olam, the repair of the whole universe.

HERE, then, is the real reason why American Jews are not to be seen in Jerusalem: "They stay where they are, reject the return, because they await the larger Redemption." They reject the earthly Jerusalem for the "Jerusalem that remains a yearning, answer to Exile, home." Some Israelis, unspiritual beasts that they are, have accused American Jews of falling in love with the fleshpots of the Diaspora. Not so, Fein retorts. Their love affair with Exile is less an attraction to its comforts than a Jewish thriving on "marginality" and "limited liability," symbolized for Fein by no less a figure than Woody Allen—who, considering his notoriously craven statement of dissociation from Israel in the New York *Times* last January, could hardly be a more fitting emblem of "limited liability."

One wonders, indeed, how to square Fein's celebration of Exile and "limited liability" with his insistence that American Jews are an "empowered community"; for if they are empowered, surely they must take responsibility for *something*. Are they, perhaps, to be held responsible for the actions of those among their fellow Jews of whom Fein never tires of boasting, as when he writes with pride that "more than half the delegates to the 1965 national convention of SDS . . . were Jews," and so was Mark Rudd, "and so were Abbie Hoffman and Jerry Rubin, and so were I.F. Stone and Noam Chomsky and Herbert Marcuse, . . . and so were William Kunstler and Leonard Boudin"? Any nurse who has ever lifted a bedpan has done more for *tikun olam* than all the world-betterers listed by Fein. This whole sorry discussion should put us in mind of the young idealist who asked Thomas Carlyle how best to go about the task of reforming the

---

* The sexual boundary is particularly galling to Fein, who has tried to placate Big Sister by writing his book in Feminese. Not only does he strive for equal-opportunity pronouns—"his/her," "he/she"—in dealing with mere mortals; he even urges us "to love God whether or not He (or She, or It) exists."

world, and was told: "Make an honest man of yourself, and then there will be one rascal less in Scotland."

CONTEMPTUOUS of American Jewry's "obsession with survival," insistent on a specifically American Judaism based on "values" congruent with American Left-liberalism, Fein has resurrected for the 1980's (and more specifically for the election year of 1988) a suitably updated version of the "mission" theology of 19th-century Reform Judaism, according to which the Jews have a moral duty to carry the universal ethical content of their religion to a world that has not yet realized the culture of monotheism. Only that mission, argued the Reformers (in a bogus theology that has been exploded a thousand times over*), justifies the continued existence of Jews as a religion and a culture. For Fein, too, this mission remains the only acceptable *raison d'être* of future Jewish existence. "It is unlikely the Jews can survive, and *it would be unseemly if they did* [emphasis added], except as a community organized around values and committed to *tikun olam*," he writes in perhaps the most presumptuous formulation in this book.

To this does liberalism always seem to come with respect to the Jews. Only they must serve a higher meaning, a "mission," if they are to be permitted to carry on. When Orthodox Jews assert, "This is *the* way," Leonard Fein is profoundly offended; but he for his part does not hesitate to specify the only admissible grounds for the survival of a people who may, just may, wish to go on living without being able to articulate or "justify" this mysterious urge. "Political activism," "Lofty utopian ambitions," Liberty, Equality, Fraternity/Sorority—or Death: such is Leonard Fein's ultimatum to the American Jewry he has come to rescue from the clutches of Israel.

To recover the real meaning of *tikun olam*, a meaning grossly distorted not just by Leonard Fein but by a host of current exploiters, one can do no better than to turn to the theologian Emil Fackenheim.† *Tikun*, a notion of some intricacy, refers not to the crude utopianism of a Leonard Fein (anyway a mere cover for a highly specific politics) but to a mending of what has been broken, a reunion of ruptured historical and cosmic realities. In *To Mend the World* (1982) Fackenheim, while eschewing any attempt to "justify" the Holocaust retrospectively, asks what sort of *tikun* might repair that catastrophic rupture:

What then is the *tikun*? It is Israel itself. It is a state founded, maintained, defended by a people who—so it was once thought—had lost the arts of statecraft and self-defense forever. It is the replanting and reforestation of a land that—so it once seemed—was unredeemable swamps and desert. It is a people gathered from all four corners of the earth on a territory with—so the experts once said—not room enough left to swing a cat.... It is a City rebuilt that—so once the consensus of mankind had it—was destined to remain holy ruins. And it is in and through all this, on behalf of the accidental remnant, after unprecedented death, a unique celebration of life.

This *tikun*, far from being "parochial" or "particular," has within it the potentiality of being a true *tikun olam*, because the Holocaust "called into question not this or that way of being human, but all ways." It is no exaggeration to maintain that to mend that rupture would be to offer consolation and hope to the whole world.

SOME of the practical consequences of having Jews carry their utopian zeal into the public square have been suggested in a recent debate between Fein and Milton Himmelfarb on "The New Jewish Politics." (The debate took place at this year's annual meeting in New York of the American Jewish Committee.) Himmelfarb urged that Jewish voters recognize themselves as, among other things, a special-interest group, and vote accordingly. Noting that in recent electoral campaigns the Democratic party has "conspicuously refused to be anti-anti-Semitic"—by refusing, that is, to utter a word that might be construed as critical of Jesse Jackson— he warned that a failure by Jews to react strongly to such provocation would be "pretty near suicidal for the American Jewish community."

Fein, for whom Jewish history follows an arrow-straight course from "Sinai" to the left wing of the Democratic party, responded to Himmelfarb by urging Jews "not to vote just on the basis of narrow interests." (It was, of course, just their ability to rise above their "narrow interests" and give their unstinting support to Franklin D. Roosevelt that led to what Fein himself, in *Where Are We?*, terms the "shameful silence" of American Jews during the Holocaust; needless to say, this is a contradiction he neglects to explore.)

Himmelfarb's view of the conflict between Jewish liberalism and Jewish pragmatism in America is expressed more fully in a little volume titled *Jews in Unsecular America*,** which contains the edited proceedings of a conference held in 1987 under the auspices of the Center for Religion and Society. Of the many shrewd things Himmelfarb has to say both in his formal address and in the ensuing discussion, perhaps the shrewdest is his insight into the apparently incurable tendency of Jewish liberals to allow ideology to drown prudence and common sense, whether the issue at hand is school prayer, or Israel, or abortion, or welfare. He notes that three out of four Jews polled in 1984 supported govern-

---

* "Prior to the time of [Moses] Mendelssohn ... I challenge you to produce a single Jewish text ... in which the idea of a state of universal social justice is more than a marginal concern or messianic afterthought; and I challenge you to find *anywhere* the concept of a Jewish mission to help bring about such a state. Nothing in fact could be further from the traditional Jewish mentality, which has always looked upon the Gentile world as an arena of blindly chaotic and idolatrous forces.... One might as well seek to pacify earthquakes and floods. In such a view ... social justice in the world is anything but the proper worry of a Jew." Hillel Halkin, *Letters to an American Jewish Friend* (1977).

† For a fuller discussion of Fackenheim's thought, see "Judaism According to Emil Fackenheim" by Robert M. Seltzer, beginning on p. 31 of this issue—ED.

** Edited by Richard John Neuhaus and Ronald Sobel, Eerdmans, 120 pp., $8.95.

ment programs of welfare and food stamps, even though two out of three believed that these programs have many bad effects on the very people they are supposed to help. These are Jews whom Fein, using a repellent expression which means exactly nothing, repeatedly calls "caring" people—i.e., do-gooders who think they are doing good when they feel good about what they are doing.

THE conference took off from the premise that any assessment by the Jewish community of its relation to society at large must begin with the recognition that (as the editors put it) America is "incorrigibly and increasingly religious," and that "the religion in question is overwhelmingly Christian." The Christian participants in the conference, including evangelicals, genuinely wished to hear Jews speak to them *as Jews* about their relation to American society. The most striking response to their request for instruction came from Rabbi David Novak, a spokesman for traditional Judaism and—probably to the surprise of many—a spokesman as well for the idea of the "Mission of Israel" within America.

Novak recalls that this Reform idea, at first strengthened among some American Jews because of its resemblance to the "Social Gospel" of certain Protestant groups, eventually lost favor and was discredited because it always trailed obediently after liberal political programs whose outlook was wholly secular. Neither was it helped by the fact that nearly all its advocates were anti-Zionists. But now, Novak maintains, something like the Mission of Israel has emerged among the most traditional Jewish thinkers in America, although they avoid using the slogan.

Whereas the liberal Fein derides traditional Judaism because "it ignores the circumstances, the culture, the consciousness of each generation," Novak insists not only on its capacity for doctrinal development but on the genuine concern of traditional Jews with the moral and spiritual life of the general society. Although such Jews remember that "the *raison d'être* of Judaism is not to teach the Gentiles but to obey God's Torah, whether the Gentiles are interested in it or not," they are now (he argues) a sufficiently integral part of America to formulate opinions on issues of public debate and thus to help America develop along "ethical and religious lines that are not antithetical to Judaism's *theocratic* view—namely, that the revealed Law of God is to be the basic norm for every society."

Novak sees clearly that the Judaism espoused by the Enlightened Jew, eager to diffuse light among the nations, was not Judaism at all, but the particular mode of egress he had chosen from Judaism: specious theories, seductive utopias, new idols. It is, instead, only by being true to themselves, which for Novak means being true to the recognition that ethics is law and cannot be removed from theology, that Jews can expect to be taken seriously by American Christians and aid in bolstering democracy by means of shared religious values.

Unlike Fein, Novak is thus not impelled to invent a specious theory of American Jewish life, and he is certainly not impelled to do so mainly for the purpose of fending off Zionism. Nevertheless, he too must understand that the very notion of a special Jewish mission in America—even if that mission is defined more modestly, honestly, and cogently than liberals past and present have been wont to do—cannot help drawing Jews away from Zionism and Israel. Where the liberal Jewish missionaries are busy offering prophetic visions of freeing the oppressed and clothing the naked, the traditional Jewish missionaries offer lessons, drawn from experience, about "the danger of depersonalization," "the danger of deculturization," the dialectic between faith and history. Neither the one nor the other seems much interested in putting on the "new agenda" (a phrase used with alarming frequency by these writers) that form of *tikun olam* adumbrated by Fackenheim, a mending of the world that begins in the earthly Jerusalem.

MEANWHILE, as all this missionary activity is being planned by some Amercan Jews for the benefit of their fellow-citizens in the spiritual Jerusalem, the earthly Zion is burning, not metaphorically but literally. Several times in his book Fein subscribes to the metaphor of Jews as "a family," yet when he quotes his favorite passage from Isaiah 58 he emphasizes only the socially visionary lines about clothing the naked and feeding the hungry, not the line that follows them: "And not to ignore your own kin." To anyone who truly believes that American Jews belong to the same family as Israeli Jews, the text to be pondered today is not Isaiah 42:6 ("I have given you as . . . a light to the nations") but Song of Songs 1:6: "They made me a keeper of the vineyards; but my own vineyard I have not kept!"

Liberalism and Zionism

Edward Alexander

"LIBERALISM is always being surprised." That was how Lionel Trilling used to describe the characteristic liberal failure to imagine what reason and seductive common sense appeared to gainsay. During the past century, few things have surprised and offended the liberal imagination more than the weird persistence of the Jewish nation.

Liberal friends of the Jews expected that their emancipation would put an end to Jewish collective existence. Count Stanislas de Clermont-Tonnerre, the French revolutionary, told the French National Assembly in 1789 that "the Jews should be denied everything as a nation, but granted everything as individuals." Wilhelm von Humboldt, the great liberal reformer of Prussia, whose ethical idealism is celebrated in John Stuart Mill's *On Liberty*, considered the disappearance of the Jews as a distinct group a condition for taking up the cause of their emancipation.

When the Jews failed to live up to their sponsors' expectations, the reaction against them could be fierce. George Eliot wrote in 1878 that modern English resentment of Jews for maintaining themselves in moral isolation from their fellow citizens was strongest among "liberal gentlemen" who "usually belong to a party which has felt itself glorified in winning for Jews . . . the full privileges of citizenship." George Eliot had herself once belonged to that party, and in 1848, when her revolutionary ardor was at its height, predicted that the Jews as a "race" were "plainly destined to extermination." But between 1848 and 1874, when she began to write *Daniel Deronda*, her liberalism had been tempered by a wider experience of mankind and a deeper reflection on the meaning of nationality in general and of the organized memory of Jewish national consciousness in particular.

George Eliot came to cherish the idea of "restoration of a Jewish State planted on the old ground," not only because it would afford the Jews a center of national feeling and a source of dignifying protection, but because it would contribute to the councils of the world "an added form of national genius," and one of transcendent (though not Christian) meaning. At the conclusion of her essay on the Jewish problem ("The Modern HEP! HEP! HEP!"), she pleads with John Stuart Mill's liberal disciples to enlarge their master's ideal of individuality to nations: "A modern book on Liberty has maintained that from the freedom of individual men to persist in idiosyncrasies the world may be enriched. Why should we not apply this argument to the idiosyncrasy of a nation, and pause in our haste to hoot it down?"

The relation among liberalism, democracy, and the Jewish nation is directly addressed in two ambitious new books by liberals on Zionism and Israel. In one of these, Bernard Avishai, author of *The Tragedy of Zionism** and self-styled elegist of Zionism, has cast himself in the role of Epimenides coming to Athens or Plato to Syracuse, sternly ignoring the contemptible traditional and local idiosyncrasies of the natives in order to bestow upon them the blessings of the "British liberal tradition," "secular democracy," "liberal decency," and "a written constitution."

In his prologue Avishai describes how, in 1972, he and his wife left Canada to become Israelis. But by 1973 they began to feel that they were victims of "cultural enslavement" whose "English spirit" was being blotted out by Hebrew. The instrument of their deconversion from Zionism was American and English television programs which revealed to them that they were "living among foreigners" and that their true home, to which they soon returned, was Canada and the English language. Although he momentarily blamed himself for failing to become an Israeli, Avishai quickly decided that the blame lay with Israel, which, if you are American, turns your children into strangers, and with Zionism, which, "like old *halakhic* [Jewish legal] norms," represses "individual life . . . equivocation, sexuality," desiderata of the "culture of liberalism" that he now pursues as a teacher of writing at MIT.

Five pages after describing how he saved himself from the clearest and most dangerous siren

---

EDWARD ALEXANDER is professor of English at Tel Aviv University and the author of *The Resonance of Dust: Essays on Holocaust Literature and Jewish Fate*, among other works. His article, "Operation Moses," appeared in our July 1985 issue.

* Farrar, Straus & Giroux, 389 pp., $19.95.

call he had ever heard, Avishai announces that it is time "to retire" Zionism in favor of democracy. Ten pages later he contemptuously describes early political Zionists such as Leo Pinsker, Theodor Herzl, and Vladimir Jabotinsky as people who invented an ideology to assuage "personal disappointment," for they "were themselves people who had tried to assimilate and ... failed." The ironic vision of this tragedian-elegist does not extend to himself.

Conor Cruise O'Brien also begins his massive study of Israel and Zionism, *The Siege*,* by describing those elements in his national, religious, and family background that drew him to the subject. In the late 1950's that most unphilosophical principle called the alphabet conspired with destiny to situate O'Brien, as Ireland's UN representative, between Iraq and Israel, a revealing perspective for a shrewd observer. In 1961 he left Ireland's foreign service but subsequently went into politics at home, where he served four years in opposition and four years as a member of the Irish government.

O'Brien is a liberal, but it was not his liberalism that made him see the Return to Zion, which took place under "harsher necessities" than any ever imagined by liberals, as "the greatest story of modern times." As an Irish Catholic he had no trouble recognizing, at the heart of Zionism, a powerful bond between religion and nationality. As the child of a lapsed or "enlightened" Catholic father, whom he labels a *maskil* (Hebrew for "enlightened one"), O'Brien grew up sufficiently "alienated" from Catholic society to feel yet another link with Jews living as strangers in Exile. Finally, he was moved by the conviction that "Irish Catholics ... have had a greater experience of persecution, oppression, and stigmatization than any other people in Western Europe *except* the Jews."

Throughout his book, O'Brien freely and candidly uses his experience as an Irishman and a diplomat to shed coruscating light on the story of the Zionist movement as well as on the play of forces around that movement. This means that in his view of the British Mandatory government that ruled Palestine from soon after the end of World War I until 1948, the British Anglo-Saxon constitutional system, which to Avishai is a second (and superior) revelation from Sinai, sometimes appears to be just what Matthew Arnold called it: "A colossal machine for the manufacture of Philistines." O'Brien remarks that among such Philistines, "anti-Semitism is a light sleeper," and offers as an instance the use in British official circles, starting in 1941, of the epithet "Jewish Nazi state." For Avishai, anti-Semitic remarks by the British Foreign Secretary Ernest Bevin are "tactlessness," something akin to eating soup with a fork.†

O'Brien's saga of Israel and Zionism is in two parts. The first recounts the story of Zionism from the assassination of Czar Alexander II in 1881 through the expiration of the British Mandate in 1948 and includes detailed analyses of the whole spectrum of Zionist ideologies, portraits of such central actors as Herzl, Chaim Weizmann, David Ben-Gurion, and Jabotinsky, and accounts of the Dreyfus Affair, Eastern European pogroms, and British motives and actions in Palestine. The second, longer part tells the story of Israel from its bloody beginning through the completion of the withdrawal from Lebanon in summer 1985. It comprises lengthy chapters on the inner life of Israel as expressed in its literature, on Israel's Oriental Jewish population, on the Arabs of Israel and the administered territories, and on the complex relations between international diplomacy and Israel's wars. *The Siege* is the work of a writer of flexible intelligence and boundless curiosity. The book therefore has a kind of noble imperfection, like that of large Victorian novels lovingly called loose and baggy monsters.

Avishai's "tragedy," by contrast, has the completeness of a limited mind. The first part of the book analyzes the development of Zionist ideas, especially in relation to certain crossroads in the development of the *yishuv* (Palestinian Jewish community) and with favorable emphasis upon cultural, as opposed to political, Zionism. The second part traces, in just three chapters, the rapid disintegration of Labor Zionism from its victory at the 1931 World Zionist Congress to "the end of Zionism" on the eve of the Six-Day War of 1967. The last, most aggressively polemical section of the book presents what Avishai sees as the various tragedies and failures, from 1967 to the present, that resulted from Ben-Gurion's "post-Zionist matrix" of "power, Bible, defiance, settlement, economic growth."

Avishai's is a much narrower book than O'Brien's in scope because it tells comparatively little of what the Gentiles, apart from Palestinian Arabs, are thinking and doing. His description of the 1938 Evian conference on Jewish refugees, for example, includes a polite, passing allusion to the failure of the Western democracies to accept Jews, followed by a detailed, acerbic description of Labor Zionist hopes that the conference would fail. This is also a narrower book in its quality of mind. O'Brien's discussion of Israeli literature ranges widely from Abba Kovner, Aharon Appelfeld, David Shahar, and Yehuda Amichai to Amos

---

* Simon and Schuster, 800 pp., $24.95.

† Avishai is equally charitable toward the constitutional democracies of the U.S. and Canada, which, he says, closed their doors to mass immigration "in the depths of economic depression." In fact, those doors were closed in the boom years of the 20's. Irving Abella and Harold Troper (*None Is Too Many*) have demonstrated that Canada's distinction of admitting fewer Jewish refugees from Hitler than any other Western country had nothing to do with economics, everything to do with that "tactlessness" called anti-Semitism.

Oz and A. B. Yehoshua, Avishai's is limited to books and plays that illustrate "the liberal, post-Zionist curve of Israel's leading writers," especially if these "leading writers" deal with an Arab-Jewish love affair or depict Israelis as Nazis.

Both books are unusually personal and enlivened by anecdote. O'Brien's invocations of experience often reveal the hypocrisy or hatred that is part of the burden Israel must bear. Recalling how in 1974 the UN delegates of every Western European nation, including Ireland, joined in the standing ovation for Yasir Arafat, O'Brien writes: "I asked our Foreign Minister, Garrett FitzGerald, whether it was altogether wise for Ireland to be so fulsome about the PLO: might there not be a precedent in relation to the IRA? Garret thought not. . . . Arafat and his Fatah were the moderates." On another occasion, as Ireland's representative at the 1946 conference on refugees in Geneva, O'Brien had to meet with a Monsignor representing the Vatican who frankly told his interlocutor of his feelings about Jews: "I'm not anti-Semitic. I just hate them."

Avishai's anecdotes, by contrast, serve mainly to cast a warm glow over his debating skills marshaled in combat against illiberal, supposedly paranoiac Jews. In Israel, he vanquished a taxi driver whose experiences in Lebanon had embittered him toward Palestinian Arabs. In North America, he joined an Israeli in heaping scorn upon Diaspora Jews who still brood over the Holocaust and "now need to invent anti-Semites to feel like Jews, to perform the commandment of Auschwitz." (It is characteristic of Avishai to suppose that the power exercised over ordinary Jews by this commandment—as Emil Fackenheim phrases it—not to give Hitler posthumous victories is merely that of a smart syllogism, on the order of "since Hitler didn't want Jews in Germany, we must live there.")

THE stark contrast in method, tenor, and tone between the two books is everywhere apparent. For O'Brien the Jews, for all their political inaptitude, are a great people, and the state of Israel, despite its "Panglossian" professors, its proud, overweening politicians, and a national character "so democratic as to be almost unworkable," is the culmination of a movement whose power over Gentiles as well as Jews is a "mystery" that cannot be explained except by the divine power of the Bible. For Avishai, full of acrid contempt for those who sense "something mysterious and wonderful about Jewish history," the Jews are a small people, but a nasty one. Their country has become the devil's own experiment station, where the state is "superior to all other moral values," where young people increasingly succumb to their primordial instincts for "domination, lockstep, revenge," and where the Bible impedes peace by deluding "new" Zionists into calling the West Bank Judea and Samaria (always enclosed by the author in quotation marks) and impedes "liberal democracy" by imposing upon Hebrew speakers an archaic vocabulary in which the word for freedom *(cherut)* is national rather than individual in meaning.

O'Brien expresses admiration for the heroism of the outnumbered Jewish defenders of the early settlements of Yad Mordechai, Degania (helpfully identified, by Avishai, by its Arab name Umm Juni), and Geulim. Citing several sources, he writes that in the War of Independence, "the numbers actually engaged on the two sides seem to have been about equal. But the Arabs had a huge initial superiority in . . . equipment and firepower, heavy weapons, armor and aircraft." Avishai, judging the paltry efforts of the Jews by the high and severe conceptions of gallantry that obtain at MIT, is unimpressed. He writes, citing no sources at all, that "Jewish forces outnumbered the combined strength of the Arab forces and Palestinian irregulars by 2 to 1—a fact which should dispel misty notions about how courage alone vanquished the Arab Goliath."*

In both books the large immigration to Israel in the 1950's of Oriental Jews, strangers to democracy, receives detailed attention. O'Brien describes the lives these people had led as second-class citizens in their lands of origin, where they were held in contempt by the aggressive "triumphalist creed" of Islam. He argues persuasively that they were something more than a mixed multitude, incapable of appreciating the socialism and atheism of Israel's founders. Rather, they were Zionists, from "national traditions kept alive through religious observance."

For Avishai, the Oriental Jews were not merely, like many of the children of Labor Zionist veterans, not Zionists—they were also destitute of liberalism, hence poor material for secular democracy. It was in order to mobilize such a rabble, he argues, that Ben-Gurion had to sacrifice the revolutionary ideas of Labor Zionism in favor of statism and militarism, and diplomacy in favor of retaliation. Their best people, i.e., their "liberal intelligentsia," having gone to Montreal or New York rather than Israel, the Oriental Jews were deaf to the blandishments of socialism and democracy. They had come to Israel because of their "vivid understanding of the modern world's tribal and dark side."

No hint is given by Avishai of what is abundantly provided by O'Brien: namely, evidence that Oriental immigrants responded to this "chance to be strong against the Arabs" not from some metaphysical glimpse into the modern heart of darkness but from living among them. Explicitly, Avishai bewails the fact that so few Yemenite cobblers and North African policemen

---

* According to the American military historian Trevor Dupuy, the Arabs committed 40,000 men to the conflict, the Jews had 30,000 men under arms, 10,000 more ready for mobilization.

have learned the true, "European" meanings of democracy and freedom at Hebrew University; implicitly, what bothers him is that so many have learned about Arabs from experience and not from, say, one or another of the country's institutes of Middle East studies, where they could receive instruction in how to hallucinate moderation in their enemies.

ASCRIBING moderation to Israel's enemies and willful extremism to Israel's leaders is characteristic of Avishai's approach. (There are assorted "tragedies" scattered through his account of Zionism, starting with the establishment by the Histadrut [General Federation of Jewish Workers] of a "dictatorship of the proletariat." But the underlying meaning of the title is that the protagonist, Zionism, has brought about its own destruction by *hamartia*, or arrogant pride.) He describes King Feisal of Iraq in 1919 "offer[ing] protection for Zionism under a united Arab state." O'Brien points out that the real intent of this offer was, as even the British Royal Commission Report of 1937 confirmed, that "If King Hussein and Emir Feisal secured their big Arab state, they would concede little Palestine to the Jews." The agreement, wrote the British intelligence officer Colonel French at the time of its signing, "is not worth the paper it is written on."

Avishai depicts the present King Hussein of Jordan intrepidly (if vainly) arguing for recognition of Israel at the Khartoum conference of Arab nations following the Six-Day War. But how, asks Avishai, could he dream of making peace without getting back Jerusalem? We are not told why Hussein showed no interest in peace or recognition between 1953, when he came to the throne, and 1967, when he led his country into war against Israel. In any event, the ascendant political figure in Israel by this time was Moshe Dayan, who, allegedly, made any settlement impossible.

For Avishai, Dayan is "a modern pharaoh" who virtually created Palestinian Arab "radicalism." So fond is Avishai of this conceit whereby Arabs become Jews and Israelis their Gentile oppressors that he tells how Dayan's heart, presumably like Pharaoh's in the Bible, "had been hardened by terrorist attacks such as the one [on a school] at Ma'alot." This is to say that Arafat does not murder but only executes divine sentence. Avishai claims that "in 1968, Arafat was still an unlikely guerrilla, criss-crossing the West Bank on a motorcycle. ..." O'Brien, however, reminds us that in March 1968, at Karameh, this pathetically enterprising cyclist, in league with a Hussein who now called himself a *fedayeen* (commando), murdered 23 Israeli soldiers.

Avishai indignantly reports that in 1976 only the dovish Israeli politician Yossi Sarid recognized that the newly elected pro-PLO mayors of the West Bank, graciously willing to set up a state "in whatever part of the homeland would be liberated," represented "a new opportunity for Israeli diplomacy." O'Brien, on the other hand, quotes "moderate" Palestinian Arabs who unblushingly declared that "the step that follows liberation is the dismantling of the racist . . . structure of Israel as a state." He offers too the sobering reminder that the organizers of the massacre of Israeli schoolchildren at Ma'alot "were well-known Palestinian 'moderates' who had been in dialogue with Israeli 'doves.'"

Avishai's generosity toward Israel's adversaries is epistemological as well as political. He sneers at the argument of Revisionist Zionists that most Palestinian Arabs were as much immigrants to the country as most Jews were. He does not deny the fact, but maintains that Arabs who moved to Palestine from Damascus or Amman were, "in their own eyes, . . . doing no more than moving from one part of the Arab homeland to another." How such people could consistently also claim, after 1948, to be homeless refugees if they lived anywhere outside the borders of Israel is not a question to interest Avishai, though he castigates Labor Zionists for causing the displacement of Arab residents "from their country." Later he refers gingerly to Joan Peters's "highly controversial book" about Arab immigration to Palestine, *From Time Immemorial*, promising that a friend of his will soon explode Peters's thesis. But in the meantime we must rest content with the view that "the number of Arabs who came, and their actual place of origin, beg the question of the subjective feelings of the people who came to call themselves Palestinians." In other words, it does not much matter what things are in themselves, only what they appear to be to Arabs.

O'Brien points out that, among the "subjective feelings" of Israel's Arab adversaries, belief in Enlightenment principles of secular democracy barely exists. Nevertheless, it is in this language that they have chosen to make their case to the West, knowing that it will be music to the inward ear of liberals. "In terms of the governing code of debate, based on the Western Enlightenment value system, this puts the Arab states—and the cause of Government by Consent—permanently in the right, and Israel—with its archaic Right of Return and Jewish State—permanently in the wrong." Of course, O'Brien adds, Muslim spokesmen who appeal to Enlightenment principles "are engaging in doubletalk, masking the realities of what is fundamentally, on both sides, a religious-nationalist culture conflict." He notes that the terrorist group Fatah, whose spokesmen repeat "secular democratic state" with the regularity of a steam engine, is an organization whose name means the opening of a country for conquest by Islam.

The archetype of the relation of Palestinian Arabs to democracy is, for O'Brien, their outright rejection of the Palestine Constitution proposed by Palestine High Commissioner Herbert Samuel and then-Colonial Secretary Winston Churchill in 1922. Although Weizmann accepted this commitment to representative democracy, the Arab majority scorned an arrangement that did not abolish the Balfour Declaration and bestow on the Arabs the power to exclude Jews from Palestine. Then as now only "the prestige of the absolute" could enrapture Palestinian Arabs.

For both writers the nature of democracy in Israel is bound up with religion; beyond that point they diverge in every particular. In the first part of his book Avishai insists, often to the point of absurdity, on denying Jewish religion any role in the development of Zionism; but his account of events after 1948 alleges that religious influence poisoned Zionism, prevented territorial concession, and maimed by compression, like a Chinese lady's foot, every libertarian impulse of Israeli citizens. On the very first page of his "tragedy," Avishai states that Czar Nicholas I "had been dismayed by Jewish sympathies for Napoleon's occupation."

The statement is typical Avishai for two reasons. First, it is wrong. Nicholas, not famous for his love of Jews, wrote of them in his diary: "Surprisingly . . . in 1812 they were very loyal to us and assisted us in every possible way even at the risk of their own lives." Secondly, it is wrong because Avishai cannot admit that, given the choice, many Jews preferred their traditional religious observance under a tyrant to emancipation under the aegis of French Enlightenment.

Avishai's account of the origins of Zionism is diametrically opposed to that of O'Brien, who insists that Jewish nationalism drew its ultimate strength from the Jewish religion and that even Ben-Gurion and Weizmann were, and could not but be, essentially religious Jews. Avishai never even mentions such early religious Zionists as Yehuda Alkalay and the widely read Zvi Hirsch Kalischer; declares that the *Eretz Yisrael* of religious Jews "corresponded to no actual territory," even though Weizmann had somehow got the impression that Jews who in the East End of London prayed for dew in the summer and rain in the winter were attached to Palestine (and not Atlantis); and reports (falsely) that all religious Zionists at the Zionist congresses supported Herzl's scheme for emergency settlement of Jews in Uganda.

Avishai lashes Ben-Gurion and Golda Meir for not entering into a *Kulturkampf* against religious forces. He depicts Rabbi Abraham Isaac Kook, who as chief rabbi of Jaffa from 1904 held out a welcoming hand to Labor Zionism, as a parasite, but reserves his harshest epithets for the new, religious Zionists who do work the land. Although Avishai's single reference to Jewish daily prayers—"the daily prayers stated that Jews had been exiled 'for their sins'"—indicates he has not said them for a long time, he is filled with a visceral loathing for those who do, which reminds one that the French Enlightenment whose child he is was not only liberal and secular, it was also anti-Semitic. "Scripture hawks," "ultra-nationalist settlers," "fringe romantics": these people have, in Avishai's view, lost their human status.

The relatively small number of religious Jews in the fledgling state and the much larger number of citizens for whom religious symbols had become, through the agency of the state, a kind of civil religion, kept Israel from becoming a secular, democratic state in two ways, according to Avishai. First, they made it impossible to promulgate a comprehensive bill of rights and constitution, and thus enabled the discriminatory Law of Return, which grants citizenship to all Jews who request it, to be passed and maintained. In the long list of liberal nostrums prescribed by Avishai for the de-Judaization of Israel, abolition of the Law of Return has a high place. He is not, however, a dogmatic egalitarian. He does not want Arabs to be bothered with that little matter of serving in the army from eighteen to fifty-five, and he does not object to the principle of "affirmative action" as such: in fact, he recommends it—for the Arabs. Secondly, the religious and their allies stand accused of fostering an atmosphere of intolerance, especially in Israeli schools, that permeates all aspects of society.* His complaint that "Israeli schools have taught children much more about the tribes of Israel than about the Enlightenment" will elicit a bitter laugh from people whose children have actually attended these schools, the kind of laugh invited by one who cries fire in the midst of a flood.

In his epilogue to *The Siege*, O'Brien argues cogently against exchanging the territories of Judea and Samaria for an illusory peace. This notion, he implies, can be espoused only by well-intentioned fools or ill-intentioned rogues. By a strange irony, O'Brien adds, "Those in the West who urge that the effort to rule over large numbers of Arabs may eventually destroy Israel itself might do well to note that Meir Kahane is making the same point, while drawing from it an inference radically different from what the Western critics have in mind."

Avishai, who favors yet another partitioning of Palestine ("the only democratic solution"), is not exactly making "the same point" as Kahane, yet there is an uncanny resemblance between the mental worlds they inhabit. In both, the opposition between Zionism and democracy is inevitable and Manichean. In both, the "problem" of marriage between Jew and Arab is obsessive. Kahane

---

* For his information on the "anti-democratic views" of Israeli high-school students Avishai relies on the tendentious polls conducted by Jerusalem's Van Leer Institute. The biased, unreliable character of these surveys has been analyzed by Shlomo Sharan of Tel Aviv University. See *Ma'ariv*, International Edition, September 27, 1985.

wants to outlaw it, and Avishai, speaking for those few Israelis who combine the liberal craving for forbidden fruit with the liberal craving for legality, wants Israel to institute civil marriage.

In flagellating Israel with half-understood, misapplied, and uniquely inappropriate slogans about the "tyranny of the majority" that he has gleaned from Tocqueville and Mill while demanding that Israel surrender its Jewish character, Avishai shows a poor grasp not just of his liberal sources but of something far more important. John Stuart Mill once wrote that in the makeup of every state there must be *"something which is settled, something permanent, and not to be called in question: something which, by general agreement, has a right to be where it is, and to be secure against disturbance."*

In the state of the Jews, a state (as O'Brien keeps stressing) under siege and likely long to remain so, that "something" can only be Jewish religion and not liberalism—not necessarily the Judaism of the Orthodox parties but a Judaism freely and variously interpreted and always including the conviction that Jewish life leads somewhere because it began somewhere. This religion may not suit the most refined tastes, and some of its devotees may be raw and blind in their gropings. But men live and, if need be, die for values, not for procedures; for beliefs, not for conclusions. Early Labor Zionists seemed to do very well without religion because, as O'Brien recognizes, they were sustained by the very Judaism they denied. The same was not true for their children and grandchildren, for whom no traditional faith existed that could endow gestures of rebellion with meaning.

It is a gloomy thought that the enemies of Israel neither slumber nor sleep. But there is comfort, too, in remembering that the first elegist to crow over the demise of Zion was a fellow named Merneptah, a ruler of Egypt who announced that "Israel is desolated; its seed is no more." That was in the year 1215 B.C.E.

Zionism as Americanism

JEROLD S. AUERBACH

The legend is compelling: the renowned Progressive reformer, who became the first Jewish Justice of the Supreme Court, shed his identity as an assimilated Jew and, past the age of 50, proclaimed his commitment to Zionism. His personal conversion triggered the momentous transformation of a moribund movement — without members, leaders, ideas, or resources — into the powerful, respected voice of American, even world, Zionism. American Zionism was the institutional shadow of the most revered American Jew of the 20th century, Louis D. Brandeis.

Like most legends, however, this one mixes fact with fantasy. Brandeis's Zionist identification — prolonged, spasmodic, and hesitant — seems to defy explanation. He grew up in a family whose primary ethnic affiliation was German, and so it long remained for Brandeis himself. The limit of his participation in Jewish affairs, until shortly before his fiftieth birthday, was an occasional charitable donation. But in 1905, responding to an invitation to commemorate the 250th anniversary of Jewish settlement in the United States, Brandeis first addressed a Jewish audience. Warning that there was no place in the United States for "hyphenated Americans," he demanded loyalty to "American institutions and ideals." Good Jews, Brandeis insisted, already displayed energy, perseverance, self-restraint, intelligence, and austerity — precisely the traits that distinguished loyal Americans. His character profile, a revealing self-portrait, celebrated the loyalty of Jews to the United States.

Five years later, after a prolonged silence on Jewish issues, Brandeis was called to New York to mediate a garment workers' strike. Captivated by the exuberance of the Lower East Side, he heard Jewish Socialists and capitalists denounce each other in Yiddish while citing biblical authorities to justify their negotiating positions. Brandeis experienced a shock of recognition. He discovered among these immigrants "the qualities which to my mind, make for the best American citizenship.... a true democratic feeling and a deep appreciation of the elements of social justice." Once again, Brandeis had extracted distinctively American meanings from his exposure to the culture of immigrant Jews.

Soon after the strike, Brandeis was the subject of an interview that significantly expanded his identification as a Jew. He commended the enduring prophetic mission of the Jewish people "to struggle for truth and righteousness today just as the ancient prophets did"; and he even declared that Zionists were "entitled to the respect and appreciation of the entire Jewish people." But he reiterated his concern that Jews demonstrate "above all things loyalty to American institutions," warning once again that "habits of living, of thought which tend to keep alive difference of origin or to classify men according to their religious beliefs are inconsistent with the American idea of brotherhood and are disloyal."

Brandeis's ambivalent pattern of Jewish identification and withdrawal persisted. In 1913, he was exposed to a cross fire of criticism when he was considered for a position in Woodrow Wilson's Cabinet. Business and banking interests, offended by his passion for corporate regulation, tinged their hostility with anti-Semitism. Prominent Jewish leaders were diffident about his appointment. In a cryptic letter, Jacob Schiff of the American Jewish Committee declared that while Brandeis was "without doubt, a representative American," Schiff could only provide "a qualified reply" to the question of whether Brandeis was a representative Jew. Too Jewish for the Brahmins and insufficiently Jewish for Schiff, Brandeis lost the support of both — and the appointment. Stung by anti-Semites and rebuffed by Jews, he again withdrew from participation in Jewish affairs.

Within the next year, however, two fortuitous encounters decisively molded Brandeis's conception of Zionism, persuading him of its compatibility with American values.

In the spring of 1913 he met Aaron Aaronson, a Palestinian immigrant from Rumania, whose engaging personality and Zionist passion deeply stirred the austere Boston lawyer. Until Brandeis met Aaronson, his encounters with Jewish immigrants had left him profoundly ambivalent. For Brandeis, as for so many German Jews, the Eastern European newcomers were too Orthodox, too radical, too poor, too uncouth, or simply too numerous for comfort. Aaronson, by contrast, was a brilliant agronomist, a self-reliant pioneer, and a proud Jew. His descriptions of "the little communities" of law-abiding Jews that flourished in Palestine fascinated Brandeis, who described Aaronson as "one of the most interesting, brilliant, and remarkable men that I have ever met." Brandeis imagined that Palestine could instill pioneering virtues and progressive ideals in tens of thousands of Jews who might otherwise languish in

Eastern Europe — or emigrate to the United States.

Captivated by Aaronson, Brandeis still hesitated, searching for safe passage through the treacherous shoals of Jewish identity and American loyalty. A chance meeting with Horace Kallen, the American philosopher of cultural pluralism, finally persuaded him that he could strengthen his patriotism, paradoxically, by deepening his Zionism. Kallen, the son of an Orthodox rabbi, had considered his own Jewishness "an outmoded burden" to be discarded for universal principles of liberty and justice. He attended Harvard (where he first met Brandeis) to become "educated and Americanized." There, ironically, Kallen encountered a literary historian who taught him that the Jewish prophetic tradition had inspired the American founding fathers. Once Kallen discovered the Bible as the source of American freedom, equality, and democracy, it was easy for him to become a Zionist. Substituting tolerant images of diversity for the prevailing metaphor of the American melting pot, he proclaimed the United States "a commonwealth of national communities." In its orchestra of national groups the discordant notes of cultural dissonance would become the inspiring melodies of patriotic harmony.

Kallen and Brandeis met again in August, 1914, on their way to the Zionist conference in New York where Brandeis was elected leader of the American movement. The outbreak of war in Europe weeks earlier had already crippled the World Zionist Organization, shifting the center of Zionist gravity to the United States. Literally on the eve of his assumption of leadership, Brandeis was persuaded by Kallen that Zionism was entirely compatible with Americanism. With Kallen's guidance, he discovered the most congenial approach to Zionism, which he expressed in the remarkable *non sequitur* that became his Zionist credo: "To be good Americans, we must be better Jews, and to be better Jews, we must become Zionists."

"Throughout long years which represent my own life," Brandeis conceded as he accepted the mantle of Zionist leadership, "I have been to a great extent separated from Jews. I am very ignorant of things Jewish." The wish to be a good American, not the depth of his Jewish identification, shaped Brandeis's conception of Zionism. So his Zionist references were suffused with American, not Jewish, allusions. Recasting Zionism in American terms, he even transformed Zionists into New England Pilgrims. Referring to "our Pilgrim Jewish Fathers" in Palestine, he described Zionism as "the Pilgrim inspiration and impulse all over again." Once Zionists and Pilgrims were indistinguishable, Brandeis could extend his own roots (as a Zionist) back to 17th-century New England, the very source of American civilization. His Zionist identification tapped his yearning for acceptance as an American. If "we must become Zionists" to be "good Americans" (the ultimate goal), Brandeis would make the commitment. As he explained to a journalist in 1915: since Zionism repeated the Pilgrim experience, New Englanders who were descendants of "the Pilgrim Fathers should not find it hard to understand and sympathize with it." (As always, Brandeis wanted Brahmin acceptance.) The interview, appropriately, was published on July 4.

Brandeis expanded the appeal of Zionism by contracting its Jewish content. Rarely reflecting upon "things Jewish," he was dedicated, above all, to organizational efficiency. (Perhaps his most characteristic gesture was the installation of a time clock in the Zionist office.) His correspondence testifies to his passion for organizational precision: instructions for pledge campaigns; insistence upon monthly, even daily, reports of activities; consuming concern with accurate financial records. Even during the euphoric weeks at the end of 1917, when the Balfour Declaration and the British conquest of Jerusalem sent Zionist hopes soaring, Brandeis tempered his pleasure with reminders about organizational details. Learning of the Declaration, he telephoned "joyous congratulations" to Chaim Weizmann, but he stressed the need to "strengthen the organization in (1) Members (2) Money (3) Discipline." A rapturous message from one of his aides about the fall of Jerusalem to General Allenby elicited the reply: "I note your telegram, fall of Jerusalem creating 'Big Sensation.' Is it creating big 'Money and Members'?"

The Brandeis emphasis upon men, money, and discipline galvanized the American Zionist movement after 1914. But his organizational priorities depleted American Zionism of Zionist content. Brandeis cared little for the issues that agitated European Zionists or for their answers, whether cast in political or spiritual terms, to the Jewish Question. At home, his impatience with the Orthodoxy of Mizrachi and the Socialism of Poale Zion isolated them at the fringes of the Zionist movement. All ideologies — including Zionism — were suspect. Brandeis was primarily concerned with securing the place of Jews in American society. His crowning achievement was the demonstration that Zionism was entirely compatible with Americanism. As he expressed it with intense personal satisfaction, after his nomination to the Supreme Court, "in the opinion of the President there is no conflict between Zionism and loyalty to America."

Zionism as Americanism captured a large following in the American-Jewish community. But its emphasis upon liberal reform and patriotism rearranged Zionist priorities. Before 1914, the Federation of American Zionists had attracted a small but knowledgeable group of Hebraic scholars and Zionist intellectuals. These Zionists, most of whom have disappeared into the oblivion cast by Brandeis's shadow, were deeply committed to the national liberation and spiritual regeneration of the Jewish people. They struggled thoughtfully with the most tormenting issue for American Zionists: how to define Diaspora Judaism in relation to Jewish national revival in Eretz Israel. Clustering around Solomon Schechter at the Jewish Theological Seminary, they developed conceptions of American Zionism in *Jewish* terms that retained the historical connection of Jews, even in the *goldene medinah* of America, to their

Promised Land. Schechter grasped the function of Zionism as a bulwark against "the Galut of the Jewish soul," withering under pressure of assimilation. He insisted that the "rebirth of Israel's national consciousness" and "the revival of Judaism" were inseparable. Zionism must not only address the problem of Jews (arguably confined to Eastern Europe), but the problem of Judaism — nowhere more glaring than in enlightened Diaspora communities.

Under Brandeis's leadership, these issues all but vanished from the American Zionist agenda. While Schechter's classic statement of his Zionist credo reverberated with echoes of Herzl, Ahad Ha'Am, Nordau, and even Rabbi Kook, Brandeis's addresses, by contrast, were replete with references to classical Greece. He came to Zionism, as he conceded, "through Americanism" — not through Judaism. It is no small measure of the power of Brandeis's leadership (and, of course, the concerns he shared with many American Jews) that he could transform American Zionism into a movement that sought legitimacy in American terms.

It was one thing for Brandeis to proclaim the compatibility of Zionism and Americanism in the abstract. It was altogether different — more urgent and complicated — once the Balfour Declaration transformed the fantasy of a Jewish homeland into a formal promise. To be sure, a haven for Jews in Palestine might siphon the immigrant flow from the United States. That was a welcome prospect to Brandeis, who wondered: "Is it desirable that America should be practically the only country to which the Jews of Eastern Europe may emigrate?" But if Palestine was the obvious alternative after 1917, it was also disturbing, for it raised precisely those dangerous issues of multiple loyalties that the Brandeis formula had been designed to eradicate. "I am but expressing the views . . . of all Zionists with whom I have personal relations," Brandeis wrote on the day the Balfour Declaration was issued, "when I state that they and I neither advise nor desire an independent state." Indeed, statehood was "a most serious menace." (Louis Lipsky, leader of the Eastern Europeans within the American Zionist organization, understood why: "The nearer Palestine is brought, the more devoted the American Zionist must become not to the Stars and Stripes . . . but to the blue and white flag, and that land.") Once again, the nagging question had surfaced: Was Zionism Americanism or was it, ultimately, un-American?

To resolve their dilemma, Zionists elevated philanthropy above politics. Jews must give their "complete allegiance" to the United States; Zionism, therefore, "can exist as a philanthropy but not as a political motive." Palestine, for Brandeis, remained most inviting as an investment for American Jews, beckoning with "opportunities for inspired millionaires." He proposed that American Jews form "investment companies" to channel funds to Palestine; American Zionists must, nevertheless, assume "no moral responsibility" for developments there.

Philanthropy can better be understood, however, as an evasion, not the fulfillment, of Zionism. That was precisely why (with Brandeis's active encouragement) prominent anti-Zionists like Jacob Schiff, Louis Marshall, and Felix Warburg (who feared that Palestine would become "a trash basket" filled with a "Hebrew-talking mob") made common cause with American Zionists on philanthropic grounds. An infusion of funds, controlled for purposes deemed worthy by American donors, might (in Warburg's words) "save Eretz Yisroel from the Zionists." The Zionist movement, Brandeis concluded in 1919, most needed "businessmen — financial and managerial ability," supplemented by "some good practical legal ability." Once the Zionist organization resembled a business or a corporate law firm, American Jews could be comfortable with their Zionism. American Zionists, financially generous but frightened of involvement, were primarily concerned with protecting their investment in the United States.

For a moment, in the summer of 1919, Brandeis almost seemed to waver. On his first (and only) visit to Palestine, he was deeply moved, especially in Jerusalem where he was thrilled by that "wonderful city." As he traveled, passion supplanted accounting precision in his correspondence. "The ages-long longing, the love is all explicable now," he confided to his wife. "It is indeed a Holy Land." Palestine, he told Chaim Weizmann, "has won our hearts. It is no wonder that the Jews love her so."

Brandeis left Palestine after two weeks, inspired by his visit and convinced that he understood the major problems and possibilities. But he quickly repressed his strong feelings. By the time he reached England, to address the Zionist General Council, his faith in Progressive virtues had been restored. In London, to the stunned surprise of his Zionist audience, he declared that the transcendent issue in Palestine was — sanitation. He dismissed mass immigration as chimerical; the first priority must be to eradicate malaria and install proper sanitation facilities. Brandeis, sounding like a Progressive reformer aghast in an urban slum, would delay immigration, Shmarya Levin complained, "until the last mosquito is wiped out."

By then Brandeisian Zionism, lacking enthusiasm for a Jewish state or for the ingathering of exiles, had reached a dead end. Within two years the Brandeis leadership was decisively repudiated by the Eastern European followers of Chaim Weizmann. Hearing in Zionism "the echo of our innermost feelings as Jews," they were not prepared to sacrifice fundamental precepts of Jewish national unity to American principles of efficiency or trepidations about divided loyalty.

Weizmann once conceded that it might not be absolutely necessary to be mad to be a Zionist, but it surely helped. American Zionist leaders, by contrast, were quite sane. The professional men, predominantly lawyers, whom Brandeis recruited to the inner circle of Zionist leadership, were a remarkably homogeneous group of acculturated Americans. Their Jewish roots were accurately described as "thin and feeble"; their primary qualification was respectful awe for their leader. Most were graduates of Harvard Law School — the only institution that evoked in Felix Frankfurter "quasi-religious" feelings. They shared Brandeis's sensitivity to issues of Jewish identity, American loyalty, and the appropriate relationship between them. Zionism commanded their energies as long as it was compatible with their liberal reform agenda. They tended to be indifferent to Jewish issues unrelated to their own status as Jews in American society. Insinuations of divided loyalty provoked angry denials, coupled with ringing patriotic affirmations. The lure of Bolshevism for Jewish revolutionaries stirred deep apprehension. The diversion of immigrants from the United States to Palestine was a pleasing prospect. Philanthropic ventures (especially a university in Jerusalem dedicated to Western liberal values) inspired enthusiasm. But Zionist precepts were consistently rearranged to suit their American priorities. Only in America could Jews who rejected the idea of a Jewish state enhance their qualifications for Zionist leadership.

Why should so assimilated a Jew as Brandeis have identified with the most nationalistic expression of Judaism, especially when the norms of Brahmin Boston were so evidently appealing to him? How could Brandeis and his associates have imagined that Zionism could serve their needs as Americans? And why, above all, was their judgment unerring — even though so many other assimilated German Jews, with precisely their concerns, turned to Reform Judaism? Everything about Brandeis — his German antecedents, social position, and apprehensions about acculturation and loyalty — perfectly qualified him for quiet affiliation with a Reform temple. Instead, he chose public identification as the leader of American Zionism. Why, then, did Brandeis become a Zionist?

The Brandeis "conversion" can best be understood not as a conversion at all, but as the culmination of a persistent effort to define loyal Americanism. Between 1905 and 1915 — from his warning to "hyphenated" American Jews to his enunciation of Zionism as Americanism — Brandeis searched for a formula that would assuage uneasiness — including, no doubt, his own — about the loyalty of Jews to the United States. After the garment workers' strike he no longer chastised Jewish immigrants for their un-Americanness. But he did not find the terms for reconciling Jewish identity with American loyalty until his fateful meetings with Aaronson and Kallen. Once Brandeis could identify Zionism with "his" New England forebears, it was sufficiently anchored in the American experience to capture his allegiance. (Reform, by contrast, may have been too Jewish for him.) Once Zionism was an instrument of immigrant acculturation, rather than an expression of Jewish nationalism, Brandeis was a Zionist.

Brandeis continues to fascinate us because his translation of the dilemmas of Jewish identity into an American vernacular resonates powerfully among American Jews. Loyalty was not merely *a* problem; if Brandeis's preoccupation is an accurate indicator, it was *the* problem. Brandeis felt, acutely, the latent tension between Judaism and Americanism, and tried to alleviate it with his redefinition of Zionism. But Zionism as Americanism, severed from connections to the distinctive experience of Jews as "a covenant people," came perilously close to Americanism without Judaism.

American Jews fervently hoped that the complicated identity issues raised by freedom and Zionism, even by anti-Semitism, could be resolved within a framework of American values. Brandeis, by word and deed, was an exemplary model, for his conversion to Zionism was an affirmation of his Americanism — and a measure of his distance from Judaism. His accession to power within the American Zionist movement is usually interpreted as the legitimization of Zionism in the United States. It was, instead, a decisive moment in American Jewish acculturation, for it draped the American flag over the most nationalistic expression of Judaism. As Harvard lawyers replaced Judaic scholars in Zionist councils, the transformation was complete. This pattern replicated a shift of profound cultural significance, a century earlier, when public leadership in the United States had passed from the ministry to the bar. By World War I, the American Jewish community had experienced a parallel transfer of authority, from rabbis to lawyers. The law would not go forth from Zion but from Washington, where Brandeis, revered as the American Isaiah, sat on the Supreme Court.

Yet Brandeis should not be isolated from the main currents of Jewish national revival in his time. He did, after all, follow closely in Herzl's footsteps. Both men were successful assimilated Jews from the periphery of Jewish life who inspired the Jewish masses to identify with Zionism (and with them). They offered creative responses to the Jewish Question *despite* their distance from Jewish tradition. Just as Brandeisian Zionism was progressive Americanism tinged with New England Puritanism, so Herzl's *Judenstaat* was a liberal, not a Jewish, utopia. The "urbane assimilationist," in Europe as in the United States, "became the savior of the suffering chosen people." That is why Ahad Ha'Am, who rejected Jewish normalization for spiritual Zionism, wrote sorrowfully (but presciently) just before the turn of the century: "Almost all of our great men, those, that is, whose education and social position fit them to be at the head of a Jewish State, are spiritually far removed from Judaism." His assessment of Herzl applies as aptly to Brandeis, the Zionist as American. ■

JEROLD S. AUERBACH, *Chairman of the History Department at Wellesley College, is currently writing* Rabbis and Lawyers: Dilemmas of American Jewish Identity.

American Jews and Israel:
Two Views

II. JUDAH M. EISENBERG

"Our Rabbis taught: One should always live in the Land of Israel . . . for whoever lives in the Land of Israel may be considered to have a God, but whoever lives outside the Land has no God. . . .

Rab Judah said:
Whoever goes up from Babylon to the Land of Israel transgresses a positive commandment. . .; whoever lives in Babylon is accounted as though he lived in the Land of Israel."

[Babylonian Talmud, Kethuboth, 110b–11a].

THE STUDENT SEVERAL places in front of me on line at the Tel Aviv University cafeteria was well over six feet tall, and therefore almost certainly an American. A second student, just as tall, brushed past to join the first. As he crossed in front of a petite Israeli girl he quite politely and with a heavy American accent asked to be excused; clearly, he felt that his friend was saving him a place in line. The girl protested to her own companions, more in good-humored exasperation than in real anger, "As if I have a choice!"

This minor incident in many ways contains the main ingredients of an increasingly vexing problem. In the past few years, American Jews (many of them students) and Israelis have been encountering each other with growing frequency, and it is becoming increasingly obvious that many of these contacts are producing a mutual recoil. Is this merely part of the normal level of incompatability between people of different national backgrounds, or does it suggest the existence of deeper currents in conflict? Many signs would seem to indicate the latter.

To place this problem in perspective it is worthwhile to note that of the 13,875,000 Jews now living, according to the latest estimates given in the American Jewish Yearbook, 5,870,000 live in America and 2,620,000 in the Soviet Union; 2,497,000 are Israelis. Since prospects for the Jewish community in the Soviet Union are currently cause for anxiety, this means that the future of world Jewry rests almost completely with those in America and in Israel. Thus any potential tendency for these two groups to grow apart must be a source of profound concern for us.

It is altogether too easy to note, with a certain tone of complacent trust, that American Jews and Israelis still have a great deal in common, that Jews have survived for a long time and endured successions of near-fatal calamities, and that they have through all of this maintained strong bonds. Yet if we consider the changes that have taken place in American Jewry and in Israel within a single generation, there is little cause for complacency; both groups are rushing away from their points of common origin at a great rate, nor is the movement in the same direction. Few of us could claim with certainty that fifty or seventy-five years from now our American children or grandchildren will feel any significant special relationship with Israelis.

The present gap between American Jews and Israelis is based in part on the sharply different realities in the two countries. I suspect that it is also a product of two different mythologies held sacred by the two groups, sharply contrasting with each other and with reality. But let us start with the more objective components of the divergent attitudes. There is first of all that most insurmountable of barriers to understanding: the fact that America is a rich and secure country, while Israel is poor and menaced. It is often difficult to determine whether Americans are unique because of certain innate national characteristics, or because they are the first national group in history to have to confront the problem of what to do with great and widespread prosperity. (Tevye the Dairyman would no doubt point out that this is a problem he is prepared to cope with; but it is a problem nonetheless.)

Now while Israelis, on the one hand, are often incapable of grasping either the degree to which America is wealthy or the implications of that wealth, Americans, on the other hand, by and large are blind to the economic situation of the average Israeli and the impact this has on his attitudes. A plumber in Israel once said to me, "You know, Americans are not generally well liked in Israel. People think they are too rich and want to know why they are there and not here. But recently I went to the wedding of my son who is studying at Cal Tech, and suddenly I realized what a country that is! What a land! You have everything there!" It somehow becomes more possible to forgive the American his wealth and his desire to go on living amidst it by seeing it at first hand in the American context. American cars—even the more modest ones—look monstrous and incredibly luxurious in Israel, but measured against the American landscape they fit better. And much the same can be said of Americans themselves.

IT IS EVEN MORE the case that Americans cannot readily perceive the economic problems of Israelis, even if they have visited Israel. While driving through Tel Aviv one evening, an Israeli friend of mine who had just returned from a long stay in America looked at the throngs of lively and stylishly-dressed people all around and asked, "Can you really believe the State is about to go bankrupt?" The illusion is gratifying, but no American should succumb to it before he has tried working out the budget of his Israeli counterpart, making allowances for such things as the terrible uncertainties of living with no financial nest eggs, the rapidly upward spiraling costs and taxes, and the fact that one is at the mercy of arbitrary and capricious bureaucracies which can suddenly upset one's financial plans with a random ruling. Lastly, he must estimate how the high level of military reserve service in Israel would cut into his professional achievement.

The differences due to economic level between America and Israel are compounded by differing economic systems and their corresponding sets of values. Israel, with its socialist leanings and relatively planned economy, calls for a high degree of self-sacrifice for the common good on the part of its citizens, while America professes a capitalistic, free-enterprise system in which what is good for the individual or aggregates of individuals is supposed to be good for the country. In many contexts this disparity in views can be a rich source of misunderstanding.

Apart from those differences in outlook between American Jews and Israelis which stem from non-Jewish aspects of their formative experiences, there also are a variety of divergent attitudes which arise from the distinctive ways in which these groups see their Jewish identity. In America, Jews tend to view themselves as forming an entity based primarily on common religion, and secondarily upon ethnic bonds. (As other American groups place greater emphasis on ethnic ties, this latter component will no doubt receive greater weight amongst

31

the American Jews as well.) To a degree truly unprecedented in their history—the experiences of German and of French Jews in the late nineteenth and early twentieth centuries notwithstanding—Jews in America have been able to identify with and internalize the dominant ideals and national aspirations of the country they live in. Israelis on the other hand have as their main common experiences the many-faceted struggle for Jewish national survival, and their strongest loyalties are to the concrete manifestations of the Jews as people and nation. There is, as is well known, a relative indifference on the mass scale to matters of religion. Furthermore, the ethnicity of American Jews, which often assumes the form of a nostalgia for specifically European exilic legacies, arouses a certain contempt on the part of Israelis who would rather derive their folk customs from the actualities of the Land, and from the last period of major contact with it as a national entity.

For a visiting American Jew, there is always a certain shock at the degree to which the Israeli's Jewishness expresses itself through nationality. He is also often a little baffled at the fact that a majority of Israelis simply do not hold in awe a number of the things which American Jews have been brought up to see as sacred. It is all perfectly fine to realize that many Israelis are non-religious—so are many American Jews—but it still often catches one unawares when a primary school class is marched off to a nearby synagogue to see the quaint cultural relics of Jewish folkways.

There is also the other side of the coin: while many Israelis are essentially not involved in organized religion, the degree to which religion and the religious bloc enter as concrete political components in their lives is difficult for many Americans to accept. The latent feeling of the Americans is that Israel should embody all those virtues of Western political liberalism which Western Jews have come to feel as partly their own—especially so that it should not be the cause of any embarrassment to them with respect to non-Jewish holders of liberal ideals. After all, the mere existence of a Jewish state challenges a simple and neat view of the significance of his Jewishness to an American, and this problem has recently become somewhat more intense because of agitation calling for the replacement of Israel with a "Palestinian state" having no special relationship to Judaism. In this context, Israel must all the more be a paragon of liberal virtue for the American Jew to present to his non-Jewish friends.

In general Americans tend to be disturbed when they encounter attitudes and behavior in Israel which do not correspond to the long series of myths they have woven about the Israelis. Americans have come, for example, to hold an image of Israel as a highly efficient, Western country. (This image is strongly fostered, of course, by Israel's military successes.) Now, while this may be the case when measured on a global scale duly weighted with heavily-populated developing nations, it is not so when seen against the background of America. The initial shock which Americans feel when they make their first entry into Israel's bureaucratic jaws, and the constant irritation and denigration of the individual which they may subsequently experience, is made even more sharply intolerable by its contrast with their preconceived image.

The myth of Israel's Western efficiency is often accompanied in American minds with the notion that Israelis are a community of cheerful and colorful pioneers who see themselves as responding to the great challenges and opportunities of building a new nation. This may actually be true to an astounding degree in proportion to the usual human attitudes elsewhere, but it is not true to anything like the extent travel agents and youth group leaders would have one believe. As a result, the sudden confrontation with reality can be disturbing for visiting American Jews, especially when it is coupled with an appeal to their altruism as grounds for thinking of settling in Israel—to a level of idealistic motivation, in other words, which is in fact at odds with much that one encounters in Israel. (This myth also has a deleterious effect on the attitudes of Israelis towards their American cousins, in that it leads American Jews to send their problem teen-agers to Israel in the hopes that "they may get caught up in the excitement there." Well, they may indeed do so, but they may also present Israelis with a rather strange view of America in the process.)

IT IS IN THE picture of Israel as a somewhat pastoral and idyllic place where life has not yet become so complex and far removed from essential roots of humanity as it is in the West that the American mythology reaches a peak. The fact is that many of Israel's most challenging problems have been exacerbated by the elaborate ramifications and convolutions they have managed to acquire in the relatively short history of the State. What is disastrous about this myth of bucolic simplicity is that it tends to call to Israel so many Americans who expect Israel to help them in the resolution of their own particular aberrations, when in reality it may take an unusual steadiness of purpose coupled with flexibility of tactics to deal effectively with the Israeli scene. Moreover, virtually all of the troubling problems in America have their counterparts in Israel.

But myth-making is as two-sided as are the other sources of misunderstanding between Israelis and American Jews. Israel, for its part, has a rich and embroidered collection of legends concerning life in America. As one might expect, these legends are also not without some basis in reality; but, like their counterparts, they derive their destructive powers not only from their degree of exaggeration, but also from their tendency to freeze people into inflexible postures which cannot be modified to deal with a changing picture of reality. The foremost of these, it seems to me, is the belief that American Jewry feels the imminent threat of massive physical hostilities on the part of their non-Jewish neighbors, and that consequently Jews cannot really feel secure or at home in the United States. An attitude which naturally accompanies this is that the *only* way to lead "a full Jewish life" is in Israel. The inevitable conclusion from these axioms is, of course, that all American Jews are potential "olim" (immigrants to Israel), who need only be brought to a proper realization of their own perilous situation. Moreover, the only obstacle to this proper understanding is the self-seeking materialistic greed of American Jews.

If these two groups have elaborate sets of myths about each other, their response to this is very often in the form of counter-myths about themselves. Those aspects of Israeli reality which the American is inclined to view as flowing from a clumsy, all-pervasive bureaucratic mentality, from doubtful manners, and from repeated invasions of the private domain of the individual and his personal dignity are often interpreted in Israel as manifestations of warm human concern, a kind of turbulent, democratic, fermenting bath of Jewish humanity. True, there are abrasive elements, but even the abrasions are Jewish. And the Land is Jewish, a fact which is a source of never-ending amazement—quite rightly so—and leads to the creation of its own special mystique.

THE ISRAELI-AMERICAN confrontation is a testing ground for each group's conception of itself, and it forces, with great power, a reassessment of their respective realities and ideals. In this sense the two groups are mutually threatening. There is the obvious threat to Israel of "yeridah" (emigration) to America, especially on the part of the technological elite who are generally exposed to life in America for long periods of time and who can more easily find jobs in the United States. Reciprocally, American Jews may feel some alarm (which the lines at the head of this article from Tractate Kethuboth suggest was shared in Babylonia almost two millennia ago) at the prospect of losing to Israel the potential leaders of the American Jewish community—and losing with them the hope of realizing their own particular dream for Jewish life in America.

The two groups are now engaged in what must of necessity be a lengthy process of delineating and hardening their respective identities. It is essential that this process be carried out as much as possible in an atmosphere which permits a high level of exchange and flow between the groups, or else we risk growing irrevocably apart —and this could lead to disaster for Jewish life in both countries. How then can one minimize the many divisive forces at work in the American-Israeli encounter?

It seems to me that one must start by recognizing the existence and severity of the problem. It is not likely to benefit at this stage from benign neglect. It will not be solved unless some active steps are taken towards its solution. Both parties are going to have to devote some of the same kinds of energy which they now expend in cultivating American support of Israel to the matter of developing stronger ties and deeper understanding between the groups.

The standard solution to all intergroup problems these days is to assert that we must have more communication. In the case of the American-Israeli encounter this may well be valid, but if they are to be effective the interchanges will have to start taking on a somewhat different character from the present ones. American leaders will have to make a concentrated effort to school themselves in the realities of Israel, including those problematic areas of its existence which, once they are acknowledged to a prospective United Jewish Appeal donor or Israel Bond purchaser, will have to be discussed in careful and balanced detail. This schooling cannot be the product of casual two-week or even two-month visits. There will have to come a time when anybody who professes to a role of leadership in the American Jewish community will have to plan on regularly spending a half a year or a year in Israel, and not in the shelter of a special American program, but immersed in the actualities of Israeli life.

AMERICAN JEWS MUST be made more aware of the long and difficult road which still lies ahead of Israel in getting fully established as a nation. They will have to help her on this road, and they must come to a greater realization of their own interest in this effort: ultimately the existence of Israel is quite as vital to the meaningful existence of American Jews as theirs is to hers.

In a similar fashion, Israel will have to come to terms with the realities of the presence of an American Jewish community. It exists, and it is supremely unlikely suddenly to metamorphose into a rich source of olim. A significant minority may find Israel to be a more natural homeland for them, but the vast bulk of the community will stay here, at least for the foreseeable future. Therefore they must be dealt with as what they are—Jews in America with whom Israel must have a very significant relationship not only on the scale of decades but into the indefinite future. Israeli personnel will ultimately have to be trained to make a contribution to American Jewry as such, just as now they are trained to recruit for purposes of aliyah.

Such programs have to come to be regarded ultimately not as luxuries but as vital components of our joint survival as Jewish communities. The common bonds and interests between us are after all still of a transcendent character. If our concept of Jewishness is to retain a universal significance in the future, we must see to it that we assiduously cultivate our commonality. This is the special challenge of our generation, and one to which we must rise. The uniquely brilliant features of Jewish existence which have allowed us to survive to this time make no automatic guarantees for the future.

JUDAH M. EISENBERG *teaches in the Physics Department at the University of Virginia.*

An Agenda for Conservative Judaism in Israel

HERTZEL FISHMAN

THERE ARE TWO BASIC WAYS TO EXPRESS Conservative Judaism in Israel. The first is to establish a distinct Conservative framework — the Mesorati movement — and to enlarge the number of its synagogues, organizational activities, and projects. Inasmuch as Dr. Tabory and others deal with this approach — with which I, too, am identified — I direct my attention to the second, more all-embracing route of Conservative Judaism in Israel.

Religious Authenticity

This second approach is more ideological than organizational. It relates to *klal yisrael*, one of the cardinal principles of Conservative Judaism. In the Jewish state, this term must be interpreted to mean the mainstream of the Israeli society.

The bulk of Israel's Jews mistakenly view themselves as "non-religious" and the very first task of Conservative Judaism is, therefore, to correct their mistake. By teaching and serving as an example of enlightened religion, we may hope to restore many Israeli Jews to their religio-national heritage. This is not merely an academic exercise, but an imperative service to a citizenry which desperately requires the Jewish religion to provide it with a sense of belonging, faith and perspective. This distinctive Conservative message and religious philosophy can be conveyed within existing, indigenous Israeli frameworks — schools, youth movements, teachers colleges, community centers, adult education classes, kibbuẓim, etc., and through the public media of newspapers, radio and TV.

While most Israeli Jews do not consciously express a positive relationship with religion, basic religious concepts such as God (a transcendent or personal Divine Power who, *inter alia*, can readily be identified with our people's historic supreme ideals and values), faith in such a power ("the eternal of Israel does not deceive," I Sam. 15:19), belonging (to *klal yisrael*), a developing *halakhah* (which gives direction and order to our religio-national society) — not to speak of Sabbath, holidays, customs, ceremonies and prayers — are inherent and immanent in the life of Israel's national society. Very few people can live in Kiryat Shmonah, walk the streets of Jerusalem, serve in the army reserves, or have a son or daughter

HERTZEL FISHMAN *is the representative of the World Council of Synagogues on the Jerusalem Executive of the World Zionist Organization and on the Board of Governors of the Jewish Agency.*

AN AGENDA FOR CONSERVATIVE JUDAISM : 411

in the Defense Forces, without an accompanying sense of faith whose source is beyond mortal limitations. Without question, in Israel, one's relationship with the Divine is more consistent and real than that of many sociologically-oriented religious Jews in the Diaspora who participate only occasionally in a religious experience. Precisely because the future of the Israeli society is so uncertain, its citizens must root their inner strength and *bitaḥon* deep within Judaism's national religion.

And yet, the majority of Israelis consider themselves "non-religious," because they do not accept Israeli Orthodoxy, and because they are unaware of the significance and direct relevance of the historic Jewish religion to their lives. It is up to Conservative Judaism to explain, untiringly, the difference between the historically developing authentic Jewish religion and the tendentious partisanship of the politically-motivated Orthodox religious establishment in Israel. For what most Israelis seek, without being able to express it, is a viable religion which responds to their deepest spiritual needs and national-ethical aspirations, and provides *halakhic* anchorage in historic Jewish peoplehood. Without cultivating an ongoing commitment of belonging to a worldwide Jewish people, the three and a half million Israeli Jews remain isolated and vulnerable in a hostile world and, inevitably, their feelings of loneliness and insecurity are accentuated.

On yet another religious plane, Conservative Judaism's role in Israel is to stress the category of *miẓvot* between person and person as publicly and consistently as Orthodoxy emphasizes the religious category of *miẓvot* between a person and God. The Jewish life of an Israeli is not limited to the synagogue or to religious ritual as it is in the Diaspora, but may be expressed in daily life — on the street, the bus queue, the supermarket, the bank, the clinic, the factory or the government office. In their teachings and, above all, through personal example, Jews in Israel are in a strategic position to project and underscore the profound belief that all persons are created in God's spiritual image and are therefore to be treated with respect, sensitivity and integrity. They would thereby be making a major religious contribution not only to Israeli society, but to the realization of *l'or goyim netatikha*.

Religious Alternatives

The present status of religion in Israel is, to a large extent, a result of religious ignorance. Non-Orthodox children are raised to understand the word *dat*, religion — a term that remains honorable and respected in most cultures — as a pejorative and antiquated concept. The great bulk of the population knows religion only as certain types of Orthodoxy, be they east-European and Hasidic versions, or those of Muslim lands. Even so-called "non-religious" Jews relate (negatively) only to a religious Orthodoxy which monopolizes the country's media. Ignorant about the historic development of the Jewish religion and *halakhah* they know of no authentic Jewish alternative to the current status of religion in Israel.

One way to change this unfortunate situation — for Judaism's sake as well as for the sake of Israeli Jews — is to have Israeli society exposed to varied ideologically and halakhically religious possibilities. There are notable examples of enlightened Zionist Orthodox approaches among ideologues in HaPoel HaMizrachi kibbuẓim and reputable religious philosophers at the Hebrew University and Bar-Ilan University. But neither their viewpoints and teachings nor those of non-Orthodox halakhic spokesmen are known to the broad Israeli public. Surely the Israel national radio and TV and the country's daily press owe it to Israel's citizens to have such viewpoints heard clearly and often. Are these views any less legitimate than those represented by the anti-Zionist spokesmen of the extreme religious right?

The challenge facing Israeli society is to change the climate of understanding with respect to the Jewish religion which has always incorporated and respected differing theological and philosophical outlooks. The halakhic options advanced by the stricter Bet Shammai and by the more lenient Bet Hillel are both acknowledged by Jewish tradition as reflecting "the words of a living God." Both represented Jewish religious authenticity though, indeed, practical necessity required the preferential legal recognition of one viewpoint over the other. Israeli society can be sensitized to the legitimate necessity and precedent of incorporating into its religious thinking varied halakhic views that are relevant to a modern, sovereign Jewish state. Only then is there a chance that the Israeli public will consider religion in positive and desirable terms.

Ethical Nationalism

The unbalanced presentation of Judaism in Israel is not limited to *halakhah* but affects the entire moral ethos of Israel's national life. Religion in Israel cannot only be a matter of relations between an individual and God, and between one person and another; it must also include the relationship between the national society and its individual citizens. If Zionism, *inter alia*, means the conversion of a private Jew into a public Jew — with the needs of the nation taking precedence over private or parochial interests — so, too, does it mean amending Reinhold Neibuhr's famous thesis to read: "Moral man, *moral* society."

The teachings of Aḥad Ha'am contributed to the ideology of Conservative Judaism. His emphasis on the distinctive collective moral ethos which permeates historic Judaism became integral to the movement's platform. To date, however, Israeli society has not imbued its citizens with norms and standards reflecting this national ethos; it has not forged the

AN AGENDA FOR CONSERVATIVE JUDAISM : 413

civic personality who projects it. As a secular nationalism, Israeli Zionism has proven wanting. The *miẓvah* of aliyah becomes pedestrian if it is limited to a normal immigration process to Israel; i t takes on the significance of a supreme religious obligation if it represents *aliyah bik'dushah* — ascending to Israel in order to create a model ethical society. Conservative Judaism must clearly enunciate the religio-national thesis that Zionism is an organized quest to implement the Sinaitic covenant through which we became a people for the purpose of creating an exceptional national community, an *am segulah*. Most Israelis have forgotten, or never were aware of, this covenantal relationship; they must be constantly reminded of it. Such a continuing challenge can become a powerful morale-booster in Israel's national life and guide its people's sense of national destiny.

By systematically seeking to influence the sovereign instruments of Jewish statehood in Israel, Conservative Judaism can teach the society that the role of the miẓvot, is, indeed, to refine human nature (*Bereshit Rabba* 44a). This idealistic, though admittedly uphill, national educational task can become the crowning contribution of Conservative Judaism in the Jewish national homeland.

American Jews and Israel:
Two Views

I. ROLAND B. GITTELSOHN

MANY WORDS HAVE already been written on the relationship between the Jewish communities of the United States and Israel. But most of them unfortunately have dealt with the problem in terms which are simplistic and which almost preclude any real mutuality. There are certain things we are supposed to do for the Israelis, other things they are expected to do for us; but too often our respective transmissions pass each other somewhere along the way without meeting at all.

Let me be specific. We, on our part, are expected to provide a maximum of financial aid as well as political support for Israel. This we have pre-eminently accomplished. The Jews of Israel on their part, export to us various kinds of cultural enrichment: songs, dances, paintings, books—elementary Hebrew conversation for the many, and excellent Hebrew literature for the few. They also provide us with the vicarious thrill of having achieved a series of spectacular military victories without exposing ourselves to anything more dangerous than occasional UJA dinners. Having said this much, however, we have covered the whole of our interchange as far as the average Jew thinks of it either there or here. Each community travels toward the other on its own one-way route, with implied signs facing the other that say: "ONE WAY—DO NOT ENTER."

We therefore need to examine our relationship with Israel in greater depth than we have in the past. There will come a time when Israel will be strong and secure enough not to need the kind of fiscal and political help for which it now relies on us. If our relationship is to be reciprocal, if it is to count for more than a footnote in the chronicle of Jewish life, there must be much more to it than most of us have recognized thus far.

The first two-way road which must be opened is that of Jewish identity and definition. At the first Israel convention of the Central Conference of American Rabbis on Mt. Scopus, I put the matter this way: ". . . in authentic Judaism religion and nationalism have always been inextricably intertwined. Where other peoples have found it possible to separate them surgically, for Jews each has been like a seasoning, pervasively penetrating and permeating the other. . . . Anyone who distorts the tradition to make it appear as only religion or only nationalism will have concocted an aberrant monstrosity which will not be authentic Judaism. . . . We must remember that without either religion or nationalism there is no historically valid Judaism."

Because I was a guest in Israel, I refrained from being as explicit then as I shall try to be here. Many Israelis—judged superficially, most Israelis—have sinned in ignoring the religious component of our corporate identity. They see religion as something tedious and outmoded because—to be truthful—the only kind of religion to which they have been exposed has in fact been tedious and outmoded. They see themselves as an ethnic collectivity, as a nationality not innately different from all other nationalities. They have mutilated the corpus of Judaism by excising one of its vital organs.

And we have done precisely the same thing by severing another of its vital organs. We American Jews have too often acted as if Judaism were only a religion. We celebrate the holidays—or talk about celebrating them; we participate in public worship—or talk about so participating; but we ignore the reality that much in Judaism goes beyond what the world normally calls religion, that we constitute a community and a people whose civilization must be actively lived—in the synagogue, in the home, in every corner of life, if it is to survive.

There is a special danger in our distortion of Judaism. We live in a time when the influence of theology and firm religious faith as such is waning. I am convinced that if we boldly accept the challenges for change that our age thrusts upon us, this period of decline could prove to be transitory, that new kinds of theology could play at least as great a role for our grandchildren as the old beliefs did for our grandparents. But the fact remains that the immediate temper of our time is not theological. If we persist in identifying Judaism with religion alone, we are inviting many of our most promising young intellectuals to abandon it.

What we need, then, is continuing collaboration between the Israelis and ourselves to maintain the organic integrity of Judaism. We must persistently remind them of its religious component and they must repeatedly remind us that it possesses extra-religious dimensions as well. Only thus can the synthesis which has historically given Judaism its uniqueness in the past be sustained for the future.

This brings us to another route along which our one-way avenues must be transformed into a two-way boulevard. American Jews and Israelis have much to teach each other about the precise nature of religion itself in modern Judaism. Each of us is subject to his own peculiar myopia in this matter. I have had many conversations with self-designated irreligious Israelis. When I tell them about the availability of a new option in their country in the form of eight or nine so-called Progressive congregations, and one or more Conservative groups, their immediate tendency has been to scoff. You call this Jewish religion? they ask with a poorly-disguised mixture of hostility and derision. And they answer their own question by asserting at once that religion means the *N'turay Karta* and *Meah Sh'arim* and the *Heychal Sh'lomo*—the ritualistic remnants of medieval ghetto life still extant in the new land.

This kind of religion they reject, even as many of us have done. But since they close off any valid alternative, to discard this brand of religion means, in effect, to repudiate all religion. Ours is the inescapable responsibility to show them—no matter how much effort and time it takes—that now, as in the historic past, there are varieties of authentic religious expression within Judaism. The Progressive congregations in Tel Aviv, Jerusalem, Ramat Gan, Haifa and elsewhere are only one possibility. The ultimate forms of non-Orthodox religious Judaism for Israel have yet to be worked out by the Israelis themselves. Our task is to persist in convincing them that they can have at least as many religious options as we have, that Jewish spiritual expression must develop and grow today, even as it always has in the past, that their choice is not limited to one between rigid Orthodoxy or no religion at all.

This must not be misconstrued as an attack on Orthodoxy or a desire to supplant it in Israel or elsewhere. Orthodoxy must be retained and strengthened for those who choose it and whose spiritual needs are met by it. There must be, as a matter of fact, a variety of orthodoxies available to those who want or need them. But Orthodoxy, for all its admirable virtues and strengths, cannot be allowed to maintain a stranglehold or exclusive monopoly over Jews anywhere.

W<small>E MUST EXERT</small> another influence too on the meaning of religion in Israel. The official rabbinate there has concerned itself exclusively with such matters as *kashrut*, Sabbath observance, laws dealing with marriage and divorce—with what we might call ritual minutiae. There has been no attempt to exercise a broader concept of religion, one which would offer counseling to congregants in their personal traumas or stimulate them, in the name of faith, to implement the social ethic of traditional Judaism. The *rabbanut* has had nothing to say about the treatment of Arab refugees, about integrating oriental Jews into Israeli society, about the disparities of wealth between rich and poor, about business ethics or political corruption. All these issues of morality, on which the ancient Hebrew prophets preached with such eloquence, have been defaulted by Israel's rabbis and left to secular influence. We American Jews, especially those of us who insist that religion must be applied in every public arena of life, have much to say in this respect to our Israeli brothers.

Does it sound as if I am going back to the old one-way traffic pattern in urging that we instruct the Jews of Israel on the true nature and responsibility of religion? I am not. For in a strangely paradoxical way, while they need us for one kind of religious liberalization, we need them for another kind. We are limited by religious narrowness too. We have unwittingly become so Protestantized in the United States that many of us tend to think of the religious life as something which occurs only within the walls of the synagogue. When we search for spiritual allies in Israel, therefore, we are likely to look only toward the several congregations which have been established more or less in our image.

We who belong to the Central Conference of American Rabbis made a fascinating discovery during our Jerusalem convention. One of our most illuminating sessions took place when we met for half-a-day with leaders of several non-religious kibbutzim. We learned that we have a great deal in common with these socialistic secularists who, until very recently, would have been scandalized at the thought that what they are doing could in any sense be designated religious.

We found that they have been asking the same questions which intrigue us: What does it mean, in spiritual terms, to be a Jew? How do men in general, Jews in particular, relate to the meaning of the universe? Is there an innate, prevailing purpose in cosmic reality? What higher, ultimate loyalty can a man have, even above the establishment and defense of the State? Our respective vocabularies have differed so vastly that only when we sat down together, and especially when we started listening to one another for the first time, did we realize that in significant respects we and they are on the same quest. During intervening months that impression has been strengthened—so much so that last July a small group of rabbis representing the Central Conference and a similar delegation from the Kibbutz movement met for three days in Haifa to explore these matters more deeply.

Much can be learned from the several revisions already made in the *Haggadah shel Pesach* published by Hashomer Hatzair. Some of their earlier *haggadot* resembled the *Communist Manifesto* more than anything in Jewish tradition. But the most recent edition is amazingly different. To be sure, it is still a strange document from a religious point of view—among its other peculiarities, it doesn't include a single *b'rachah!* The only mention of God is in excerpts from the Bible, where it would have been clumsy, to say the least, to expurgate the Divine Name. The four cups of wine are introduced with toasts rather than blessings. And yet these pages breathe with the Judaic spiritual essence. Somehow, the men and women who edited them with such loving care—writing some passages themselves, selecting others from the Bible, the Talmud and modern Hebrew poetry—without saying *Baruch atah Adonai* even once, have come as close to the essential religious meaning of Judaism as any Jew alive! This is what I mean when I say they can teach us too. While we are trying to impress them with the dynamic quality of Jewish religion, with the variables and alternatives it encompasses, they in turn can help us understand that new forms and formulas may be emerging for expression of ancient truths.

I believe that something of this truth has impressed itself upon Prime Minister Golda Meir. While for obvious internal political reasons, she must be circumspect in what she says publicly about non-Orthodox Judaism, there could be little doubt as to how she really felt when she addressed the closing session of the 1970 CCAR convention, or when she entertained a small group of us afterward in her home. This was more than just perfunctory politeness on her part. She revealed a sensitive understanding of the mutual spiritual need existing between Israel and the non-Orthodox Jewish religious community of the United States. And last spring, at a time of extremely tense international pressure in the Middle East, on the day the Egyptian truce was due to expire, Mrs. Meir met at length with Alfred Gottschalk, President of the Hebrew Union College-Jewish Institute of Religion, to negotiate for the gift of additional property in Jerusalem to the Reform movement. Even though a tempting offer had come from a major international hotel corporation for this valuable property between the King David Hotel and the Jerusalem School of HUC-JIR, the Prime Minister had arranged for us to receive it as a gift. Here we plan to expand our College-Institute and, together with the Central Conference of American Rabbis, the Union of American Hebrew Congregations, and the World Union for Progressive Judaism, build a major center for non-Orthodox Judaism in Israel. Here we shall learn and teach, and promote the two-directional highway we badly need.

This would not be the first time such traffic prevailed. During one of the most creative periods of our past, precisely when the Talmud was being formed, two-way traffic flowed between Palestine and Babylon. Neither community then could have attained its fullest success without the other. Here is a paradigm for the proper relationship between the Jewish communities of Israel and the United States today.

ROLAND B. GITTELSOHN *is Rabbi of Temple Israel in Boston, Mass. His article "Women's Lib and Judaism" appeared in our October, 1971 issue.*

A Strategy for non-Orthodox Judaism in Israel

ALFRED GOTTSCHALK

I READ EPHRAIM TABORY'S "REFORM AND Conservative Judaism in Israel: Aims and Platforms" with interest and disappointment. The interest stems from a constant and abiding concern with the problems raised by Dr. Tabory. The disappointment flows from his very limited perceptions of the history of at least the Reform Movement in Israel and the peculiar sampling of opinions and documentation which he has assembled. It is strange that he does not state or seem to know that the Reform Movement in Israel or, as it is known there, Progressive Judaism, goes back much further than a decade, having its roots in Palestine prior to the establishment of the State of Israel.

I have written at considerable length on the subject in an article entitled "Israel and Reform Judaism: A Zionist Perspective" in *Forum* (No. 36, 1979). There I document that there were, indeed, from the mid-1930s on, Progressive Synagogues in the three main cities of Palestine, as well as some which developed in other towns. Their budgets were always insufficient; their constant need for financial aid was spelled out in hundreds of supplicating letters sent to the headquarters of the World Union for Progressive Judaism. A handful of pioneering rabbis received pitifully little remuneration from their work and were often compelled to take clerical jobs on the outside to earn a living. Yet they fought hard and did not give up their principles of attempting to establish in Erez Yisrael a non-Orthodox Judaism which would be in harmony with the modernist tendencies of the Yishuv. Israeli Chief Rabbi Kook even permitted Rabbi Wilhelm to officiate at marriages, an action that was not to be repeated by any of the subsequent Chief Rabbis. One certainly cannot forget the pioneering efforts of Rabbi Elk of Haifa, who envisaged a school built on the principles of Progressive Judaism. This institution would be the educational center where not only Progressive religious instruction would be offered, but also where the general curricular thrust would be determined by Liberal religion. Rabbi Elk, as is well known, established the Leo Baeck School in Haifa, which today is one of the leading institutions for secondary education in Israel.

It is also somewhat strange that Dr. Tabory does not understand, or know of, the role of the Hebrew Union College in Jerusalem vis-à-vis the development of the Reform Movement there. In the mid-fifties, Dr. Nel-

---

ALFRED GOTTSCHALK *is president of Hebrew Union College — Jewish Institute of Religion.*

son Glueck announced his plan to build in Jerusalem a counterpart to the American School of Oriental Research. He indicated that the building was to have a Synagogue in which non-Orthodox services would be held. This resulted in a massive confrontation and an exhaustive effort on the part of the Orthodox establishment to prevent even a modicum of Reform Judaism from receiving official sanction. To say the least, the failure of that pressure meant that the cause of religious pluralism in Israel was not lost. The Orthodox brought up all their forces to obstruct and prevent the establishment of Reform synagogues. The press polemics and personal calumnies against Dr. Glueck were unrestrained. Yet Glueck prevailed, even over the threat of Rabbi Yekutiel Halberstam, who told Prime Minister David Ben Gurion that the Orthodox Jews of Jerusalem were prepared to go all out to prevent the introduction of Reform services, even to the point of open war.

The establishment of the Hebrew Union College Synagogue, with its indigenous service, has served as the spiritual center for Progressive Judaism in Israel, and continues to do so. Thousands of Israelis and non-Israelis alike have worshipped within its walls, participating in religious services that are read from Siddurim and Maḥzorim especially written for the College's services in Jerusalem.

In 1971, I developed at our Jerusalem School an intensive Jewish Studies program leading to the ordination of Israelis as rabbis for the Progressive Movement in Israel. To date, three young men have been ordained, and eight others are presently in the course of study.

Dr. Tabory does, however, point to certain abiding questions which require continuous study and clarification, namely, what is to be the continuing, identifiable core that will differentiate Reform Progressive Judaism in Israel from the other more dominant Jewish religious experience there. I am not at all concerned that Reform Judaism will remain the smallest of the religious movements in Israel for a time to come. It was that when Isaac Mayer Wise founded it in America. I am concerned, however, that Progressive Judaism retain a distinctive nature so as not to permit its classification as being "less" than the other contemporary religious expressions in Israel. It certainly will be different. It is undeniably a correct assertion to hold that Progressive Judaism in Israel cannot be solely imparted as an ideology; neither can Conservative Judaism. It must develop along indigenous lines, and it must engage in a process of continuing self-definition. The greatest asset, and problem, of Progressive Judaism is that it is non-dogmatic in nature; that it appeals to voluntary rather than compulsory belief; that it is, in fact, concerned with the larger world in which it finds itself and does not merely attempt to replicate narrow-gauged ritualistic expressions of the various Jewish Orthodoxies afloat in Israel today.

What has distinguished the Reform Movement outside of Israel, and in Israel as well, has been its concern for the dimension of social justice in particular. As a religious grouping in Israel, it is unique in that respect. That passion is, in fact, its appeal to the various kibbuz movements which have expressed interest in developing a variation of Progressive Judaism of their own.

One aspect regarding Progressive Judaism which continues to intrigue me is that despite our relatively small numbers in Israel, which I believe are growing, the quality of the person who is attracted to the Progressive Movement in Israel is quite compelling. The profile I find is that of an intellectual, caring Jew, wishing to enter the lifestream of Judaism on some significant level for him/ or her/self. The younger generation reflects an individual who comes with more questions than we have answers, interested less in organizational affiliation than in intellectual and spiritual stimulation. It is from this group that we receive continuing moral and spiritual support.

The Reform and Conservative Movements in Israel have, in the current government coalition, their most implacable foes and opponents. Bellicose advertisements in Israeli newspapers indicating that Israelis have not fulfilled their religious obligations if they worship in a Conservative synagogue for the holydays is but a showpiece example of this hostility and obstructionism. If our Conservative brethren were even more committed to halakhah, it still would not matter to the Orthodox whether they were Conservative or Reform. As far as they are concerned, we are both intrinsically *tref*. It is incumbent upon Jews of the Diaspora, particularly the American Diaspora, to place counter pressure on the Israeli government to avert even more serious incursions in our religious freedom and the hard-won status quo, tenuous as it may seem, that we now have.

I believe that the Reform and Conservative Movements in Israel will share a common destiny. One will not flourish at the expense of the other. Both will either find a solid rooting or both will eventually blow away. My own conviction is that both will find solid rooting but will, of necessity, remain limited in size, unless the movements can find a way to make inroads into the large Sephardic sector of the Israeli population through a conscious and strenuous effort of outreach. I also believe that the Russian-Jewish immigration provides a rich opportunity for the Conservative and Reform Movements to win for Judaism the members of this aliyah who, by and large, reject Orthodoxy and who would, I think, be responsive to an integrated modernist approach to Judaism.

I strongly disagree with Dr. Tabory when he states, "It is the relative failure of Reform Judaism to make a greater impact in Israel that has led it to undergo introspection to determine for what it stands." I think that the case is just the contrary. Because Reform Judaism has had an impact, however one defines that, it has led to introspection not only among its own adherents but among other Jews as well and to the probing of the direction of Judaism in the so-called totally Jewish society which is Israel. There is no question, however, that Reform Judaism has not yet nurtured a sabra who is a Reform theologian, capable of addressing the Israeli mind in a compelling and articulate manner; neither has the Conservative Movement. Sadder yet is that it is especially true of the Orthodox Movement which, despite its brandishing of secular power, has not developed in this generation a great spirit and moral personality such as Rav Kook.

It must further be pointed out that the Reform Movement in the last decade has made an extraordinary effort to create a new center for its spiritual being. The World Union for Progressive Judaism has its headquarters at the Hebrew Union College in Israel. The College itself has initiated a rabbinic training program, as well as other programs, that will prepare lay leadership for an indigenous Reform Judaism for Israel. The Reform Movement, in establishing its rabbinic and teacher training institution, is laying a sure and stable foundation for the future of its Movement in Israel.

Cooperative ventures with the Conservative Movement from time to time have been effected, but largely in areas of political action and not in joint cultural or religious activities. There still seems to be the notion among Conservative Jews that a full-blown association with the Reform Movement will stigmatize it and prevent its own development. The more numerous Conservative congregations, comprised largely of Americans, Canadians and American Conservative rabbis who have made aliyah to Israel, present a special enclave in Israel today. The question is whether aliyah can sustain that growth or whether the Conservative Movement also must give thought to creating its own religious leadership in Israel predominantly for Israelis and not for Americans who have made aliyah.

If Conservative Judaism, as well as Reform, is not to remain a flash phenomenon of a first generation of immigrants, it will have to secure stronger foundations than now exist with respect to its future growth and development. Both Movements have an extraordinary mission — one I believe to be nothing less than securing Judaism in acceptable garb for Jews living in modernity who want to remain religious but who do not wish to be Orthodox. Such a Judaism is in process in Israel, perhaps inchoate in form to our eyes at the moment, but moving with sure steps to definition.

Judaism and the Land of Israel

ARTHUR HERTZBERG

AS A POLITICAL FACT THE STATE OF ISRAEL IS a unique creation. Though its legal existence has been recognized by all of the major powers and by most other states, all of its immediate neighbors, the six Arab states on its borders, continue to insist that its presence in the Middle East is a political and moral affront of such magnitude that it entitles them to try to effect its destruction. There have been many revolutions in the twentieth century in the name of national self-determination; Israel is the only example of a new state created by a largely non-resident people returning to the homeland of its ancestors.

In our century the tendency of political states, both old and new, has been to conceive of themselves as secular arrangements which represent no particular religious tradition. The State of Israel is indeed largely secular. For that matter, one of the avowed purposes of its creators was to make it possible for Jews to lead completely secular lives as Jews, within their own polity. Nonetheless, Israel was created by Jews to be, and to remain, an essentially Jewish State, that is, to represent something more than a conventional, secular, political arrangement to serve the needs of its individual citizens of whatever condition or provenance. This mystique pervades even the secularists in Israel and is deeply felt among the majority of the Jews of the world, regardless of the nature of their religious convictions or commitments. The multiplicity of often clashing forms of life and value appears, from this perspective, to be the confusion of creativity, the necessary turmoil which attends the effecting of a synthesis between the old and the new. The present is seen as an age of becoming, and the sometimes even bitter internal conflicts of the moment are part of some larger harmony. The national mood in Israel is one of attempting to encounter the twentieth century in terms of its own historic tradition.

The most unusual characteristic of the life of Israel today is its connection with the Jewish community of the world. This theme was stated by one of its earliest constitutional acts, the Law of Return, under which any Jew is a citizen of the State of Israel from the moment of his arrival as an immigrant. Such a law is not entirely unprecedented among modern irredentist movements, but the whole complex of connections between the State of Israel and the world Jewish community is, indeed, unique. Support, both moral and financial, by the majority of the Jews outside of its borders is critically necessary to the development of Israel. The State of Israel regards itself, and is universally regarded, as the

ARTHUR HERTZBERG *is Rabbi of Temple Emanuel, Englewood, N.J. and a lecturer in the Graduate History Department of Columbia University.*

spokesman for some Jewish interests, such as the rights of the Jews of the Soviet Union, which are not immediately related to its own position and which, sometimes, in terms of narrowest self-interest, Israel would be best off avoiding. The leadership of Jerusalem remains dedicated to the task of helping to preserve Jewish loyalty and consciousness among the Jews on all five continents.

It is too narrow and even unjust to view this concern as the desire of an embattled nation to keep alive a maximum reservoir of good will and support or even, ultimately, of potential new immigrants. The preservation of the Jewish spirit is the fundamental purpose for which the State was conceived by its founders, and this commitment is even more important than the immediate needs which the Jewish settlement in the Holy Land has served during this tragic century, as the major place to which Jewish refugees from persecution could come as of right and not as an act of foreign grace. In turn, the Jews of the world look upon Israel as the major contemporary incarnation of many of their own hopes for continuity. The depth of the emotion which Israel evokes among them is, to be sure, affected by recent memories of Auschwitz. Israel is, indeed, in its very strength, a symbol of the end of Jewish passivity and lack of power to resist slaughter; it does represent an open door for Jews who do not easily, in this present age, trust anyone else but themselves with the keys to their safety. At the very root, however, Israel, and the world Jewish concerns which help sustain it, are both based on some of the grand and ancient themes of Jewish religion and of Jewish history. One cannot understand the present unless it is viewed as both a contemporary re-evocation of elements of faith and hope peculiar to Judaism and, paradoxically, as a contemporary tension between this older outlook and newer modes of thought and life.

II.

All of the elements of Jewish religious consciousness were present and, indeed, defined, in the very first encounter, in the Biblical narrative, between the One God and Abraham. The account needs to be recalled, both for what it affirms and for what it excludes: "And God said to Abram, go forth from your land and from your place of birth and from the house of your father to the land which I will show you. And I will make of you a great people and I will bless you and make your name great; and be a blessing." In the next verse the last promise is amplified: "and all the families of the earth will be blessed through you." Abraham obeyed the command and entered the land, where the One God appeared to him, reiterating and amplifying the promise: "and to your children I will give this land" (Gen. 12:1–3). In these encounters Abraham was taken away from all of his original relationships. Community, land and even the family within which he arose, all represent ties which were broken for a fresh beginning, a covenant with the Lord, in which a new community was to be created which Abraham was to found. It was to arise in a particular place, the land of Canaan, which had been set aside for the authentic encounter between the seed of Abraham and the God who founded their community. The life of this community in this land was to exist for a purpose: to demonstrate to all other people how human life is to be lived at its most moral. The implication already exists in the original sending that any falling away from such a standard will represent a breach in the covenant and a defilement of holy soil. Exile is already conceivable as punishment and the ultimate return is already in view as laden with messianic meaning, of redemptive quality for Jews and for mankind.

One can skip the centuries and quote a modern writer from almost our own time, to find these most ancient themes reappearing essentially as they were first pronounced. Solomon Schechter wrote in 1906, in New York: "The selection of Israel, the indestructibility of God's covenant with Israel, the immortality of Israel as a nation, and the final restoration of Israel to Palestine, where the nation will live a holy life on holy ground, with all the wide-reaching consequences of the conversion of humanity and the establishment of the Kingdom of God on earth—all these are the common ideals and the common ideas that permeate the whole of Jewish literature extending over nearly four thousand years."

Both as a fact and as a promise the relationship of Jews to the land of Israel thus appeared as an indispensable element in the original covenant. Jerusalem appears later, at the time of David. It is clear from both of the Biblical accounts of its conquest, in Samuel and in Chronicles, that making the city into the capital is the act which set the seal on the creation of the Jewish Kingdom. The city did not belong to any individual tribe, not even to the tribe of Judah: "And David and all Israel went to Jerusalem" (I Chronicles 14:4), thus acquiring it by action of the entire people and making of it the place to which all Israel would turn. It certainly does not need to be demonstrated that all of the Biblical writers looked to Jerusalem as the essence of the meaning of their faith, life and hope. In the later years of the existence of the Second Temple, Jerusalem was the center of pilgrimage not only for the Jews in the Land of Israel but also for the increasingly scattered Diaspora. The evidence for this is to be found in all the literature of the period, in Josephus (*Wars* I, 4, 13), Philo (*Laws* 1, 68) and the New Testament (*Acts of the Apostles* 2:5). The literature of the Talmud is, of course, laden with accounts of masses from all the Jewish world coming to the Temple, especially to celebrate the Passover. There is a tale, no doubt exaggerated, that on one Passover, King Agrippa had the priests count the number of paschal lambs that had been offered up and he found that the total exceeded 1,200,000 (*Pesaḥim* 64b). It is well known that in those days, in the century before its destruction by the Romans, the Temple was visited by gentiles as well as by Jews and there is Talmudic evidence that in the sacrificial cult there was regular provision for acts of prayer and atonement for all of the "seventy nations" of the world.

The connection between Jews and the land was not broken by the Exile. By the third century, the Babylonian Jewish community had begun to overshadow the one which remained in the land under the Romans, and yet Babylonian authorities ruled, as firmly as those in the Holy Land, that either party to a marriage could force the other, by appeal to Rabbinic courts, to move from the Diaspora to the Land of Israel (*Ketubot* 110b). Dwelling in the land remained, in the view of most of the later Rabbinic authorities, a Biblical commandment of continuing validity, and those of the medieval writers who did not insist on this as a religious good absolved themselves and the people of their generation because of the dangers to life that the journey involved (*Responsa* of R. Isaiah Trani II, 25). This point is perhaps best made by quoting a tale from the third century: Two rabbis were once on their way out of the Land of Israel to Nisibis, where the great teacher, R. Judah ben Batyrah, dwelt, to learn Torah from him. They got as far as Sidon and there they remembered the Land of Israel. They began to weep, they rent their garments, and they remembered the Biblical verses which promised the land to the seed of Abraham. The rabbis turned around and went back to their place in the land, pronouncing that dwelling in the Land of Israel is, in itself, an act equal of religious significance to all of the Commandments in the Torah (*Sifrei, Re'eh*).

In aspiration and in memory the connection of Jews with the land was, thus, not broken by the Exile. On the contrary, the destruction of the Temple and of the Holy City, Jerusalem, and the absence of Jews from their land, were regarded as a punishment. Life outside of the Holy Land was possible for Jews, but it was less than the full life, in perfect obedience to God, which could happen only with physical restoration. What has increasingly appeared with the progress of historical research in the last century is that these religious commitments were more than merely visionary. Some Jews continued to remain in the land even during the most dangerous and disastrous times and in every century there were returns to it, sometimes by small handfuls of leading spiritual figures and, on occasion, by substantial communities.

In the early centuries of the common era, access to Jerusalem, itself, was denied to Jews, though there is some evidence that the Roman emperors of the second century and the one thereafter did permit them to visit the city and to worship on the Mount of Olives and, sometimes, even on the Temple Mount itself. The situation became even more difficult by the fourth century, and there is contemporary evidence from

Christian sources that Jews had the greatest difficulty in buying the right to come to pray near the Western Wall, at least on the Ninth of Ab, the anniversary of the destruction of the Temple. The Pilgrim from Bordeaux, the earliest Christian visitor whose written account of his visit to Jerusalem has survived, tells that in the year 333 Jews came every year to that site to "bewail themselves with groans, rend their garments, and so depart" (*The Bordeaux Pilgrim*, pp. 21–22). There are comparable accounts by the Church Father, Gregory of Nazianzus (*Orat VI de pace*, p. 91), and by Jerome, in his commentary to Zephaniah written in the year 392 (*Migne, Patrologia*, XXV, Col. 1354). But with the end of Roman rule in Palestine the prohibition against Jews living in Jerusalem was lifted, and after that there is evidence for an often flourishing Jewish community in that city. During the Crusades the great traveler, Petaḥiah of Regensburg, was in Jerusalem in the years 1180–1185, and he reports that at the time there was only one Jew, a dyer, resident there, but after the era of the Crusades the community began to rebuild.

It is instructive in this connection that, ever since 1844, a half-century before the first stirrings of modern Zionism, Jerusalem has been the one city in the Holy Land which has consistently had a Jewish majority in its population. According to the 1844 edition of the *Encyclopedia Britannica* the population figures of the time were 7,120 Jews, 5,530 Moslems and 3,390 Christians, and all of them lived within the walled city. By 1896, when much of the Jewish population was already outside the wall but the city as a whole was still a unit, there were more than 28,000 Jews and some 17,000 Christians and Moslems, combined into roughly equal halves (*Luaḥ Eretz Yisrael*, 1896). The first government census by the British, that of October, 1922, found almost 34,000 Jews and about 38,000 Moslems and Christians in the whole of the city. Even at that point, with the Jewish population growth taking place entirely outside the wall, there were still 5,639 Jews in the Old City itself. In 1931, Jews were a majority of 51,000 in the city out of a total population of 90,000, while by 1939 the Jewish population of all of Jerusalem was an even more pronounced majority. However, almost two decades of riots and pogroms by Arabs against Jews in the Old City had made it a dangerous place in which to live, and Jewish numbers in the Old City itself had declined to something over 2,000.

In the last two millennia of its history Jerusalem has been the most dangerous and difficult place for Jews to dwell in of any of the cities of the Holy Land, yet this sampling of population figures is evidence that physical connection to the city remained so precious to Jews that they were willing, throughout the ages, to risk the dangers and to submit to the suffering. All of the chronicles and contemporary accounts of the Middle Ages substantiate the import of the figures for the last century:

whenever the barest possibility existed, even under hostile powers, enough Jews were to be found to cleave to Jerusalem so that, across the centuries, theirs was the largest continuing presence there. Memories of the past, messianic hopes for the future, and modern Zionism in all its contemporaneity are, indeed, the heirs of the major continuing physical connection with that city.

This clinging by Jews to Jerusalem, even more than to the whole of the rest of the Holy Land, is no accident; it has the deepest roots in the continuing religious tradition and folk consciousness of Jews. It is "the city which I have chosen unto me" (I Kings 11:36) and the one "upon which my name is called" (II Kings 21:4). It was, of course, the place where the Temple stood, the seat of God's presence, even though the heaven and the heaven of heavens could not contain Him. In the imagery of prophecy Zion and Jerusalem are often parallel to all of Israel; both these names are often used to represent not only the whole of the people but also all of its land. For example, "Speak unto Zion, you are my people" (Isaiah 51:16) or "Comfort ye, comfort ye, my people; speak to the heart of Jerusalem" (Isaiah 40:1). The synagogue poets of late ancient and medieval times made much of these themes, and of the hundreds of examples that could be given, the most famous is also the most characteristic. Writing in Spain in the eleventh century, Judah Halevi cries out: "Zion, wilt thou not ask after the peace of thy captive children?" Ironically, this poet and philosopher ended his life as a pilgrim in the Holy Land, where he was killed soon after his arrival.

In the daily prayers of Jews to this day, one of the benedictions of the silent devotion is a prayer for the rebuilding of Jerusalem; that paragraph represents the hope for the restoration of Jews to the Holy Land as a whole. In the grace which Jews say after every meal, morning, noon and night, the third benediction reads: "And rebuild Jerusalem, the holy city, speedily and in our day; blessed art thou, O Lord, who builds Jerusalem." All synagogues throughout the Jewish world, from the first one in antiquity to those being erected this very day, have been built in such fashion that they face towards Jerusalem. Its very name has always evoked the memory of a time when all was well, when Jews lived on their land and worshipped God in His holy temple, and the hope for the day when some of this glory would return. To be buried on the Mount of Olives, no matter where one dies, has been regarded for two millennia as the surest hope of the Resurrection, and bodies were being returned from Rome some 2,000 years ago for that purpose. To kiss the stones of Jerusalem, even in its destruction, was to be as close to God as man could be. To participate in its rebuilding was the hope of the ages.

In the Holy Land, as a whole, the Jewish presence after the fourth century was, in terms of numbers, of relatively lesser importance. Nonetheless, the realities of Jewish history during the nineteen centuries of the Exile are misstated if there is no emphasis on the important existence of Jewish communities in the land itself throughout the centuries. The Talmud of Jerusalem was created by important schools of Jewish learning in the Holy Land, and these declined only in the fourth and fifth century under Christian persecution. The fixing of the vocalization of the Hebrew Bible, the Masoretic Text, was done by Jewish scholars in Tiberias between the eighth and tenth centuries. At that time, and for the next century or so, both the Karaites and the followers of the Talmudic tradition had important communities in the Holy Land, and, for a while, around the year 1000, academies of rabbinic learning were reconstituted in Jerusalem and Ramleh. These were of such consequence that they shared leadership in the Jewish world, as a whole, with the schools in Babylonia, though the Babylonian academies had by then, enjoyed an uninterrupted tradition of almost a millennium. Even under the Crusaders, Jewish communities continued to exist in the cities of Acre and Ashkelon as well as in a variety of other places, particularly a number of villages in the Galilee, in several of which Jews have dwelt without interruption since before the destruction in the year 70 c.e.

At the beginning of the thirteenth century there came the first organized attempt by Jews in Europe to return to the Holy Land, when three hundred rabbis of France and England came there. Some of these men were of the highest intellectual rank. Naḥmanides left Spain after an unfortunate disputation in Barcelona, which was forced upon him by Pablo Christiani, and spent the last three years of his life from 1267 to 1270, reconstituting a Jewish community in Jerusalem. Towards the end of the fifteenth century, the almost equally important Obadiah of Bartinora, the author of the standard commentary on the Mishnah, left Italy for the Holy Land and he, too, reinvigorated the Jewish community in Jerusalem.

From the beginning of the sixteenth century, there was an important growth of the Jewish population in the Galilee and, especially, in the town of Safed. Exiles from Spain, after the final expulsion of Jews in 1492, arrived in the country in some numbers and within a century there were no less than eighteen academies of Talmudic studies and twenty-one synagogues in Safed alone. Indeed, the most important spiritual stirrings and creativity within Jewry during the sixteenth century took place there. There was even an abortive attempt to reconstitute the authority of the ancient patriarchate, which had lapsed under Roman persecution. The studies of both Kabbalah and Talmud were pursued with renewed creative élan, and it was in Safed, in 1567, that Josef Karo published the *Shulḥan Arukh* which was almost immediately accepted by the bulk of world Jewry as the authoritative summation of Jewish law and practice.

Until the end of the seventeenth century, the overwhelming majority of the Jews in the Holy Land were either Sephardim, of Spanish extraction, or Orientals. Central and East European influence, however, became prominent in the year 1700, and has existed in unbroken continuity into the contemporary era. A group of several hundred people arrived from Poland under the leadership of Rabbi Judah the Pious, and even though the destiny of this community was not a happy one, these immigrants were followed by others. Toward the end of the eighteenth century there were disciples of Elijah of Wilno, the greatest Talmudic scholar of the age, as well as a major group of relatives and other followers of his great antagonist, the founder of Ḥasidism, Israel Baal Shem Tov. Both legalists and ecstatics within East European Jewry could not then imagine the continuity of Judaism without a living link to the soil of the Holy Land.

Throughout these centuries economic conditions in the country were generally difficult, and the Jews suffered perhaps more than did other communities. Those in the Holy Land were constantly sending letters and even personal emissaries to their brethren in the Diaspora asking for support, and one of the prime sources of our knowledge of medieval and early modern Jewish history is in what remains of these exchanges. It was a well established tradition throughout the Jewish world that these continuing requests from their brethren in the Holy Land took priority even over local charitable needs.

The Jews in the Holy Land were, to be sure, living largely from foreign alms, and in this they were seemingly parallel to Christian pilgrims and monastic orders in the land during that era. But there were two important points of difference: Jews who came to the Holy Land did not cluster around a variety of holy places, for from Jewish perspective, dwelling in the land, anywhere, was the fulfillment of religious commandment. In the second place, their very presence in the land had radically different resonance among the Jews of the world than the Christian or Moslem presences had among their brethren elsewhere. This often embattled and struggling Jewish community, repeatedly reinforced by new arrivals and always in connection with the whole of the Diaspora, was a constant reminder to the majority that it was living less than the ideal religious life and that return to the land was the ultimate goal. Maimonides, in the twelfth century, had defined this consummation as not necessarily an eschatological event attended by miracles and cataclysms. The restoration would happen in a natural way, by a change in the political situation which would allow Jews to return to their homeland as part of a universal process ushering in a final age of justice and peace. This view did not become the dominant one, for Messianists continued to dream of a cataclysmic "end of days."

Hopes of immediate return were aroused more than once through the ages. For a brief moment in the sixteenth century, when the melodramatic David Reubeni appeared in Rome to offer some supposed military support to Pope Clement VII against the Turks, there was even talk of such a restoration in the highest Christian quarters. The false messiah Shabbetai Zvi had half the Jewish world, and even some Christians, convinced that the miraculous restoration would take place in the year 1666. During Napoleon's campaign in the Middle East in 1799, he summoned the Jews to rally to his banner with the promise that he would help restore them to their land. We know that this offer resulted from some conversation with younger elements of Jewry in the Holy Land. For that matter, the first stirrings towards making an end of living essentially on alms began before the middle of the nineteenth century. Sir Moses Montefiore, the leader of English Jewry, and various forces of the French Jewish community, especially the Rothschild family, worked to teach Jews in Palestine to become artisans and even farmers. Central European philanthropists even created a school for these purposes in 1854 in Jerusalem. It was followed in 1870 by the founding of an agricultural school, Mikveh Israel, and within the next two years two Jewish farm colonies were established. The career of modern Zionism began in 1881, as a direct result of large scale pogroms in Russia, but already in that year, before any of the new immigration to the land began, the American Consul in Jerusalem, Warder Cresson, wrote to his government that there were then a thousand Jews in the country who were deriving their livelihood from agriculture.

III.

This ancient and ongoing connection to the land and the messianic hopes which this connection both exemplified and helped to keep in being were the spiritual and emotional climate within which modern Zionism arose. In the immediate situation of the last decades of the nineteenth century the bulk of the world Jewish community, which was then to be found in Europe, found itself confronted by three situations. The most searing and immediate was virulent hatred of Jews, and not only in their major place of settlement in Russia. While millions were on the move from that country after 1881, it occurred to several of the intellectual leaders of Russian Jewry that in their newer homes these emigrants might ultimately be as much in danger as they had been in the places from which they were fleeing. Such phenomena as French and German anti-Semitism towards the end of the century raised the question whether the more liberal part of Europe, in which Jews had been formally emancipated, would honor, in bad times, the promise of equality for all.

In the second place, what seemed then to be the most hopeful of contemporary political ideas was the example of those peoples who were working toward their own national independence. Liberal nationalism was being proclaimed, not in the name of dominance over others, but of a creative future for all the historic communities which would be both autonomous and live in concert with each other. This was the great dream of Mazzini, and the earliest major theoretician of Zionism, Moses Hess, responded to it as early as 1860 with acceptance and profound emotion.

The third situation, and the one perhaps most difficult to define, was the inner spiritual estate of Jewry itself. The dissolution of older values and identities, and especially of the religious, which was engulfing the younger intellectuals of all the traditions of the Western world, was felt with particular poignancy among Jews. The new age was revolutionary and upsetting of the older faiths, but for the Christian majority the continent of Europe, its monuments and most of what men had built on that soil, and its very languages represented the continuity of Christendom. The revolution was occurring for Christians in a context which could ultimately assimilate even these tensions into some new synthesis. But from the Jewish viewpoint, though Western secularity required an act of personal conversion to the mode of life which descended from the majority tradition, those Jews who were willing to undergo this conversion, such as Heine and Disraeli, found themselves less than completely accepted. The nineteenth century, thus, taught some Jews that it had been possible for them to be authentically themselves in the century before, while still in the ghetto, apart from society, whereas in the new, half-emancipated age that followed, it was much more difficult to find their own mode of encountering modernity, either as individuals or as part of their own historic community. The nineteenth century was sufficiently open to Jews, intellectually, for them to experience all of its problems; it was sufficiently closed to deny them the possibility, even if they had wished, to disappear as individuals in modern society. They remained sufficiently rooted in their own older heritage to regard their community as an ultimate spiritual good, worthy of both survival and inner refreshing. They were sufficiently men of their day to feel that their own involvement in their particular past and in the land sacred to their spiritual tradition was in keeping with the contemporary belief that historic communities and peoples were worthy of preservation, for their own sake and for the service of humanity.

The tragedies and torments of the twentieth century and the achievements of the Jews of Israel have confirmed the direst of these predictions and some of the greatest of these hopes.

It cannot be emphasized enough that even the greatest of opportunities that the open society made available to Jews raised for them severe questions of spiritual survival. The rights of equality, wherever they have substantial meaning, were given to Jews as individuals, and the continuity of their community perforce had to be defined as a matter of private belief or, at its most organized, as a religious association parallel to that of contemporary Christian churches. From the Jewish perspective such redefinition, enshrined in the modern slogans of the separation of Church and State or of religion and culture, was a far more difficult and devastating charge than it was for the Christian majority in the Western world. For Jews, the holy congregation of all Israel, which means the reality in this world of all that Jews do in community, is the fundamental premise of their identity and tradition.

Classic Jewish interpretation of the Bible has always insisted that Israel "according to the flesh" is what is meant by Isaiah's prophecies concerning "the suffering servant." It is the individual Jew's experience of the Jewish people, of its corporate life, way and history which mediates for him between the individual and God. When the richness and inner integrity of the life of that community is attenuated by either persecution or assimilation, or when belonging to the tradition becomes so privatized as to represent a bewildering variety of personal choices, that which is specifically Jewish in the consciousness of Jews will act, as it had acted in the last century, to recreate a living Jewish community on the land of Israel. For the rest of world Jewry this community represents the indispensable contemporary center which ties Jews to one another and which encourages them to believe that their own lives, though cast in different molds and under minority circumstances, are viable. Its very creation some two decades ago represented a turning away from despair in the aftermath of the Nazi years and the rekindling among Jews of belief in the future. To use one of the clichés of the contemporary "theology of hope," the Jewish people in the 1940's had ceased believing in either the *humanum* or the *futurum*. It regained belief in both in 1948, when the State of Israel was established.

IV.

There can be no doubt that the Zionist reconstitution of a national Jewish community in Palestine in our time was an act which derived both from the ultimate well springs of the historic Jewish faith and from the immediate necessities of a stormy contemporary age. This does not mean that all the trappings of political statehood and all the acts of sovereign power are here being presented as commanded, valid or necessary. On the contrary, what saves any nationalism, any sense of historic community and kinship, from becoming exclusivist, from the arrogance of "blood and soil," is conscience. It is even more wicked to assert that there is no salvation outside one's own nation than to pronounce that there is no salvation outside one's own church. The conscience which protects us from both such assertions has become manifest in the modern age both in secular forms, such as the United Nations Declaration on Human Rights, and in religious pronouncements by all of the major Western faiths. This most fundamental of our moral convictions has as its source

Biblical prophecy. It was Amos who said to the Jewish people of his time that in the eyes of God, chosen though they were by Him, they had no more rights than the children of the Ethiopians, and that his bringing the Jews from Egypt was paralleled by his bringing the Philistines from Caftor and the Arameans from Kir. Here we are confronted by the universal element, the command of the living God of all the world, which enters as a radical demand into the midst of every human particularity and keeps it under judgment. Indeed, the meaning of community for Jews is that they live in the real world of action and choice, in this world, and the meaning of their chosenness is that they are subject to the most severe and searching of moral judgments: "Only you have I known from all the nations of the world; therefore, I will visit upon you all your iniquities" (Amos 3:2). For men of religion, indeed for all men of conscience, both elsewhere and in Israel, its acts, like those of any other people, are under judgment.

It needs to be remembered in this connection that the Zionist movement has itself, at least during part of its history, been of two minds about the demand for a sovereign Jewish state. Statehood, as such, was not even in the Zionist program from the days of the Balfour Declaration in 1917 until almost all the Zionists, with the doors of Palestine completely closed to Jews, had little choice but to opt for sovereignty in 1948.

In accepting, in 1917, the last reformulation of the Balfour Declaration, Weizmann and his colleagues knew that they were agreeing to some form of bi-national existence with the Arabs in Palestine. This was all clearer in the exchanges of 1919 between the Emir Feisal and both Felix Frankfurter and Chaim Weizmann. It was against any increase in Jewish numbers in Mandate Palestine, and not against a Jewish State, that Arabs made riots in 1921. For that matter, the repeated stoppages in Jewish immigration by the British authorities under Arab pressure, especially during the 1930's while Hitler was becoming an ever more murderous menace, was what made it clear to the Jews that any increase in their numbers, any possibility of having the legal right to buy land, or even the ultimate safety of their community could not be left to the good will of others, of which there was all too little. From the Jewish perspective, partition, and even statehood, were not hoped-for consummations but, rather, dire necessities. For that matter, even the very military might of Israel is less a source of pride and of national chauvinism than of fear of the constantly threatened destruction. It is certainly beyond doubt that the present choice of Israel is either its own sovereignty or its ceasing to exist, not only as a state, but also as a community. What is equally true is that, for the continuity of Judaism and of Jews, the State of Israel is today a prime necessity for all men who care that the Jewish ethos should flourish and make its own kind of contribution to all of mankind.

Israeli Imperatives and Jewish Agonies
IRVING LOUIS HOROWITZ
and MAURICE ZEITLIN

THE THOROUGHNESS OF THE ISRAELI MILITARY success over the combined efforts of the Arab states raises more problems than it resolves. Indeed, before the month of victory, June 1967, let out, the defeated were making all sorts of demands, and the winners were making all sorts of concessions. As Israeli Foreign Minister Abba Eban wryly remarked: "This is the only war in history where the victors sued for peace and the vanquished demanded unconditional surrender."

The David-and-Goliath imagery is weakened by the extraordinary thoroughness of the defeat of the Arab armies. Numbers do not add up to power. The many were beaten by the technologically sophisticated few. The politically oriented army was defeated by the professionally competent army. Arab states without a sense of nationhood were beaten by the Israeli nation they had not accorded the legitimization of statehood. These are not simply scholastic paradigms but a set of outcomes that illustrate the continued ambiguity of Israel's political context, however decisive its military success. This ambiguity extends to the political reaction of world Jewry to the Israeli victory. This could hardly have been otherwise, since the Jewish people have been marginal members, with multiple loyalties, of all states throughout recent history, whereas in Israeli society this situation has been entirely reversed: not only is Israel a Jewish state, but the Israelis have come to behave as marginal members of the international Jewish community, despite Israel's constant protestations of concern for that community.

1. Ambiguities in the Israeli Victory

THE VICTORY OF THE ISRAELI ARMY in June 1967 may be the great historical watershed separating the Jew and the Israeli. In place of the Jew as victim stands the Jew as victor. Paradoxically, it is this very victory on the battlefield, the vision of the Jew as military strategist and citizen-soldier, that has caused widespread reactions not of joy but of hostility among statesmen, intellectuals, men of the left, right, and center. The Jew as aggressor, as *Real*-politician, as "imperialist," has both replaced and fused with the usual stereotypes in the lexicon of

---

IRVING LOUIS HOROWITZ *is a professor of sociology at Washington University in St. Louis and senior editor of* Trans-Action. *He is director of Studies in Comparative International Development, and the author of, among other works,* Three Worlds of Development. MAURICE ZEITLIN, *associate professor of sociology at the University of Wisconsin, is the author of* Revolutionary Politics and the Cuban Working Class, *and (with Robert Scheer)* Cuba: Tragedy in Our Hemisphere.

hostile images of the Jews. Tragically, this new lexicon is restricted not to the big-power statesmen, whether British, American, or Soviet, but finds its most vociferous voices in representatives of the newly independent ex-colonial and even revolutionary régimes.

Anti-Semitism was once, as August Bebel called it, the "socialism of fools." Now anti-Zionism performs the same role. Zionists once dreamed that the territorial concentration of the Jewish people in Palestine, their historic homeland, would abolish the conditions of insecurity and hostile surroundings in which they were compelled to live while in the *Galut*. But the concrete reality is that of a small nation caught in the conflicts of the Cold War, and trapped into becoming the cement between the legitimate national aspirations of the Arabs and régimes which misrepresent and pervert these aspirations.

The "Jewish Revolution" of our times is the profound distinction between nationalism and cosmopolitanism, or, perhaps, Zionism and Judaism. The Israeli authorities have shown the same contempt for those choosing to ignore or minimize the importance of territorial imperatives that the Soviets have displayed for "rootless cosmopolitans"— their special language for Diaspora Jews.

There is a sense in which the radical has reacted to Israeli victory not as a problem in Jewish identity, so much as a problem of identifying with victory itself. For the current behavior of Israel is notably that of a matured nation. On the battlefield, in the United Nations debates, in various policy utterances, Israelis have definitely not behaved like representatives of a "small nation" or an "underdeveloped nation." Like any big power, Israel insists on the geographic spoils of victory. She desires a rationalization of her boundaries: the Jordan River, the Straits of Tiran, the Suez Canal. She insists that the rights of her citizenry take precedence over the rights of Arab refugees. She desires not just *de facto* gains but *de jure* status, i.e., the recognition by the Arab states of Israeli legitimacy. In such insistence, in the act of forging a united national front from within, Israel's military victory has fractured its support abroad. For if radicals, particularly those dedicated to a "thermonuclear pacifist" position, are discomfited by military success, the ruling conservative elements—and here we can include the established positions of ambivalence taken by the United States and the United Kingdom, as well as the anti-Israeli militance pursued by the Soviet Union in the United Nations debates—are self-righteously indignant over a state daring to lay claim to big-power status by the use of classical big-power techniques of armed violence. The United States is markedly ambivalent toward the Israeli military victory—for while the U.S. does not suffer any immediate loss of influence in the Near East, it clearly places the Americans on the periphery rather than at the center of policy-making in the area.

Both radical and reactionary critics of Israel's military victory have sensed, rather than articulated, that a new nation has been born in 1967. The period between the writing of *The Jewish State* by Herzl and its actual creation was inconclusive, comprised as it was of a patchwork of bribes, land purchases, and hard labor. The Arabs could claim that Israel's existence was guaranteed first by the United Nations in 1947 and by Great Britain and France in the Suez debacle in 1956. The 1967 conflict, however, was comprised of Israeli military might and *Realpolitik*. To be sure, not even world Jewry was particularly convinced otherwise. Their great fears that the latest round of Arab threats and blockades would result in the decimation of Israel, and their consequent impulsive rallying to the Israel cause, even to the point of demanding United States armed intervention, indicate that the Soviets were not alone in their underestimation of Arab weakness and Jewish might. Now that Israel has become a realized state, a first-rate, albeit small power in the Middle East, the need for sovereignty rather than support could drive a wedge between Israel and Judaism that might be deeper than any in the past.

Beneath the current euphoria of troubled pride in a military victory gained by Jews, unparalleled since the legendary victory of the Maccabees in the pre-Christian era, is the fear that, far from unifying the Jewish people, Israel's recent victory will establish a relationship between Israel and Jews much like that between other nations and their own dispersed national minorities. The victory of Israel, if it endures, compels a re-evaluation by all sectors of world Jewry of its *freedom from* Israel, just as the defeat of Israel would have compelled re-evaluation of Jewish *responsibility to* Israel.

The problem of "dual loyalty" for the individual Jew tied to two nations was far more intimate before the Israeli victory. For the American Jew, a generalized sentiment in favor of kith and kin will now have to yield to the realization that Israel is a prime military force. The Soviet Jew, for his part, is faced with the greater dilemma that any show of support for Israel would even more likely be construed as anti-Soviet behavior. In other words, support for a powerful nation (other than one's own) is not the same as philanthropic underwriting of a poor nation.

It is a tragic fact that today's most vociferous, if not virulent, anti-Israel advocates are to be found (aside from those in the Arab world) in the governments of the Soviet Union, China, and Left-of-Center Third World nations. Anti-imperialists and revolutionaries seem at last to have found an issue on which they can unite. However, the coexistence of "dual loyalties" to the struggle against imperialism and to the national aspirations of oppressed and exploited peoples, whether they be Jew or Gentile, Arab or Israeli, African or Vietnamese, cannot allow us to stand by in silence.

It is a fact, to which many radicals are apparently impervious, that the "Arab world" contains within it not only such supposedly "progressive" régimes as the Nasserist Egyptian and the Ba'athist Syrian, but also the Hashemite monarchy of Jordan, ruled by King Hussein, and the feudal backwater of King Faisal in Saudi Arabia. Can revolutionaries legitimately ignore, nay deny, such facts while attacking Israel, a relatively democratic state built by its citizenry in the face of diplomatic, political, economic, and military harassment by its neighbors, as well as by the former colonial power dominant there, Great Britain? How, in the name of revolutionary politics, can a new state, mobilizing its citizenry to defend itself against a foreign aggressor and emerging victorious, be condemned by the very world that ordinarily would applaud such an event? This would be unfathomable were it not that neither the Cold War nor nationalism allow for political rationality.

2. Israel and Colonialism

ISRAEL'S INCONTROVERTIBLE RIGHT TO a peaceful national existence and her expedient alignment with the Western powers must be clearly distinguished. The ultimate and irreducible issue is whether Israel has the right to exist. The Arab position, in defeat or otherwise, has been clear and unequivocal. Is was stated by General Abdul Rahman Arif, Head of State and Government Chief of Iraq. "The existence of Israel," he said on June 28, 1967, "is in itself an aggression and must therefore be repulsed, and there must be a return to a normal situation." The Arab definition of "normality" is a Palestine without Israel. No matter how many times the Arabs have repeated these sentiments, there is resistance to taking them seriously. Perhaps this stems from the apparent distinctions they make between Israel and Jew, Zionism and Judaism.

This is not the place to argue neat ideological distinctions. The American Council on Judaism has made similar distinctions, and so has the Soviet government. In fact, probably a good many Jews living in the Diaspora would prefer a less strident definition of the complete Jew than provided by David Ben-Gurion—namely, to live in Israel. However strained the continued identification between Jews in exile and Jews in torment, the anti-Zionist view implies an eternal Diaspora without a temporal center. It implies a return to a condition of Jewish life in the interstices of society—monetary maneuvering, intellectual competition, and political dependence. The question is not whether the Jews can survive without an Israel; even granting that they could and would, the question has shifted from the *survival of* to the *quality of* Jewish life. This quality has been profoundly influenced by the Nazi experience of mass murder, the Soviet experience of betrayal, and the American experience of mindless absorption.

Even were the existence of the State of Israel to encourage negative tendencies in Jewish identity, should that mean that Jews have less right to a national state than Arabs do? Would the Moslem peoples be willing to entrust their survival to religious and cultural forms alone, without territorial reinforcements? The frequent Arab proclamations of sovereignty over Palestine indicate that to the Arab leaders Israel represents a national threat and not a religious or cultural threat. Indeed, Arab propaganda has sought to make this distinction central.

That the leaders of states themselves struggling for nationhood should attack another people's right to exist as a nation—a "people which," in Israeli Foreign Minister Abba Eban's eloquent words, "had given nationhood its deepest significance and its most enduring grace" —indicates only that incredible myths about Israel have been accepted as truth even by otherwise critical and independent minds, or subscribed to for reasons of *Realpolitik*. They would deny the right of national existence to a people almost destroyed in the gas chambers and ovens of Dachau, Buchenwald, and Auschwitz. They attack a state built by the labor and sacrifice of several generations of one of the most brutalized peoples history has known. They attack a state which, even at the termination of the war, when hundreds of thousands of refugees were homeless, ill, and spiritually destroyed, could not absorb the remnants of a murdered people without a life-and-death struggle for existence against the combined maneuvers of imperial England and the armies of corrupt feudal regimes. How can a nation be defined as beyond the pale once again, but this time by the very movements and régimes which claim to be leaders of national redemption and social liberation? There are so many issues intertwined in the Arab-Israeli conflict that it is necessary to re-examine fundamentals.

At the center are issues of colonialism and nationalism in all their manifestations. The truth about Israel is not so simple as the delegates assembled in Cairo early in July, representing fifty states, would have it. Is Israel a "treacherous aggressor" and the "spearhead of imperialism"? The question can be resolved into two parts: first, the connection between Israel and the struggles of the former colonial world for national sovereignty; and second, the role of colonialism in Israel's establishment. Was Israel, from its inception, an act of "aggression" and of colonialism? Does Israel constitute a European imperialist excrescence amidst the indigenous people of the Middle East, pushing them from their ancestral lands and exploiting those who remained? The historic facts cannot be reconciled with such a simplistic interpretation of Israel's birth.

The Soviet Union itself was able to put aside in this instance its own formulas, and recognize the historic right of the Jewish people to a homeland in Israel, and the great obligation of the United Nations to aid in that undertaking. The Soviet Union was the first to give Israel its *de jure* recognition, and its ally Czechoslovakia was Israel's major source of arms to defend itself against the invading feudal armies of the Farouks, Sauds and Husseins. Great Britain not only abstained from voting in favor of Israel's admission to the United Nations, it did all within its power, diplomatically and even militarily, to abort the new state before its birth and then to aid in "strangling it in its cradle." At the time of the Palestinian partition, Bartley C. Crum, a member of the Anglo-American Committee of Inquiry on Palestine, commented in his book, *Behind the Silken Curtain*, that

> Fully seventy per cent of the British colonial officials whom I met in Palestine were either, at worst, openly anti-Semitic, or, at best, completely unsympathetic and resentful toward Jewish hopes in Palestine. . . . [Britain placed] Palestine under the Colonial Office, with administrators taken from the ranks of the Colonial and Indian services, where their experience had been almost totally that of overlords dealing with subservient and illiterate natives.

It was Chamberlain who returned from Munich to announce that there would be "peace in our time"; the same Chamberlain was responsible for imposing limits on Jewish immigration into Palestine, for using British troops to prevent the early refugees from Nazism from entering Palestine, and for disarming and imprisoning members of the Jewish self-defense forces. He did so at the behest and under the pressure of the Grand Mufti and oppressive Arab régimes which were allies of the Nazis. Little wonder, then, that the present pious British attitude toward the "Jerusalem issue" is discounted by Israelis.

3. Arab Policies

IN THE 1930s ARAB TERRORISTS and "guerrillas" waged a continuous war against Jewish settlements in Palestine: arson, destruction of wells and of pipelines, and murder. Then as now they were part of the apparatus of "Arab liberation." It was with the active propaganda and financial support of the Nazis and Fascists that Haj Amin al-Husseini, Mufti of Jerusalem and Nazi propagandist, advocated mass murder of the Jews. Ahmed Shukeiry, present head of the so-called Palestine Liberation Organization, is a large landowner, an unmistakable heir of the revanchist chauvinism of the pro-Nazi Arab, who dares to proclaim himself leader of a national liberation struggle and offer "support" to the Vietnamese Liberation Front. One day the head of the reactionary Syrian delegation to the UN, another day leader of the Saudi Arabian delegation, on yet another day he heads "guerrilla war" against Israel, a war against individual citizens, with "guerrillas" who never dare attack a military force, a "guerrilla force" which is, in fact, not a guerrilla force at all but a band of mercenaries in the pay of a foreign power, Egypt. And Nasser? He has a dream of destruction, a dream which in June 1967 took the shape of a "final battle that will bring Israel's defeat. In this battle the dream of the Arabs to exterminate Israel will come true." This "progressive" has spoken of the *Protocols of the Elders of Zion* with favor, and his government has published a series of National Books, one of which bears the title *Talmudic Human Sacrifices*, resurrecting the blood-ritual myth. The rhetoric of anti-imperialism disguises an irrational messianic drive to destroy a neighboring country— a drive which, if successful, would inevitably lead to the murder of its citizenry. What sort of socialism encourages the publication and use of university texts in which such examples of "socialism" as "Hitler's German Socialism" (*Arab Society and Arab Socialism*) or the "Nazi experience in attempting to achieve progress and build the new society" (*On Socialist Society*) are offered, and in which Marxism is attacked "because Karl Marx decided to take as his starting point a certain social phenomenon, when the truth was that the problem existed inside man himself . . . " (*Arab Socialism*), and Marxism is "rejected root and branch as a purely materialistic philosophy" (*The July 23 Revolution*), preaching such "evils as equality between man and woman" (*The Arab Ideology*). Nor is this primarily a matter of ideological disputations. For the "anti-imperialist" leadership of Nasser continues to to inflict poison-gas warfare on his fellow-Arab Yemenis.

We are not concerned here with evaluating the Arab régimes which now claim to be "progressive" and "anti-imperialist." The fact is that they are not led by revolutionaries fighting for social justice. It is a delusion to think so. One would be entitled to such a private illusion were it not for its tragic public consequences. Moreover, even were these régimes engaged in the job of revolutionary construction at home, there would be no excuse for the irrational chauvinism that characterizes their leadership. Even the Israeli Communist Party was, in its electoral campaign for the Sixth Knesset, moved to denounce Nasser's "dangerous chauvinism which threatens the stability of the entire region," and to proclaim: "Let it be known that the Communist Party of Israel . . . will be the shield of Israel's existence . . . "

Just such anti-imperialists and revolutionaries as King Farouk of Egypt, Abdullah of Jordan, and Nouri Said of Iraq launched an unholy religious war in 1947-48 against Israel with the intention of "pushing her into the sea," an intention which has remained the constant pivot of Arab policy. Precisely this policy gave birth to the mass exodus of Arab refugees from Israel. The Arab Higher Committee ordered the evacuation, the Mufti instilled an ungovernable animus into the Arab masses via radio propaganda, alternately cajoling, threatening, and warning them to leave or suffer the consequences which would be worse than death. The Arab exodus was in part a planned evacuation for the temporary duration of the war, as part of Arab military strategy, and in part, perhaps mainly, a fear-driven flight from unreal horrors. The one genuine horror, the massacre at Deir Yassin of innocent Arab men, women, and children by Israeli Right-wing terrorists (whose perpetrators were severely condemned by Israel public opinion), came *after* the great exodus had begun—though obviously it served by word of mouth as an "example" of what awaited Arabs who tarried. In fact, many Israelis viewed the exodus with dismay and tried to stem it, urging the Arabs to remain, and guaranteeing them protection and security.

4. Jews in Palestine

NOR IS THE ARAB ATTACK ON ISRAEL understandable as an attempt to recover lands usurped by a foreign conqueror that had imposed his will on the indigenous peoples. Quite the contrary, it bears repetition that the Jewish people had not only maintaind their spiritual contact with Palestine throughout the centuries in the *Galut* but also that Jews have been continuously an indigenous, though a minority, population of Palestine. In some areas of the country, such as Peki'in in the Galilee, there are even families (about fifty of them) which trace their genealogy directly back to the Hebrews; in Jerusalem and Safed they were a majority throughout this century; and they formed substantial communities in Tiberias and Hebron. For centuries after the devastating defeat of the Jews by the Romans, in the last of a series of colonial revolts against the Assyrian and Roman Empires, the Jews constituted the major population of Palestine. When the majority of the Jewish people finally became dispersed throughout the world, it was the return to Palestine which acted as a major culturally unifying bond maintaining the national existence. This remote province of the Ottoman Empire remained a center of Jewish nationalism. In fact, the first great nationalist leader of the Arabs, Prince Feisal, in a famous letter to Justice Frankfurter, had wished "the Jews a most hearty welcome home" in 1919, recognizing their link to Palestine: "We Arabs," he said, "look with the deepest sympathy on the Zionist movement." In this much debated statement, he concluded by saying: "Our two movements complete one another. The Jewish movement is national and not imperialistic . . . Indeed, I think that neither can be a real success without the other."

Throughout the centuries Jewish inhabitants formed a persistent part of the population in Palestine. As the historian James Parkes points out: "Apart from neolithic survivals and the Copts in Egypt, Jews are the longest settled of the present identifiable inhabitants in some, and have lived longer in all the others [countries of the Middle East], than Arabs have in Palestine or Egypt." The Jewish presence and immigra-

ISRAELI IMPERATIVES & JEWISH AGONIES : 395

tion into Palestine was constant, though it became of greatest significance only in the twentieth century. At the turn of the century, eighteen per cent of the Palestinians were Jews; and by World War I the Jewish population of Palestine was already 100,000. If the Jews did not become an increasing proportion of the Palestinian population, it was because Arab immigration into Palestine outran even the Jewish immigration and was stimulated by the economic opportunities opened up in consequence of the one area in the Middle East undergoing rapid economic development. In the portion of Palestine which was to become the Jewish State under the UN Partition Plan, the Jews were an even greater part of the population. What is important is that Jews constituted a continuous minority within the area from the fall of the Second Commonwealth to the establishment of Israel. They were hardly strangers in Palestine. Moreover, fully sixty-five per cent of Israel's present population are *Arab* Jews—Jews from Morocco, Tunisia, Syria, Iraq, Yemen, Jordan, and other parts of the Middle East. Of the remaining thirty-five per cent an increasing number are indigenous *sabras*. This amounts to an exchange of Arab population along religious lines.

Nor did the presence of "European" Jews lead, as colonialism has always done, to the exploitation of the Arab masses. On the contrary, from its inception, immigration inspired by Zionism was imbued with an ethic of return to the soil, of a religion of labor, and, indeed, of socialism. The cardinal principle of the agricultural settlements, the *kibbutzim*, was the end of exploitation of man by man; they refused to hire workers, Jewish or Arab, preferring to build their communities entirely by their own collective labor. Obviously, Arab workers and peasants were exploited in Palestine, as they are in contemporary Israel, and as they are in any system employing wage labor in private firms producing for the profit of their owners. But the characteristic pattern of Jewish settlement in Palestine, while separatist in form, was anticolonial and non-exploitative in substance.

The land acquired by Jewish settlers was purchased from Arab landowners with money collected from hundreds of thousands of Jews contributing to the Jewish National Fund. Land became the collective property of the entire Jewish people. Much of it was barren swampland, owned by absentee sheikhs, and usually unpopulated. Where there were tenants, the Jewish National Fund made the extraordinary effort of compensating them with other land or money. That Jewish settlement proceeded in this way can be no more condemned than land acquired by Arab landlords, and certainly less so, given the use to which it was put. The class structure, in which a few sheikhs ruled the agrarian population, exploiting their labor and living comfortable lives in the cities on their "earnings" from lands tilled by subsistence peasantry in the villages of Palestine, was, in fact, increasingly altered as Jewish settlement and agricultural and industrial development impinged on the feudal ruling patterns.

When the State of Israel was established in 1948, Jews owned only 8.6 per cent of the land, and Israeli Arabs 3.3 per cent, with another 17 per cent abandoned by Arab owners. Seventy per cent of the land in Israel's part of Palestine, in fact, had been "Crown lands" owned by the British under the Mandate, taken from the crumbling Ottoman Empire, most of it in the Negev, a barren and uninhabited desert.

5. British Colonialism and Jewish Zionism

NOT ONLY WAS THE PATTERN OF JEWISH SETTLEMENT in Palestine non-colonial, it was, in fact, anti-colonial. The end of British rule in Palestine came largely as the result of the Zionist movement, Jewish settlement, and the Yishuv's (Palestinian Jewry) struggle against the British. Britain, the classic colonial power in the area, resisted the establishment of the Israeli State, abstaining from voting in favor of its admission to the UN, and doing all within its power until then to forestall independence. The British consistently opposed and thwarted Arab-Jewish attempts at *rapprochement,* inflaming Arab chauvinisim to defeat Arab and Jewish nationalism.

When the British Mandate came into effect in 1922, there were numerous meetings between Jews and Arabs at Cairo, Geneva, and London, to work out political and economic cooperation between them. Negotiations between representatives of the Zionist Executive (among them Chaim Weizmann, future President of Israel) and Arab spokesmen were stopped under British compulsion. A year later, similar attempts at direct negotiation with Arab leaders were thwarted by the British. As late as 1943, there were efforts made by important Arab leaders to work out an agreement for a bi-national state with Zionist representatives. Precisely at this point (November 19, 1943), a number of repressive measures against the Jewish community in Palestine were launched by the British administration. Settlements were cordoned off and besieged by British soldiers, ostensibly to search for deserters from the Polish army (*sic!*), resulting in many Jewish casualties. In the months to follow, various *kibbutz* leaders were imprisoned, and there were repeated attempts to deprive the Jews of their defense arms. Intensified search operations were conducted, and "illegal immigrants"—victims of Nazi oppression who had managed to reach Palestinian shores—were arrested and deported. Large-scale arrests took place, designed to smash the Jewish apparatus of defense and regrouping of the exiles.

During the two years following World War II and preceding the establishment of Israel, the British colonial régime encouraged the return to power within the Arab community of the Husseini Party, most of whose principal leaders had spent the war years in occupied territories of Europe, collaborating with the fascists. The Grand Mufti, Haj Amin El Husseini, wanted in Europe as a Nazi collaborator, managed to "elude" British capture, return to Cairo, and resume direction of the Arab forces opposed to conciliation with the Jews. When the Arab Right organized paramilitary terrorist formations, the British ignored them. In every way, the most intransigent, chauvinist, reactionary elements in Arab leadership were encouraged by the British. Finally, when the State of Israel was declared, the British made a last desperate effort to provide the Arabs with strategic military strongholds, such as the famous Kastel on the Jerusalem-Tel Aviv road, and permitted British Centurion tanks mysteriously to fall into Arab hands. It was the Israeli military victory against the Arab régimes, based on the exploitation of the Arab masses, that guaranteed the end of British colonialism in Palestine and set in motion movements within some of these countries to establish genuine nationalist and reform régimes.

Nasser's Egypt, rather than choosing the path of peaceful cooperation with the new Jewish state, chose to re-assert Arab chauvinism and to divert itself from the task of completing an authentic social revolution. Moreover, while attacking "imperialist Israel" as a "monster state" and threatening to "grind [Israel] into the dust," Nasser has not disturbed major foreign investments in Egypt itself. Indeed, the increasing penetration of American foreign investment into Egypt has been a constant in the Nasser era. Imports from the United States alone roughly equal those from Europe as a whole and amount to more than twice that of imports from the Soviet Union. Aside from the seizure of the Suez Canal, in itself scarcely a major revolutionary act, though of symbolic significance, Egypt's struggle against imperialism has been largely a war of words. Holding the Tri-Continental Conference in Cairo cost Nasser little but gave him precisely the "nationalist" façade which allows him to compel many on the Left and in the Third World to support his formula of "Palestine" against Israel.

6. Guerilla Warfare in Israel

THE STRATEGY OF GUERRILLA WARFARE has now been proposed for conducting the "fourth round" against Israel. The model provided for Cuba, Algeria, and Vietnam has become the euphoria of defeat. The Algerians, mistaking their own anti-colonial struggle against France with Arab revanchism in the Middle East, have called for guerrilla warfare against Israel to regain lost national territory. The Cubans, falsely projecting their own nationalist struggles onto the "Arab peoples," and identifying the situation with their own experience with United States occupation of their country, have supported this call. Ricardo Alarcon, speaking in the UN on behalf of Cuba, began with the eloquence one might have hoped for of a revolutionary government that has had to defend its own people's right to an independent national existence:

> With regard to the Near East problem, this delegation wishes to express that the people and the Revolutionary Government of Cuba, as a matter of principle, are opposed to every manifestation of religious, national, or racial prejudice, whatever the source may be. Likewise, they believe that any political proclamation whose aim is the annihilation of any people or state is to be condemned. This principle is equally applicable to the Palestinian people, unjustly and brutally dispossessed of its territory, and the Hebrew people, who, for 2000 years, have suffered under persecution and racial prejudice and—during the not-too-distant era of Nazism—suffered under one of the most cruel attempts at mass extermination ever recorded.

These words emphatically distinguish the Cuban position from the Arab position summed up by Nasser on May 28: "We intend to open a general assault against Israel. This will be total war. Our basic aim is the destruction of Israel.'" Nontheless, the Cubans, who were clearly aware of the constancy of such Arab proclamations, were able to take a position which is neither revolutionary nor just and demonstrably incorrect:

> Our position with regard to the State of Israel in the Middle East crisis is determined by that state's aggressive conduct as an instrument of imperialism turned against the Arab peoples to settle existing problems; it has done so in the most treacherous and indefensible form: a Nazi-style surprise attack carefully prepared in advance. . . . The State of Israel enjoyed the full benefit of the agreement to an unconditional cease-fire. But this is not enough for her. She has also declared that she will maintain possession of the occupied territories. If they do not withdraw without delay, the Arab peoples have the legitimate right to resume the fighting. . . . The only alternative left for the Arab peoples—in which their future is at stake—is the same as that of the peoples facing imperialism in Asia, Africa, and Latin America: to resist and fight. *Patria o Muerte! Venceremos!*

That these words are appropriate not to the Arab but to the Israeli cause—"Homeland or Death! We shall overcome!"—seems to have escaped the Cuban delegate's notice. That they should have escaped the Soviet delegate's notice could surprise no one who is aware of the Soviet's demonstrated willingness to sacrifice nationalist and revolutionary movements—as in China, Vietnam, and Greece—for their own perceived national interests. That the Cubans, who have no national interests at stake in the Middle East and who, despite their precarious and dependent situation, have generally maintained an independent revolutionary line and international posture, should now accept Arab propaganda is particularly revealing; it underlines the extent to which the Arab leaders have succeeded in confusing the issues by the select use of anti-imperialist rhetoric.

The "occupied territories," the Gaza strip, the west bank of the Jordan, and the "Old City" of Jerusalem, were occupied and annexed

ISRAELI IMPERATIVES & JEWISH AGONIES : 399

in the first place by Egypt and Jordan in open combat against the newly founded State of Israel; these territories were intended by the United Nations Partition Plan to constitute an independent Arab state in Palestine (which was never established because of those régimes); and Jerusalem was to be internationalized. These facts seem to have escaped the notice not only of the Cuban delegation but also of the new breed of non-historical "materialists" from the Socialist European bloc.

Of more fundamental importance is the striking misperception of the real significance of Israel's military victory, and of popular "resistance" and guerrilla warfare. In Algeria, as in Vietnam, guerrilla warfare has proved an effective weapon in the hands of indigenously-based nationalist forces resisting the material military superiority of a foreign and colonial (or would-be colonial) power attempting to subject the population to its will. This is precisely the Israeli situation. Spurred by their consecration to the national cause and in defense of the "homeland," the Israelis have successfully resisted Arab aggression. They won, just as the Algerians won, and as the Vietnamese National Liberation Front will win against foreign aggression.

Moshe Dayan, Israel's Defense Minister, himself has drawn the parallel between the Israelis and the Vietcong, and cogently stated the essential meaning of guerrilla warfare:

> Guerrilla war is the weapon of the weak—but it is not a weak weapon. Whatever the ultimate outcome of the strife in Vietnam, it will remain a fact that in the previous decade the Vietcong succeeded in defeating the French forces and that now, with a small army, low-grade weapons, and extremely primitive equipment, they are holding out against the strongest army in the West, that of the United States of America. . . . There are, of course, crucial differences between the Vietcong war and the sabotage and terror operations of Ahmed Shukeiri's units. In contrast to the guerrilla fighters in Vietnam, who make use of every opportunity to attack American troops, the Arab gangs avoid all direct contact with Israeli forces. The aim of the Vietcong fighters is to drive the foreigner —the American—from Vietnam, unite the North with the South, and bring down the Saigon Government. These are not empty phrases from propaganda pamphlets, but genuine aims, for which they are willing to lay down their lives. . . . There is no similarity between [the] . . . the minelayings and quick return to Arab territory [of El Fatah terrorists] (where they are paid for these "raids") and the life-and-death struggle of the Vietcong. . . .
>
> The Arab leaders claim that . . . Israel's Jews . . . are foreigners, Europeans who have succeeded in occupying an Arab country but will be compelled to evacuate it again. Their fate, they assert, will be like that of the Crusaders who were in the end driven out by Arab forces, or the French, pushed out of Algeria.
>
> This political and military analogy fails to take into account a basic fact—that the Jews are not foreigners in Israel. This is not only true as regards their own feelings and their historical links with the land. While Israelis may be Jews who came from other countries, they did not remain tied to them. The decision to evacuate the French from Algeria was taken in Paris, and the fate of the Crusaders was decided in the capitals of Europe. But it is the citizenry of Israel who make the decisions on the

security problems that plague them, and this they do from the point of view of Jerusalem, not that of Jews of New York or London. In the Arab-Israeli dispute it is the Arab guerrilla fighters who are the strangers; the native inhabitants of Israel are the Israelis. The entire question of the war against Israel and the way in which it should be waged is decided in Cairo and Damascus.

In this remarkable document, Dayan concluded by cautioning against the intoxicating rhetoric of guerrilla insurgency: "The Arabs seek to wrest Israel from the Jews. This can be achieved—if at all—only by means of total war. Acts of sabotage and terror do not lead to this end, and in fact have the opposite effect—they tend to strengthen the nation that is attacked. *Guerrilla warfare can achieve its aim when it is used as an instrument of national struggle, against a government imposed from the outside, but it is rendered ineffective when it is used to assault a people settled on its own land.*" (our italics)

It should be appreciated, however, that Dayan's commentary on guerrilla warfare was written prior to the Second Sinai campaign. This means that with the acquisition of vast new territories, irrespective of their *de jure* status, in which Arab majorities prevail, guerrilla organizations are now in fact quite feasible. For in these newly conquered regions the special circumstances for the conduct of permanent underground violence do exist. It will thus become a prime focus of Israeli management to prevent the conditions of insurgency from emerging. This can be done in either one of two ways: treatment of guerrillas as gangsters (in which case the Israelis will be making the same mistake that the British committed in the '40s), or treatment of Arab opposition as normal, and even legitimately expressing authentic national sentiments. But a settlement of the tactical issues obviously depends on a resolution of the policy questions—a settlement which is made terribly remote because of the ideological shallowness of an Israeli policy that yet manages to bridle the organizational sophistication of the Israeli armed forces.

7. Israel and the Soviet Union

THE ISRAELI-ARAB WAR HAS TURNED INTO a postwar confrontation between Israel and the Soviet Union. Clearly, the Soviet Union must be shocked by Israel's behavior. It has a fifty-year history of treating Jews as Russians have been accustomed to treat Jews—and getting away with such treatment. This gap between stereotyped expectation and Jewish performance is what partially accounts for the violent reponse to the Israeli victory.

The Israeli military victory was a Soviet political defeat. More significant, it was a defeat for a foreign policy based on illusions and on alliances with incompetent régimes. In one sense, however, the Soviet Union has gained by the Arab defeat. It has made these régimes far more dependent on her than they were before their military defeat. This gives her even greater political leverage in the Arab world than an Arab victory might have achieved. Nonetheless, it was a blow to Soviet prestige, a defeat for Soviet military planning and weaponry, and an event not likely to inspire the confidence of other countries which may require her material and political support.

There have been shock and hesitancies on both sides. Israeli political leadership, drawn so heavily from Ashkenazic sources, from Eastern Europe and Russia, at one and the same time seemed intimidated by Soviet military might and convinced that this might would be used with restraint. After all, if Ukrainian anti-Semitism is deeply rooted in Russian rural history, so too is Socialist condemnation of anti-Semitism. The war against Nazi Germany fused Soviet and Jewish interests. And this was but the most recent chapter in a history of Socialism that intertwines with the history of emancipated Jewry from Marx and Bebel to Luxemburg and Trotsky. Even in the most bitter days of Stalinism, Lazar Kaganovich reminded world Jewry of Bolshevik connections with yesteryear. The support of the Soviet Union for the establishment of the State of Israel, however tepid and hesitant, was genuine. Furthermore, is was a compromise of the Soviet position on the "national question" consciously taken in the name of humanitarianism. It was made in the name of the Jewish people along Zionist rather than Marxist lines—not to mention an end to British dominance in the Middle East.

The extent to which the Soviet Union preserved the remnants of European Jewry from destruction and supported the rights of Jews to a nation-state should not be forgotten. However, the Israel leadership could not be expected to accept the realities of post-Stalinist Soviet policy—the extension of Russian power to the Middle East on the shoulders of Arab backwardness. Socialist dialectics and Marxism-Leninism have given way to the pragmatism of geographical determinism. Nonetheless, it is evident that the Israeli authorities were taken by surprise, were in fact stunned by the severity of the Soviet condemnation of Israeli "aggression." They were unprepared for the lopsided Soviet support of Arab military sheikhs and feudal landlords (including many who had persecuted Communists), all in the name of supporting the Third World. As recently as 1966, the *Israel Government Yearbook* referred to the Soviet Union and Eastern Europe's policy of "correctness," seeing every Soviet public utterance calling for the settlement of disputes by peaceful means as a neutralization of the Soviet foreign policy toward Israel.

So careful has the Israel government been not to offend the Soviet Union that more than one voice sympathetic to Israel has accused her of a policy of calculated indifference toward the fate of the three million

Russian Jews. The most recent, and perhaps sharpest, voice is that of Elie Wiesel, who, in *The Jews of Silence*, stated categorically that "Jewish solidarity extends to everyone in the world but Soviet Jews. The Jewish State has even begun to help nations of Asia and Africa, but toward them it displays an attitude of vague and hesitant indifference." Now these calculated hesitancies have been destroyed, along with the memory of past associations. The Israelis, too, then, have had their own shock of recognition.

8. Israel and the West

TO SOME EXTENT, ISRAELI foreign and domestic policies have probably contributed to the view that she is an "imperialist gendarme in the Middle East." The frequent charges in the United Nations debates by Arab and Communist spokesmen alike, concerning the "Hitlerite" character of the Israeli armed forces, were replied to with profound outrage by Israeli delegates and her Foreign Minister. However, the extensive militarization of Israel, its reliance on military force from the outset of its existence, cannot be seriously denied. But no commentator has demonstrated that real alternatives were available. This military determination of events has made it extremely difficult for Israel to carve out an independent foreign policy. With notable exceptions, her position has been identified in practice with the United States. It has acted in collusion with Britain and France against Nasser's "anti-colonial" régime. It has carried out systematic reprisals against Arab terrorist attacks, many of which have gone well beyond even the most generous definition of mere "defensive forays." In fact, Mapam and Achdut Ha'avodah, the Israeli Socialist parties, have consistently opposed these policies, as have leading non-Socialist figures as the late social thinker Martin Buber, and Nahum Goldmann, head of the World Zionist Organization.

Even Ben-Gurion, who was to be the architect of Israel's pro-Western leanings, recognized the rationality of non-alignment for Israel. In a speech to the Knesset in 1948, he flatly declared that:

> The State of Israel is not concerned with the internal affairs of other states. We want to live in peace with all. We are compelled to do so because we have hostages in every country, and we desire their migration to Israel. This is our orientation, and I am not ashamed of it. We shall persist in it. If some should give this orientation the foreign name "neutrality," I shall not be ashamed of that. This is an orientation based on the unity of the human race, on peace between nations, on the desire to live in peace with all peoples.

Despite its neutralist protestations, Israel did not remain idle in the Cold War. Israel became involved with policies which, perhaps expedient in the short run, could not help but alienate her from the Third World and also permit the Soviet Union to rationalize its anti-

Israeli posture as progressive. Until the outbreak of the Korean War, Israel did not identify with either bloc, and emigration of Eastern European Jewry was permitted, even encouraged, while most Jewish communities in Eastern Europe joined the World Jewish Congress. Israel's alignment with the United States in the Korean conflict put an end to this period. This was followed by the irrational anti-Zionist campaigns in the Soviet Union and the notorious anti-Semitic trials in Moscow and Prague. The policies which Israel pursued in the next several years of attempting to obtain a mutual security pact with the United States, or as an option join NATO, clearly put her in the anti-Soviet world, which in the context meant, or appeared to mean, pro-colonialism.

Caught as Israel was in the Cold War, it is not at all clear how relevant a different foreign policy would have been. In 1955, the United States attempt to impose the Baghdad Pact on the Middle East was resisted by Egypt *and* Israel. This did not stop the Soviet Union from giving unequivocal political and military support to the Arab régimes, nor the Czechs from concluding a major arms deal with Egypt. The Sinai Campaign of 1956 followed this arms build-up. The Skoda works in Czechoslovakia were supplying Israel with weapons, just as Great Britain shipped military hardware to Egypt up until the seizure of the Suez Canal. It was after the successful Israeli "campaign," however, that the geopolitical lines hardened into their present mould. For there could be no question that, if Israel's goals were internal security, those of England and France were to conduct a preventive war for the purpose of punishing and, if possible, destroying Nasser's régime. His government had just nationalized the Suez Canal and seemed to be an emerging stalwart in the anti-colonial wing within the Arab bloc. By participating in this action, Israel placed itself, as Martin Buber reputedly viewed the Sinai Campaign, on the side of the reactionary part of the world.

What choice was open to Israel at that time, even with the edge of historical retrospect, is still unclear, since Egypt was constantly threatening her with destruction and seemingly growing in military strength. The historic irony is that the Arab régimes aligned with the West (Jordan, Iraq, Saudi Arabia) were as inflamatory and threatening in their anti-Israel pronouncements as Egypt. (Ahmed Shukairy, then the Saudian UN representative, demanded the dismemberment of the State of Israel and the expulsion of the Jews.) Had these régimes then presented the same dangerous military threat, Israel probably would have acted toward them as she did toward Egypt. Her action in June 1967 against a pro-Western Jordanian régime ruled by a king, whose Legion was trained by the British and armed by the Pentagon, had no effect, however, on the cries that she is an "imperialist tool."

The constant propagandistic din over Israeli reaction and imperial control simply violates known foreign-policy decisions taken by Israel, which demonstrate not only its relative independence from the Western Bloc nations, but no less from the World Zionist community. Israel's failure to support the Algerian liberation struggle against France contributed to a strain between itself and the Socialist bloc. Again, however, her abstentions in the UN debates on Algeria, which in fact put her on the side of France, came not because of desire nor of ideological principle (even for the ruling Social Democrats of Mapai) but out of necessity. Her choice, to condemn France and risk losing her only major source of military hardware, thus making her vulnerable to Arab attack, was one few nations have faced. When the risk to her existence was less, Israel acted unequivocally against colonialism. She voted in the United Nations for sanctions against the South African régime, siding with the most militant Afro-Asian governments, despite the large South African Jewish community and past diplomatic support by South Africa.

There is the demonstrable distance Israel put between itself and the United States Vietnam policy. It did this by a measured rejection of close ties with the South Vietnam régime, and by complete neutrality in the matter of war support. Like nearly every major power, it has provided token medical supplies as a show of humanitarianism rather than affection for the war effort. Earlier, in 1962, having abstained in the past so as not to affront the United States, Israel voted for admission of China to the United Nations, although she did not support the Soviet demand to replace Formosa's seat with China's. Toward the new African states Israel has maintained a friendly stance, providing a modest but important program of technical and economic assistance that encompasses some thirty-five Afro-Asian nations, and which received warm praise, for instance, from Kwame Nkrumah when he was still considered Africa's most important anti-colonialist leader. Despite this the Casablanca "summit" in 1961 unanimously resolved to condemn Israel "as an instrument of imperialism and neo-colonialism not only in the Middle East but also in Africa and Asia." In the showdown over the General Agreement on Trade and Tariffs, and, more important, in the UN Conference on Trade and Development, Israel continually and consistently supported a Third World posture, and in so doing opposed United States policy. There was also the support officially tendered on May 15, 1966, for Polish claims on the Oder-Neisse territories. And lest this be viewed as a means to gain an ideological foothold in Central Europe, it should be understood that in so doing Israel threatened its fragile cordiality with West Germany.

The long effort of the Israeli government to achieve recognition in the eyes of the non-Arab portion of the Third World bloc has paid significant dividends. The assumption that the Israeli government is a Western outpost, an enemy in the Middle East, has not been convincing, particularly for many sub-Saharan African nations. Despite production and employment fluctuations early in 1967, Israel serves as a model of a small country effecting a healthy import-export balance and a high degree of economic autonomy despite the presence of foreign capital and industry. The Arab representation of the Israeli military victory as a huge defeat for the Third World assumes a stability in that world which is nowhere to be found.

Guinea has been the only one of thirty-one African nations to break diplomatic ties with Israel, while even Julius Nyerere, President of Tanzania, made a public statement early in June emphasizing Tanzania's recognition of Israel as a state with a right to exist. But more than this, there is an unofficial support for Israel that in effect points to a common suspicion of Egyptian aims. Kenya and Ethiopia are fighting undeclared wars against Somalia, an Arab sympathizer. Uganda, Chad, and Ethiopia are having their troubles with Sudan, which declared war on Israel and was supposed to be Egypt's channel to Black Africa. Ghana, which even under the régime of Kwame Nkrumah maintained an extensive set of economic and cultural ties with Israel, is certainly not going to support Egyptian claims, particularly since Nasser is perceived to be precisely the Arab reflex to Sekou Touré.

Of course, Israel as a small nation has limited room for maneuvering at international levels of power. However, if the charge of "lackey of imperialism" is to be treated seriously, one would have to demonstrate that any other nation of comparable size and status has fared nearly as well in developing an independent foreign policy. In a world of big power blocs, Israel has suffered from its intense isolation, yet it has also derived the advantages of turning its isolation into independence, and has not been quite so conservative or timorous as its detractors continue to claim.

Like in Dante's consignment of the Jews to the "First Circle" or "Limbo" wherein the "virtuous heathen" hover between heaven and hell, Israel belongs neither to the highly developed nor to the underdeveloped sector of the world political economy. The dilemmas and contradictions of Israel's world status are such that it is by no means clear what the pragmatic gains, in terms of a peaceful national existence, would have been of a consistent anti-colonial stance and of nonalignment in the Cold War. Policies over which she had no choice but which were necessary to her survival and which aligned her with the West have evoked responses barely distinguishable from those to her anti-colonial positions. Even those governments, like those in Africa, with which she has established ties of friendship, have often scorned her advances while accepting her favors. She exists in a limbo which wins her genuine friends in no camp, and resentment, or at least suspicion, in all.

From yet a different perspective, the fallacy of viewing Israel as a pawn in the hands of United States foreign policy can be seen by the actual outcomes in terms of support for Israel as compared with the effects on Arab unification. The French commentator, Jean Daniel, writing in *Le Nouvel Observateur*, has stated this fact most cogently:

> The kings of Saudi Arabia and Jordan are the ones who are deliberately supporting and serving the imperialist designs of the present United States foreign policy. But any support for Israel does not divide the Arabs; it unites them. The goal of imperialism, as everyone knows, is to divide. Israel has long survived, thanks to United States "charity" and French arms. It has never been a factor balancing or tipping the scales one way or the other. When we see King Faisal and President Nasser united against Israel, knowing how these two men hate each other and how each is preparing the extermination of the other, no one can conclude that the existence of Israel favors the battle of a pro-American king against a pro-Soviet president.

If such facts help to demonstrate that Israel is not the "lackey" of United States foreign policy, they do little else. Funds from American Jewry have long given Israel a special economic situation in the world of finance and business. The international character of Jewish voluntary organizations has given Israel an inordinately large voice in the councils of world Jewry. Finally, the high quality of the educated immigrants to Israel (at least those who came from Europe) also provided the young nation with external developmental inputs absent elsewhere in the Middle East. Israel may be the last new nation to develop along capitalist or neo-capitalist lines. This is a fact of paramount significance, and one that is hardly likely to inspire confidence or respect among those who define industrial development and political independence in terms of one or another form of Socialism. All of this raises anew, at the international level, the specter of the Sombartian Jew—the Jew as a creature of capitalism, who cannot survive the death of capitalism. The "inference" of some "Socialists" is that anti-capitalism is, in its very essence, a struggle against the Jewish State rather than for Socialism within it.

9. Israeli Socialism

SOCIALISM WAS INTERWOVEN WITH THE WEB of Israeli politics long before Israel's actual establishment as a state. It came as the vision of the *chalutzim*, carried with them from the *shtetlach* and ghettoes of Eastern Europe as well as the centers of "emancipated" Jewry from France to the United States. Socialism was fundamental to the dream of the Jewish State, and the physical labor of the *chalutz* aimed at one and the same time to re-create a homeland and transform the individual Jew from *luftmensch*, petit-bourgeois intellectual, trader and Talmudist, into

ISRAELI IMPERATIVES & JEWISH AGONIES : 407

a citizen rooted in the soil of his own nation. The *kibbutz* movement of collective agricultural settlements, the cooperative *moshavim*, provided the foundations of Israel. The Histadrut, the central labor organization that is cooperative enterprise and trade union fused into one, implanted a Socialist consciousness in the political culture of the Israeli working class, linking the task of nation-building and Socialism into an inseparable vision.

Dream and reality, however, have often conflicted. The Arab-Israeli war and the continual state of siege Israel has been compelled to live under—a "nervous peace, a dangerous peace," as Mapam's Yaakov Chazan put it—have created a climate wherein the most obdurate and least flexible policies, having nothing in common with either democratic or Socialist principles, continued to be put forth.

While the Israeli Left-Socialist party, Mapam, since its inception welcomed Arabs as members on the basis of common class interests and Socialist principle, in terms of Arab-Jewish understanding, it was not until 1959 that the Histadrut first gave Arab workers the right to full membership. Military government in Israel's border regions subjected its Arab citizens to persistent harassment and infringement of their individual liberties, until lifted recently under Levi Eshkol's administration. Their general conditions of life continue to be inferior, even taking into account the composition of the Arab community, most of whom are now wage-earners. The state's use of eminent domain has been disproportionately directed against the Israeli Arab community. This resulted in the expropriation of 250,000 to 300,000 dunams of Arab-owned land between 1952 and 1965, and the reduction of the per capita dunams owned by Arabs from 6.0 to 4.2 dunams.

10. The Arab Diaspora

ON THE QUESTION OF THE ARAB REFUGEES, while Israel has in many ways had a rational and correct posture, it has also been infused with the military ethos and the conception of the Arabs simply as "fifth column." If the Right wing believed merely in the imposition of a victor's solution on the Arab refugees, without regard for their fate, Israel's government did, at least, pledge compensation for abandoned lands and express the willingness to participate in rehabilitation and resettlement programs elsewhere in the Middle East. She also allowed many Arabs to rejoin their families who had not left Israel in the great exodus. Yet, in general, especially under Ben-Gurion, her policy has been summed up, in his words, as the return of "not a single refugee," with little or no attention to the possible resettlement within Israel's borders of some refugees, within the limits of her means and absorptive capacity. (Statements, like that of Egypt's Foreign Minister Salah e-Din, demanded "the restoration of the refugees to Palestine as the masters of the homeland, not as slaves." More explicitly, they intend to "annihilate Israel." This could not help but stamp the issue in its most cruel mould.) The imprisonment, on trumped-up charges of "dealings with a foreign state" of so respected and nationally known an authority on the Arab peoples as Aharon Cohen, a major spokesman for Arab-Jewish rapprochment (and leader of Mapam), was but an instance in a heavily militarized internal situation that stultified genuine continuous search for alternatives and solutions other than military ones. Israel had her own Thermidorean reaction, if not against a revolution, against a legacy which seemed so irrelevant in the context in which Israel was compelled to live—and in which, in the name of Socialism, the Soviet Union and many Third World nations attacked her sovereignty.

The Arab refugee problem has become magnified precisely because of Israeli military victory. Whether the exodus of Arabs in the wake of the 1948 and 1956 wars was stimulated as a deliberate part of Arab military strategy to maintain a vanguard anti-Israeli force, or represents a spontaneous resistance to a Jewish majoritarian state, has become largely academic. Since the extensive victory of the Israeli army involves the total occupation of Palestine, from the banks of the Suez on the West to the River Jordan on the East and the Gulf of Aqaba in the South, the question of the Arab refugees has magnified. It can no longer be argued that the Palestinian Arabs are simply moving from one part of their cultural continuity to another.

Israel has achieved a degree of security that only borders of water can provide. But, in turn, it has inherited a degree of danger that only an "enemy within" can provide. In some measure, the one million Arabs now on United Nations Relief rolls, joined as they are by at least an equal number of Arabs caught in the net of the Israeli victory, potentially offer an acute case of the "Left" or "Right" substance of Israeli politics. A Left solution would have to allow for the equal rights of the Arab peoples. Based on a population nearly equal in size to the Jewish inhabitants, the possibilities are there for a policy based on full enfranchisement of the Arabs in the political processes, bi-lingualism as an Israeli national policy, and restitution of Arab property which, by default, fell into Jewish hands at the end of the three-part Arab exodus. What is increasingly being urged by the Israeli political Right is an adaptation of the original United Nations policy of making the portions of territory occupied by Israel (but lived in by Arabs) an "autonomous Republic." The same conceit is urged of imposing a condition on Arabs that was imposed by the Soviet Union on the Jewish people in the '30s': they were "given" the autonomous Republic of Birobidjan, in an area and under conditions which guaranteed its ultimate failure. In this sense, the Zionist idea can issue into the Stalinist policy.

11. Thermidorean Reaction?

THE SOLUTION TO THE ARAB REFUGEE PROBLEM is contingent on the solution to the Jewish refugee problem. For in some measure, the question to be settled is: What kind of society is Israel—theocratic or democratic? From a sociological perspective, a great deal can be brushed aside in search of an answer. Israel is not a theocratic state, since it does not have as its ruling political directorate religious leaders. Yet the potency of the religious "zealots" can hardly be minimized, given their cultural stamp on the nation.

The Thermidorean reaction may have been inevitable in a state surrounded by enemies determined on Israel's destruction, ruled by the same political apparatus since its founding, and for much of that time by one man as its hallowed national shrine. The incorporation of theocratic elements in the state's political structure, and the inclusion of religious parties in Israel's rule, also made such a reaction highly probable. There were, of course, other factors contributing to a general conservatizing of the state. Among these were (a) the disquieting partial absorption of hundreds of thousands of refugees from Arab lands having neither political traditions nor the skills of mass participation; (b) the remnants of a European Jewry which was psychologically unprepared and socially unwilling to extract policies which would separate them from the policies decreed by the political leadership; (c) the gradual identification of the Zionist movement with its most potent economic source, the American middle-class Jew; and finally, (d) there was a *kibbutz* movement gradually relegated to a marginal role in the *enbourgeoisement* of Israel's industrialization.

Nonetheless, a nervous peace had endured for ten years between Arab nations and Israel. For example, there had not been a major incident between Israel and Egypt until the June 1967 war. Shimon Peres, Moshe Dayan, and Ben-Gurion above all, the architects of the Sinai Campaign and of Israel's pro-Western and inflexible stance toward the Arabs, had left the government. In the confrontation between the new Rafi Party of Ben-Gurion and the old Mapai led by Eshkol, the latter won a clear electoral victory. Relations with the Soviet Union were improving; Eshkol had lifted military rule of Israel's Arab citizens; new initiatives and openings on the international scene were being explored. Habib Bourguiba's hesitant but significant call for "realism" and re-examination of the Arab position on Israel, and similar statements in editorials appearing in *Jeune Afrique*, were the slightest indications that Israel might finally become a sovereign reality, an integral part of the Middle East, allowed to pursue a peaceful national existence. The June war and its aftermath have put an abrupt end to such hopes. The Arabs have become intransigent; the Israelis, imperious.

The position we have taken leads to the ineluctable conclusion that Israel cannot possibly put forth recommendations for direct negotiations with the Arab belligerents that would be tolerated, much less entertained. If even the preposterously weighted pro-Arab standpoint of Premier Tito of Yogoslavia was rejected out of hand by the Egyptian leadership, to set forth a list of proposals for negotiations would be as presumptuous as it would be futile.

Nonetheless, if Israel has made plain its desire for direct negotiations with the Arab states on a parity basis, it also served to weaken its case in the rest of the Third World. This it did as a result of its precipitous transfer of captured Soviet weaponry to the United States armed forces. *Time* magazine reported that:

> At bases in the Sinai and in Israel, the Israelis have been showing off some of the weaponry to Western technicians and, on at least one occasion, even lending it out. The United States sent transport planes to Israel to pick up three captured MIG-21's, the Soviet Union's best fighters. Two MIG-21's, the first ever to fall into United States hands, are being test-flown at Edwards Air Force Base in California. The third is being evaluated in laboratories at Wright-Patterson Air Force Base in Ohio. Since MIG-21's sometimes challenge United States pilots over North Viet Nam, the Air Force hopes to learn things that will be useful in the air war there.

Just why this loan or sale was made, whatever the *quid pro quo* may be, remains unexplained. Indeed, a rejection of the United States request for Soviet hardware could have performed two functions at one stroke: (a) point up the genuine independence of the Israeli government from United States control; and (b) indicate the solidarity of Israel with the peoples of the Third World.

The entire Middle East dilemma is now on a vicious treadmill. The intransigence of the Arabs creates countervailing hardened political arteries in Israel. The unbridled campaign conducted by the Soviet Union against Israel causes the Israelis to embrace United States economic aid even more fervently than before the Second Sinai campaign. Two decades of United Nations indifference to legitimate Israeli complaints create an internal attitude in Tel Aviv to "go it alone." Under such circumstances, it is perhaps time for a transvaluation of values: let Jewish world opinion concentrate on imperatives for settlement (including a vigorous defense of Arab human and property rights), while Israeli political life would do well to begin an "agonizing reappraisal" of the obligations imposed on it as a result of its military successes. The rational ordering of geographic boundaries is one thing; the rational taming of passions, quite another.

This is a time for testing. As the Russo-German Pact of 1939, so, too, the Arab-Israeli War of 1957 separates out those who believe in a radicalism of slavish subservience to big-power ideologies and maneuvers from those whose radicalism is rooted in the destiny of free men to define their own future.

ZIONISM THE IDEAL AND AN IDEA OF RELIGION

DOV B. LANG

Zionism—by the term I would understand the continued consciousness of the Jew directed towards a Holy Land rather than the formal movement of recent years—before the formation of the State of Israel had posed problems predominantly of ways and means. Since that time these difficulties have been transformed into ones of concept and vision. Where, prior to 1948, the difficulties of return to Israel could be subsumed under the heading of material difficulties, the present, in having the advantage over those particular obstacles, has encountered others. Is the Jew, the question runs, who lives in what has come to be known as the *Galuth* bound, now that such a trip is practically feasible, to a return to Israel? Or can he remain at once within the tradition which he has accepted and the political boundaries that mark out his so-called exile?

The question as it is introduced here has been frequently, if not popularly acknowledged. It is with two of these acknowledgements that we will be initially concerned—the first, an essay by Arthur Koestler, "Judah at the Crossroads", which appeared first in the English *Jewish Chronicle* where it was notable for the heated reader interchange that followed its publication and which was expanded in Koestler's volume of essays, *The Trail of the Dinosaur;* the second, an article by Milton Konvitz, "Zionism: Homecomng or Homelessness", that appeared in the Summer, 1956 issue of *Judaism*. The contrast in method and content between the two essays hinges finally on what appears to be an historical misrepresentation committed by Konvitz. The implications of the two postions, in spite of this or, perhaps because of it, range quite clearly from the nihilism of Koestler to certain striking methodological techniques illumined by Konvitz.

Koestler prefaces his discussion with the postulates that Judaism as a religious phenomenon has been inextricably bound up with Judaism as a nationalistic phenomenon, that the destiny of Israel the people cannot be separated from that of Israel the land and that any contrary claim to the effect that " . . . Judaism is 'a religion like other religions, a private affair which has nothing to do with politics or race' is either hypocritical or self-contradictory." Koestler cannot be blamed for failing to show a more sustained interest than he does in the religious implications of this position. The sociological consequences which he derives from it, such as the Jew's "self-segregating activities" or his establishment of "cultural ghettoes"—all emergent from this frustrated drive for nationhood—are not particularly convincing but lie beyond the scope of our discussion. What is most important, I think, is that we accept this initial proposal of Koestler; namely, that the Biblical conception of the Jew described a figure who accomplished a certain way of life making no distinction on its own terms between citizenship and religiosity, between ethic and politic, between the life of society and the life of the spirit, but rather synthesized those dualities in the intricate ties which bound the Jew at once to his God, to his people and—our immediate concern—to his land. Thus, Buber, in his introduction to *Israel and Palestine,* describes that "matrimony" out of which Zionism was to grow:

> Just as, to achieve fullness of life, the people needed the land, so that land needed the people and the end which both were called upon to realize could only be reached by a living partnership. The holy matrimony of land and people was intended to bring about the matrimony of two separated spheres of Being."

Behind such statement of a unitary destiny lies no series of miraculous events to be explained away, no webs of fiction to be de-mythologized, nothing less than the description in fact of a people's allegiance to a theocratic government in a land which brooked neither rival nor, as was to be seen, successor. The attachment is a real one; from God's original command to Abraham, *"Lech l'cho"*, through the stern reminder of Isaiah "He that is left in Zion and he that remaineth in Jerusalem, shall be called holy," the tale related is of a people's unmediated and unswerving dedication to a land and nation.

I would labor the literal inseparability of land and people for the particular reason that Konvitz, in attempting to deal with the ideological difficulties which the State of Israel poses for Judaism, appears to have transformed it into a *metaphoric* or *mythical* attachment. Konvitz holds that the bond which has tied the Jew to Israel the Land should be viewed as an extra-historical one, derived from what amounts to an ontological ordination of the Jew in the role of exile. *Galuth,* Konvitz claims, was and is still real; but it is real in the Zion-centered form by which we know it only in the sense that metaphor is real and not in the sense that the simple re-establishment of Israel the State can confute it. Not only do we, for instance, as American Jews, endure the condition of exile, but even the Jews of Israel according to Konvitz do not escape that situation. "The condition of the Jew," Konvitz writes, "every Jew, in or out of Israel, is to live in *Galuth,* in exile. Homelessness does not end with the attainment of freedom and equality in a free democratic country; nor does it end with the attainment of national independence and statehood in Israel. Like Jacob, he [the Jew] is eternally the sojourner."

I have already noted that, if only by suggestion, this description does some violence to the part that Zionism in one guise or another has played in Jewish history. The Jews who returned from the first exile, for example, held—and in the terms by which they had defined their exile, correctly—that that exile was ended. They had returned to their land, and only the lack of full political autonomy prevented a re-assertion of the Biblical image of the Jew. The same claim, even without the latter qualification, has been made by numbers of the current returnees to Israel who hold unconditionally that they have left their exile behind them. In this historical sense, at least, Konvitz's notion of the exile seems to overlook the actual force with which it operated, the literal sense in which it was believed and acted upon.

It is, however, in their more systematic effort to analyze the coming development of the Jew that the disagreement of the two writers becomes most explicit and in light of which the alternatives that they finally pose are defined. Both Koestler and Konvitz agree that the emergence of Israel the State has precipitated a crisis into the situation of the Jew. Koestler feels that now, at last, the Jew is able to arrive at a decision which has for two thousand years lain beyond his ken: he can choose to remain a Jew and in so choosing commit himself to a return to the Land of Israel; or he can free himself from what might be called the undertones rather than the ties which have until now bound him to the people of Israel and accept a place in the community and beliefs of the Western world. To decline the first alternative is for Koestler to finally cut oneself off from the community of Judaism. The Jew who would remain now in a 'foreign' land must, if he is not to betray his own interests or the interests of that land, be assimilated whole into its culture. Religious training as a form, it is granted, has a certain value, particularly in a society where social emphasis is placed on it. But Judaism in its Western setting is a distinctly minority affair, successful only in imposing on its children only the sense of 'being different' with its concommitant trauma. The Jewish child—and hence all following generations—should be sent to the neighborhood church and permitted to work out his salvation there with whatever diligence may declare itself to him.

These details of Koestler's argument betray a disquieting naivete with regard to the religious experience. But it is with Koestler's main disjunction, the either/or which demands either life in Israel or extinction abroad that issue can be most immediately taken. There is clearly no need to argue the virtues of Koestler's personal choice if, as Konvitz' proposal would indicate, we are not necessarily restricted to the alternatives on the basis of which that choice was made. For Konvitz' position on this same point would hold that the notion of exile is properly a metaphysical one and that as such its concrete, or literal embodiment is distinctly subordinate and apart from its general import. It is with this additional proposal, hinted at by Konvitz if not full developed by him, that we will be concerned; a methodological proposal which attempts, on the one hand, to re-affirm the tradition and commitment of Judaism, that part of it which speaks of a drama of exile, but which at the same time, acknowledges what it finds equally undeniable, the distinctive features of contemporary man, the singular characteristics of his thought which distinguish it and, therefore, him, from that of his forebears.

I would propose first that the concept of statehood held by the contemporary Jew is at basic variance with the notion held and submitted to by the Biblical Jew. The confluence of sources unavailable to the latter, the accumulation of historical and theoretical data over a period of 2500 years, have contributed to a concept of democratic statehood which is as clearly cogenial to the majority of contemporary Jews (those at least to whose views we have access) as it is foreign to the thought of the Bible. This discrepancy is pointed up significantly by one of the enduring political conflicts within the State of Israel. The principal obstacle, it appears, in the way of drawing up a constitution for the new country and the main reason, as E. Rackman has suggested in *Israel's Emerging Constitution*, why it was finally left in abeyance is due to a clash of interests between the religious and secular authorities, both of whom claimed jurisdiction over a number of the same spheres. No division of those spheres has yet been agreed upon nor does one seem likely to be accepted in the near future. Yet the division has, *de facto*, been made; examination of the resolution suggests that, with the exception of the *Naturei Karta* who remain aloof for special reasons, the Orthodox bloc, while still retaining a number of functions granted the civil government in other democratic states, have nonetheless conceded in the main the political primacy of a civil government and, in effect, the separation of church from state.

This Israel, then, to which Koestler would have us return on the basis of what he takes to be the Biblical definition of the Jew is not in fact the Israel of that Bible except for its physical boundaries (even these are not identical, of course) and for certain other of what might be termed its accidental qualities. I would not want to underestimate the importance of the latter properties, were it not for other considerations which seem to outweigh them. To what does a Jew, abandoning his role in 'exile', return when he arrives in Israel? He finds himself, for one, in a land whose formal structure closely resembles that of a number of other lands—perhaps, if he has been fortunate, that very land which he has called the place of his exile. There are differences of course, immediate ones such as the welcoming sign of *Bruchim HaBaim* at the port of entry and more basic ones such as the weight exerted by the Jewish tradition in establishing juridical procedure and the academic syllabus. These differences are usually exciting and moving for the new arrival, and there is no reason for denying oneself these feelings. But they should not be confused with the details of an end to the exile of the Jews, that exile which has so inevitably altered the terms of its definition in the consciousness of a people emergent through two thousand years.

I am not giving an indirect argument for the assertion of a theocratic state in Israel. The point is more simply that to return to Israel, as it is today constituted, is not to return to the Israel of which Judaism, with the Bible taken as its primary document speaks. The difficulty is not only one of facing the hard fact of the present; it is reasonably certain that were Israel theocratically organized, the argument to the exiles for a return to Zion would hardly be enhanced. To sustain the objection against a return on such terms is only to say that we are aware and conscious in ways in which our ancestors were not aware and conscious, which is a truism and not, as it might be taken, as snobbism. We have learned, after much prodding and backsliding, that the community of man does not always accept the community of God, that in the interests of the dignity with which both communities would invest man, the right to vote need be somehow divorced from the command to worship and that both ought to be conceded as rights which the citizen may make use of or decline. The state to which man comes makes certain demands and, correspondingly, grants other privileges. This in effect was the New Testament's meaning in its oft-quoted command to "Render to Caesar those things which are Caesar's and to God those which are God's." It remains to add that Jesus spoke as a Jew whose country was no longer his own, who in a sense was himself in exile and whose culture was beset by a crest of the Graeco-Roman tide which nearly five centuries earlier, in Sophocles' *Antigone*, had strikingly posed the disparity between natural and conventional law, a disparity foreign to Biblical thinking.

We have spoken thus far of what seems to be but one side of the coin. We know the tradition; we know the 'law'; we are aware of the cohesive effect which literal acceptance of the Zionist belief has had. But because of an unremittable present, we are unable to ourselves assert these terms in the same colors and lights in which others before us have seen them. Knowledge and self-consciousness have grown; they cannot be held apart from religious thought any more than they can be divorced from other cumulative facets of thought such as science and technology. To turn from this refusal to submit to biblical injunction towards formulation of a statement that justifies and even stipulates that that failure *should* be the case might seem to gloss over an objection which was raised for me by Professor Ernst Simon. Professor Simon, in reply to my suggestion that in light of the fact that the largest part of American Jewry appeared unwilling to liquidate their exile, it might be wise to re-define the terms of that exile, answered to the effect that 'there is no reason to change a law simply because some feel unable to comply with it.' I accepted this as a general answer at the time and I am willing to do so now, but only with the added and severed stricture which emerge from our discussion above. If, on the one hand, we accept the Bible in a literal sense, we are bound to admit that a return to the State of Israel is not a release from the exile which has been the experience of the Jew. The alternative on the other hand is the attempt to cast the Bible into some contemporary form of thought, some context which will satisfy the present perspective of man. There may well be, in following up this alternative, a variety of interpretations. We might, for instance take issue with Konvitz and say that a return to the Israel of today is *equivalent* even if it is not *identical* to an end of the exile; or that such a return comes *as close as we can come* to that end. Clearly, though, the difficulty raised at this point is speculative in nature, dependent on internal profundities and strengths rather than upon dogmatics, a difficulty which in a sense concedes the primary argument of this essay.

But an even more basic question may be asked of Professor Simon's suggestion: In what way do we even know the law of which he speaks? The directions offered by the Bible are no longer offered to Biblical man but to an individual separated from the former by some twenty-five hundred years. Can and should he read the Bible with the same understanding which the original readers had, if in so doing he must ignore the developments of the intervening years? My position with regard to these questions has been clear: it seems both impossible and undesirable to avoid imposing the present context on an understanding of the Judaic tradition. Even in our most conscious efforts, critical elements imbibed through ages of exposure to thought other than that of the original context must make themselves felt. Moreover, even where the question is no longer one of whether or not man *can* escape his historical position, we should ask whether it would be *desirable* for him to do so, if doing so meant, as it would seem to, that he must also divest himself of the advances in seeing and knowing which history has brought with its passage. To the last question as to the first, the specifically literalist doctrine must answer affirmatively. Our objection to the first answer remains in turn that the situation is not primarily one in which one can choose sides, but that quite automatically and with cutting disregard for the wishes or interests of man, the decision of historical participation is made for him; no matter how high in the clouds man's head rises, his feet remain earthbound. To the second answer, I again suggest that knowledge and methodologies, just as consciousness, evolve and change, and that it would be wrong and arbitrary to attempt to ignore these external factors in determining the applications of that consciousness.

What remains on these terms of the Zionist ideal? I would do no more at this point than to repeat what seems to characterize, in common, the various examples that can be cited of the Zionist spirit—the identification of individual destiny with the destiny of a particular land. This is the literal sense of the Zionist doctrine, the concrete 'myth' which demands the allegiance of the Jew to a particular land and government. But it is clear that there are other approaches than simply this concrete expression of belief which may also be considered in our openness towards the tradition out of which they have come. Thus, one looks toward the grounds of that *belief* and it is possible here to discern a variety of ideas that can be appropriated: the idea of man's finitude, his dependence on the ordination of something or Being who is far greater than he is or can be, the longing and need experienced by man for transcendence and, as a result, his current state, in Konvitz' words, as the "eternal sojourner". Though by no means exhaustive of the currents which Zionism comprehends, *these* components at least are clearly found there. Putting aside the guise which they have assumed for others, we see them in what are less concrete and yet, more significant forms.

Clearly such an interpretation of Zionism stands open to further discussion and, because of this, to possible rejection or revision. Because of the further uncertainty which seems bound to afflict *any* solution based on the method implied here, it seems the more certain that the method itself must face charges of anarchy, of attempting to reduce tradition to personal whimsy and the coordinated body of organized religion to a chaos of individual and unviable cells. This problem of authority is, of course, a great and traditional difficulty of religion in general, in a sense the very problem out of which this essay has grown. It is not by way of avoiding it to suggest initially that it must be regarded less a disruption than a continuation in the history of the essentially non-authoritarian Judaic tradition.

In spite of such reassurance, however, there remains undeniable doubt. Abuses appear to be inevitable. Less by way of answer than by way of appeal, one might reply that indeed there is no reason to hope or suspect that abuses will *not* occur. There will be *poseurs* speaking out of complacency and even out of malice; there will never, even among men of good will, be the ability to see fully the consequences or pre-suppositions of what is proposed. To leave oneself exposed to these dangers is the risk accepted by any group whose continued existence depends on its individual members; and authority in Judaism must at least partially reside with these members. But this is not yet to imply anarchy or an individualism which must sweep away the boundaries demarcated by the life and faith of a people. There remains in this group that common openness of which I have already spoken. On the continued return in good faith to that source, itself derived from the objective experience of a people rich in experience, depends any assurance we may obtain for the continued life of a tradition. In a sense, this is a trust evoked by what seem to have been the prophylactic powers of history, powers which in spite of all deviations and backsliding have witnessed the unbroken chain of the Jewish people. But it would be inadequate to regard the process in such purely passive terms, inadequate if not for the past at least for the future. It is as if, after recognizing and admitting his identity, the Jew were to accept a categorical imperative of his own: "Act as if the whole of the Jewish people, history and belief, past and future, depended upon your action." Once we can no longer trust the response to this command, the rest must truly and deservedly be silence.

Judaism and the Zionist Problem

JACOB NEUSNER

THE SUCCESS OF ZIONISM IN SOLVING THE central Jewish problems of the modern age also creates new dilemmas for the Judaic religious tradition.[1] Since Zionism functions for Jewry in much the same way as religions do for other peoples, the role and function of *Judaism*—the complex of myths, rituals, social and cultural forms by which classical Jews experienced and interpreted reality—now prove exceptionally ambiguous. Because Zionism appropriates the eschatological language and symbolism of classical Judaism, Judaists face an unwanted alternative: either to repudiate Zionism or to acquiesce in the historicization, the politicization, of what had formerly stood above politics and beyond history. The choice to be sure was recognized and faced by small reform and orthodox circles, as everyone knows. The classical reformers repudiated Zionism in the name of the mission of Israel, which, they held, required Jewry to take a decisive role in the universal achievement by all men of the Messianic age. Their last, and unworthy, heirs accurately repeat the rhetoric, but do not possess the moral authority, of the nineteenth-century reformers. Likewise, orthodox leadership in Eastern Europe and the U.S.A. quite early discerned what they understood to be the heretical tendency of Zionism: the advocacy that Jews save themselves, rather than depend on the Messiah, and return to Zion before the foreordained end of time. Their repulsive continuators present no interesting differences from the anti-Zionist reformers.

For the great mass of American Jews, who take literally the Zionist interpretation of Jewish history and innocently identify Zionism with Judaism, but regard themselves also both as Americans by nationality and Jews by religion, naive belief substitutes for and precludes close analysis. They have yet to come to grips with the inner contradictions recognized by the extremists of reform and orthodox Judaism. Indeed, they exasperate Israeli Zionists as much as Diaspora anti-Zionists. If Zionist, then why American? If the end has come, why not accept the discipline of the eschaton? If the end has not come, how to justify the revision of the Judaic consciousness and its reformation along Zionist lines? Nor has U.S. Jewry taken seriously the demands of logic and intellect for the formation of a credible ideology to explain the status quo and justify it.

---

1. My "Zionism and 'The Jewish Problem,'" *Midstream*, Nov. 1969, pp. 34–35, states the other side of the problem.

DR. JACOB NEUSNER *is Professor of Religious Studies at Brown University*

"ENLANDISEMENT"

But the problem is not American alone, nor does it face only those who articulately espouse the Zionist idea. And, rightly, understood, the problem is not a new one. The tension between ethnicism and religion, between 'enlandisement' and universality, between Jewish nationalism and the mission of Israel, characterizes the history of the Jewish people and of Judaism throughout. Take, for example, the conflict of symbolism represented by Torah and Messiah. One achieves salvation through study of Torah and carrying out its precepts. *Or* one will be saved at the end of days by the Messiah of the House of David. But if Messiah, what need of Torah? And if Torah, why the Messiah? To be sure, the two are harmonized: If all Israel will keep a single Sabbath as the Torah teaches, then the Messiah will come. So the one is made to depend on the other. For the Talmudic rabbis, the Messiah depends upon Torah, and is therefore subordinate. Torah is an essentially particularist means of attaining salvation. Its observance is the obligation of Jews. Of all the commandments therein, only seven apply to non-Jews. The Messiah is primarily a universal figure. His action affects all mankind. Both nature and the nations, as much as Israel and its land, are the objects of his solicitude. Israel first, to be sure, but everyone at last comes to the end of days.

The tension between *holy land* and *holy Torah* as salvific symbols is pointed out by 'Abd al-Tafāhum in a remarkable essay, "Doctrine," [in A. J. Arberry, ed., *Religion in the Middle East* (Cambridge, 1969), Vol. II, Part 2: *The Three Religions in Concord and Conflict*, pp. 365–412]. What is remarkable is that al-Tafāhum (who is, I presume, a Moslem, though he is not identified by the editor) writes informedly and sympathetically about all three Middle Eastern religions. He writes (p. 367), "The whole self-understanding of the Hebrews turns on 'enlandisement' and habitation and then, centuries later, on 'disenlandisement' and dispersion. Its two poles are Exodus and Exile . . . The triangular relationship is that of God, people, and territory."

With the Exile, the physical symbol is reenforced, and, in time, moved into the framework of the last things. Internalizing the effects of historical weakness, the Jews understod the exile as punishment for their sins in the land—"unrighteous tenancy"—and, as al-Tafāhum says, "The single theme of 'enlandisement' as the sign and pledge of the divine will and the human response" becomes paramount. To this is added a second understanding of Exile: "the nationhood to educate nations, the awareness of election and particularity that embraces a universal parable for all the segments of mankind and all the diversified economic and spiritual tenancies of terrestrial habitation by peoples and races in those interactions that make culture and history."

The meaning of Jewish history therefore becomes the philosophy of "experienced Zion"—an experience available both in the land and outside of it. The symbolism of Judaic religious experience was ever more shaped by having *and* not having the land. Having the land means standing in a proper relationship with the natural order. Al-Tafāhum refers to A. D. Gordon: "everything creaturely is material for sanctification. . . The land of promise is properly not merely a divine bestowal but human fulfilment." Love of Zion produces the marriage of Messiahship and kingship, land and nation. Above all, it bears the intense particularities of Jewish existence, the overwhelming love for Israel—land, people, faith—characteristic of Jews through time.

"Disenlandisement," by contrast, produces the universal concern of Israel for all people: the willingness to enter into intimate relationship with each and every civilization. Election stands over against universality, but not wholly so: "Only you have I known among the families of man, therefore I shall visit on you all your iniquities." The unresolved tension in the history of Judaism is between privilege and particularity, on the one side, and the privilege of service to men on the other. Unlike Christianity, Judaism never chose to transcend its history, its intimacy with the Jews.

Al-Tafāhum poses the question: "If Jewry disapproves the universalizing of its human mission which has happened in the Church, how does it continue to reconcile its sense of privilege with the self-transcending obligation, confessed and prized, within that very identity?" Is Israel, the Jewish people, a mere ethnic continuity? Can it equate spiritual vocation with biological persistence? "Can the 'seed of Abraham' in any case be, in these times, a physically guaranteed notion? Is destiny identical with heredity and fidelity with birth?" "Can [Jewry] either delegate its universal duty or realize it merely by the percentage of literal seed?"

In former times, these questions found a response in the allegation that Israel had a mission to carry out among the nations. Israel was a presence within the world, "absorbing its values, using its languages and participating in its life, while casting off, sometimes almost in embarassment, the distinctiveness of its own history and cultic life." But that response has its limitations, for in discounting the "historic elements of dogma and sanctity," Jews lost also all sense of particularity and readily gave up what was unique to themselves to join the commonalities of mankind. The mission ended in assimilation among those to be missionized.

Zionism, al-Tafāhum observes, "posits in new and more incisive form the old question of universality." It contains within itself "an ever sharper ambiguity about the final questions of the universal meaning and obligation of the chosen people. . . . By its own deepest convictions Judaism is committed to the benediction of all people and without this loyalty its very particularity is disqualified."

The question therefore stands: "Has the new 'enlandisement' betrayed the old? Was Diaspora the true symbol or the tragic negation of what vocation meant? Are chosen-ness and the law, identity as God's and duty to man, still proper and feasible clues to Jewish existence? Or is the land now no more than the territorial location of a secular nationality apostate from itself?" Al-Tafāhum rightly asserts that these issues are not of merely political interest, for "they reach most deeply into . . . the doctrinal heart." It would be difficult to improve upon this statement of the dilemma raised for modern Judaism by Zionism. If Zionism solves "the Jewish problem," it also creates interesting problems for Judaism.

"EXCEPT THE JEWS"

Jews, too, have recognized this paradoxical quality of Jewish existence, particularly amid a universal, international situation. Writing in *The New Yorker* (March 21, 1970, p. 42), I. B. Singer has a character state,

> The modern Jew can't live without anti-Semitism. If it's not there, he's driven to create it. He has to bleed for humanity—battle the reactionaries, worry about the Chinese, the Manchurians, the Russians, the untouchables in India, the Negroes in America. He preaches revolution and at the same time he wants all the privileges of capitalism for himself. He tries to destroy nationalism in others but prides himself on belonging to the Chosen People. How can a tribe like this exist among strangers . . .

One can hardly regard Singer's insight as mere fiction, when the Lakeville studies have shown it is fact.

There, suburban Jews, studied by Marshall Sklare and Joseph Greenblum (*Jewish Identity on the Suburban Frontier* [N.Y., 1967]), raise Jewish children in a culture of equalitarianism and send them to colleges where ethnic liberalism predominates. At the same time they expect the children to develop strong Jewish identification. To be a good Jew in Lakeville is to be ethical, kind, helpful. But moral excellence does not derive from the particular ethic of Judaism, though people suppose it does. It is a function of the generalized upper-class liberalism of the community.

The authors wonder, "Will not a sectarianism which is unsupported ideologically wither away when social conditions change? Will future generations be prepared to live with the dichotomy which the Lakeville Jew abides: a universal humanitarianism as the prime value in combination with the practice of giving priority to Jewish causes? May [future generations] not conclude that their humanitarian aspirations dictate that they place the accent on the general rather than the Jewish?"

The paradox expressed by Singer accurately describes Lakeville Jews, who espouse universal values and teach them to their children, while at the same time wanting to preserve their own particular group, to marry their children off only to Jews. If the people is unique, then what is universal about it? If the people wish to preserve its ethnic existence, then why should it claim to stand with, and for, all mankind?

A HOSTILE VIEW

Zionism solves "the Jewish problem." Its success lies only partially in politics. The more profound problems for which it serves as a satisfactory solution are inward, spiritual, and, ultimately, religious. Just as the Judaic tradition had formerly told Jews what it meant to be Jewish —had supplied them with a considerable definition of their identity— so does Zionism in the modern age. Jews who had lost hold of the mythic structure of the past were given a grasp on a new myth, one composed of the restructured remnants of the old one.

The Jew had formerly been a member of a religious nation, believing in Torah revealed at Sinai, in one God who had chosen Israel, hoping for the Messiah and return to the land in the end of days. Jews who gave up that story of where they came from and who they are tell a new story based on the old, but in superficially secular form. To be Jewish means to live in the land and share in the life of the Jewish nation, which became the State of Israel.

To a hostile observer, things looked like this: the elements of "Jewishness" and the components of "Israelism" are to be one and the same—sacrifice, regeneration, resurrection. The sacrifice is no longer in the Temple; no prophets need decry the multitudes of fatted beasts. What now must be sacrificed is the blood of Israelis and the treasure of the Diaspora. The regeneration is no longer to be the turning of sinners to repentence—*teshuvah*—but rather the reformation of the economic and cultural realities of the Jewish people. No longer 'parasites,' but farmers, no longer dependent upon the cultural achievements of the nations but creators of a Hebrew, and 'enlandised' culture, the Jews would be reborn into a new being and a new age. The resurrection is no longer of the dead at the end of time, but of the people at the end of the Holocaust.

The unfriendly witness sees matters this way: The new Zionist identity, like the old Judaic one, supplied a law for the rituals and attitudes of the faith. The old *halakhah* was made irrelevant, the object of party-politics. The new was not partisan at all. All believed in, all fulfilled the law, except for sinners and heretics beyond the pale. The new law requires of Jewish man one great commandment: support Israel. Those who do it best, live there. Those who do not, pay a costly atonement in guilt and ransom for the absent body. The ransom is paid through the perpetual mobilization of the community in an unending campaign for funds. The guilt is exorcised through political rituals: letters to Congressmen and—for bourgeois Jews, what would normally be unheard of—mass rallies and street demonstrations. The guilt of Auschwitz and the sin of living in the Diaspora become intertwined: "On account of our sin do we live today, and in the wrong place at that!" Above all, the guilty and the sinner forever atone by turning to the *qiblah* of the land: There is no land but Israel, and the Jewish people are its product. The development of an American Jewish, or Judaic, culture is seen as irrelevant to the faith. The philanthropists will not support it, for no funds are left after allocations for Israel and for domestic humanitarian institutions. The rabbis will not speak of it, for the people will not listen. The people will hear of nothing but victories, and victories are won in this world, upon a fleshly battlefield, with weapons of war.

The old self-hatred—the vile anti-Semitism of an Alexander Portnoy—is left behind. No longer weak, one hardly needs to compensate for weakness by pretensions to moral superiority, and then to pay the price of that compensation by hatred of one's own weakness. Jews no longer look down on *goyim,* for they feel like them. The universal humanism, the cosmopolitanism of the old Jew are abandoned in the new particularism. The old grandmother who looked for Jewish names in reports of plane crashes has given way to the new grandson who turns off the news after the Middle Eastern reports are done with.

The Jew no longer makes contradictory demands on society. He no longer wants to be accepted into the tradition of society. In the new ethnicism of the hour, he seeks only his share. The liberal dilemma has been resolved. Jews now quite honestly interpret the universe in terms of their particular concerns. Self-hatred, liberalism, the crisis of identity—the three characteristics of the mid-twentieth century American Jew—all fade into the background. The end of the old myths no longer matters much, for new ones have arisen in their place. The American Jews who did not want to be so Jewish that they could not also be part of the undifferentiated majority have had their wish fulfilled. Some have indeed ceased to be Jewish at all, and no one cares. Many others have found a place in the new, well-differentiated majority—so goes the hostile view.

AGAINST RELIGIOUS REACTION

In my view, it is reactionary to cavil at these developments. Only an antiquarian cares about the end of old myths and the solution of the dilemmas that followed. Zionists need make no apologies to those who point out the profound changes Zionism effects in Jewish existence. They need only ask, Is self-hatred better than what we have done? Is a crisis of identity to be preferred over its resolution? Are people better off living among the remnants of disappointed other-worldly hopes, or shaping new aspirations? Surely it is healthier for men to recover a normal life than to lament the end of an abnormal one. Granted that the Jewish situation has radically changed, I contend it is no worse, and a good deal better, than what has been left behind. All the invidious contrasts in the world change nothing.

Zionism has had a uniformly beneficial effect upon Jewry. It achieves the reconstruction of Jewish identity by its reaffirmation of the nationhood of Israel in the face of the disintegration of the religious foundations of Jewish peoplehood. Zionism indeed supplies a satisfactory explanation for the continued life of the Jewish group. It reintegrates the realities of Jewish group life with an emotional, intellectual, and mythic explanation for those realities. If Zionism really is a new religion for the Jews, then I think, on that account, it is not obligated to apologize for its success. On the contrary, Zionism works a miracle by making it possible for the Jewish group to renew its life. It redeems the broken lives of the remnants of the Holocaust. But it also breathes new life into the survivors of a different sort of holocaust, the erosion of Jewish self-respect, dignity, and loyalty throughout the Western Diaspora. Jews who want more than anything else to become Americans are enabled to reaffirm their Jewishness. Throughout the world, Jews who had lost a religious, Judaic way of viewing reality regain a Jewish understanding of themselves.

Zionism indeed serves as a religion because it does what a religion must do: it supplies the meaning of felt-history; it explains reality, makes sense of chaos, and supplies a worthwhile dream for people who find in Jewishness nothing more than neurotic nightmares. Neither metaphysics nor theology proves necessary, for Zionism explains what the people already know and take for granted as fact. Zionism legitimates what Alexander Portnoy observed but could not accept: that Jews are men of flesh and blood, that (in Portnoy's phrase), *there is an id in Yid*. What is remarkable is that the early Zionists sought to do just that: to normalize the existence of the Jewish people.

THE ZIONIST PROBLEM

In what way, then, does Zionism constitute a problem for Judaism? In my view, it is not its secularity and worldliness, but the mythic insufficiency of Zionism that renders its success a dilemma for contemporary American Jews, and for Israeli ones as well.

Let us begin with the obvious. How can American Jews focus their spiritual lives *solely* on a land in which they do not live? It is one thing for that land to be in heaven, at the end of time, or across the Sambatyon for that matter. It is quite another to dream of a far-away place where everything is good—*but* where one may go if he wants. The realized eschaton is insufficient for a rich and interesting fantasy life, and, moreover, in this-worldly terms it is hypocritical. It means American Jews live off the capital of Israeli culture. Reliance on the state of Israel furthermore suggests that to satisfy their need for fantasy, American Jews must look forward to ever more romantic adventures reported in the press, rather than to the colorless times of peace. American Jews want to take their vacations among heroes, and then come home to the ordinary workaday world they enjoy and to which Israelis rightly aspire but do not own. The 'enlandisement' of American Judaism—the focusing of its imaginative, inner life upon the land and State of Israel—therefore imposes an *ersatz* spiritual dimension. We live here *as if* we lived there—but do not choose to migrate.

It furthermore diverts American Judaism from the concrete mythic issues it has yet to solve: Why should anyone be a *Jew* anywhere, in the U.S.A. or in Israel? That question is not answered by the recommendation to participate in the spiritual adventures of people in a quite different situation. Since the primary *mitzvot* of U.S. Judaism concern supplying funds, encouragement, and support for Israel, one wonders whether one must be a Jew at all in order to believe and practice in that form of Judaism. What is 'being Jewish' now supposed to mean?

The underlying problem, which faces both Israeli and American Jews, is understanding what the ambiguous adjective *Jewish* is supposed to mean when the noun *Judaism* has been abandoned. To be sure, for some Israelis and American Jews to be a Jew is to be a citizen of the State of Israel—but that definition hardly serves when Israeli Moslems and Christians are taken into account. If one ignores the exceptions, the rule is still wanting. If to be a Jew is to be—or to dream of being—an Israeli, then the Israeli who chooses to settle in a foreign country ceases to be a Jew when he gives up Israeli citizenship for some other. If all Jews are on the road to Zion, then those who either do not get there or, once there, choose another way are to be abandoned. That makes Jewishness depend upon quite worldly issues: This one cannot make his living in Tel Aviv, that one does not like the climate of Affula, the other is frustrated by the bureaucracy of Jerusalem. Are they then supposed to give up their share in the "God of Israel"?

More seriously still, the complete 'enlandisement' of Judaism for the first time since 586 B.C.E. forces the Judaic tradition to depend upon the historical fortunes of a single population in a small country. The chances for the survival of the Jewish people have surely been enhanced by the dispersion of the Jews among differing political systems. Until World War II Jews had stood on both sides of every international contest from most remote antiquity. Now, we enter an age in which the fate of Jewry and destiny of Judaism are supposed to depend on the fortunes of one state and one community alone.

That, to be sure, is not a fact, for even now the great Jewish communities in the U.S.S.R., Western Europe, Latin America, and North America, as well as smaller ones elsewhere, continue to conform to the historical pattern. But, ideologically, things have vastly changed. With all the Jewish eggs in one basket, the consequence of military actions is supposed to determine the future of the whole of Jewry and Judaism. So the excellence of some eight hundred pilots and the availability of a few dozen fighter-bombers are what it all comes down to. Instead of the thirty-six righteous men of classical myth are seventy-two phantoms—mirages—a curious revision of the old symbolism.

A JUDAIC ANSWER

Just what is *important* about being Jewish and in Judaism? In my view, the answer must pertain both to the State of Israel and to the *Golah* communities in equal measure. It cannot be right only for American Jewry, for we are not seeking a *Galut*-ideology and no one would accept it. Such an ideology—right for here but irrelevant to Israelis—would obviously serve the selfish interests and the peculiar situation of American Jews alone. But the answer cannot pertain only to the situation of the Israeli Jews, for precisely the same reasons.

What is important about being Jewish is the capacity of the Jewish people and its mythic creations to preserve the tension between the intense particularities of their life and the humanity they have in common with the rest of mankind. That tension, practically unique to Jewry, derives from its exceptional historical experience. Until now, it has been the basis for the Jews' remarkable role in human history.

Others have not felt such a tension. To be human and to be English—or Navaho—were hardly differentiated. And why should they have been, when pretty much everyone one cared for and knew was English, or Navaho? To be a Jew in any civilization was, and is, to share the values held by everyone *but* to stand in some ways apart (not above) from the others. It was, and is, to love one's native land with open arms, to preserve the awareness of other ways of living life and shaping culture.

To be sure, before the destruction of the First Temple, Jewish people may well have been much like others. But from that time forward the land was loved with an uncommon intensity, for it had been lost, then regained, therefore could never again be taken for granted. And alongside land, the people found, as few have *had* to, that Jews live by truths that could endure outside a single land and culture. Jewry discovered in itself an international culture, to be created and recreated in every land and in every language. It found in its central moral and ethical convictions something of value for all of civilizations. Its apprehension of God and its peculiar method of receiving and spelling out revelation in the commonplaces of everyday life were divorced from a single place, even the holiest place in the world where they had begun.

But al-Tafāhum is wrong in supposing that the Jews' 'disenlandisement' was the precondition for the recognition of what was of universal importance about themselves. On the contrary, it was in the land itself that the awareness of ethnic differentiation proved the least vivid. Outside of it the group turned inward, and rightly so, for it became most acutely sensitive to its differences from others. In this respect the gentile students of Judaism do not understand what it is to be a Jew. The diaspora Jew addresses himself to the nations and in their own language, but in doing so he speaks as a *Jew*. It is the 'enlandised' Jew who sees himself as no different from everyone within his range of vision, therefore as man among men, rather than Jew among gentiles. The willingness and necessity to enter into intimate relationship with each and every civilization therefore produced two sorts of encounters, the one, between the Jewish man in his land and other men who might come there, or whom he might know elsewhere, men who held in common the knowledge of what it means to belong to some one place; the other, between the world and the always self-aware Jew living in other lands, a Jew sensitive to the language and experience of those lands precisely because he was forever at the margins of the common life.

Jewry did not disapprove the universalizing of its mission in the Church. It simply did not recognize that the Church ever truly carried out that mission. Jewry perceived no discontinuity requiring reconciliation between its sense of peoplehood (privilege) and its "self-transcending obligation." The Jews long ago ceased to be a mere ethnic continuity, and no one, in either the State of Israel or the Diaspora, regards the Jews as merely an ethnic group. One can, after all, become a Jew by other than ethnic and territorial assimilation, through *conversion*. That fact predominates in all discussions of what it is to be a Jew. The issue comes from the other side: *Can* one become a Jew not through conversion, but through mere assimilation? The dogged resistance of Jewry to the reduction of Jewishness to ethnicity alone, testifies to the falseness of al-Tafāhum's reading of the Jewish situation.

But his other question is indeed troubling: Is destiny to be equated with heredity and fidelity with birth? The answer to that question can be found only in the working out of the potentialities of both Israeli and Diaspora Jewish life.

To be sure, the old Diaspora—the one before 1948—absorbed the values of the nations and could locate no one center where the distinctiveness, hence the universality, of Jewish history and civilization might be explored. Zionism does indeed posit in new and more incisive form the old question of universality, *but it also answers that question.* In the Jewish state Jews lose their sense of peculiarity. They re-enter the human situation common to everyone but Jews. In the State of Israel everyone is Jewish, therefore no one is the Jew. And this, in my view, opens the way to an interesting development: the reconsideration of Jewish humanity in relationship with the other sorts of humanity in the world. It is now possible for the normal to communicate with the normal.

What the Israelis have to communicate is clear to one and all. They have not divorced themselves from important elements of the Jewish past, but have retained and enhanced them. The possession of the land, after all, represents such an important element. What does it mean to believe that one's moral life is somehow related to the destiny of the land in which one lives? In times past the question would have seemed nonsensical. But today no people is able to take its land, its environment, for granted. Everyone is required to pay attention to what one does with one's blessings. Today each land is endangered by immoral men who live upon and make use of it. The moral pollution of which the prophets spoke may infect not only a society but the way a society makes use of its resources. So the intimate relationship between Israel and the land is no longer so alien to the existence of other nations. And the ecological-moral answers found in the land and State of Israel are bound to have universal meaning.

I choose this example because it is the least obvious. The record of the State of Israel is, in my view, not ambiguous about "the final questions of the universal meaning and obligation of the chosen people." One need not be an Israeli apologist to recognize the numerous ways in which the State of Israel has sought to make war without fanaticism, to wage peace with selflessness. Only indifference to the actual day to day record of the State of Israel, with its technical assistance, its thirst for peace, its fundamentally decent society at home, and above all its hatred of what it must do to survive, justifies questions concerning Israel's "universal duty." On the contrary, it seems to me that Israeli society has, within the limits of its wisdom and power, committed itself to the benediction of all peoples, and with its loyalty to that very blessing its very particularity is verified and justified.

I therefore do not agree that the new 'enlandisement' has betrayed the old. It has fulfilled it.

The other half of the question pertains to the Diaspora. The Diaspora was neither the true symbol nor the tragic negation of Israel's vocation. "Chosen-ness and law, obligation to God and duty to man," are still proper and feasible clues to Jewish existence *both* at home and abroad. The land never was, and is not now, merely the territorial locus of a secular nationality. The existence of the Diaspora guarantees otherwise. The Diaspora supplies the certainty that men of many languages and civilizations will look to Zion for more than a parochial message, just as the Israelis make certain the Diaspora Jews will hear that message. But, as I said, things are the reverse of what al-Tafāhum supposes. The Diaspora brings its acute consciousness of being different from other men, therefore turns to the State to discover the ways in which it is like the others. The Diaspora contributes its variety and range of human experience to the consciousness of the State of Israel. But the State offers the Diaspora the datum of normality.

One cannot divide the Jewish people into two parts, the 'enlandised' and the 'disenlandised.' Those in the land look outward. Those outside look toward the land. Those in the land identify with the normal peoples. Those abroad see in the land what it means to be extraordinary. But it is what happens to the whole, altogether, that is decisive for the Judaic tradition. And together, the Diaspora Jew and the Israeli represent a single tradition, a single memory. That memory is of having had a land and lost it—*and* never having repudiated either the memory of the land *or* the experience of living elsewhere. No one in the State of Israel can imagine that to be in the land is for the Jew what being in England is to the Englishman. The Englishman has never lost England and come back. So one cannot distinguish between the Israeli and the Diaspora Jew. Neither one remembers or looks upon a world in which his particular values and ideals are verified by society. Neither ceases to be cosmopolitan. Both preserve a universal concern for *all* Israel. Both know diversities of culture and recognize therefore the relativity of values, even as they affirm their own.

This forms what is unique in the Jewish experience: the denial of men's need to judge all values by their particular, self-authenticating system of thought. In this regard the Diaspora re-enforces the Israeli's view of the world, and the Israeli reciprocates. Both see as transitory and merely useful what others understand to be absolute and perfected. Behind the superficial eschatological self-confidence of Zionism lies an awareness everywhere present that that is just what Zionism adds up to: a *merely* secular eschatology. No one imagines that Zionism has completed its task or that the world has been perfected. The world is seen by both parts of the Jewish people to be insufficient and incomplete.

The Israelis' very sense of necessity preserves the Jews' neatest insight: without choice, necessity imposes duty, responsibility, unimagined possibilities. The Jews are not so foolish as to have forgotten the ancient eternal cities—theirs and others'—which are no more. They know therefore that it is not the place, but the quality of life within it, that truly matters. No city is holy, not even Jerusalem, but men must live in some one place and assume the responsibilities of the mundane city. But if no city is holy, at least Jerusalem may be made into a paradigm of sanctity. Though all they have for mortar may be slime, Jewish men will indeed build what they must, endure as they have to. The opposite is not to wander, but to die.

But have Diaspora Jews strayed so far from those same truths? In sharing the lives of many civilizations, do they do other than to assume responsibility for place? Do they see the particular city as holy, because they want to sanctify life in it? Or do they, too, know that the quality of life *anywhere* is what must truly matter? Men must live in some one place, and so far as Jewish men have something to teach of all they have learned in thirty centuries, they should live and learn and teach in whatever place they love. And one may err if he underestimates the capacity of the outsider, of the Diaspora Jew, to love.

I therefore see no need either to repudiate Zionism or to give up the other elements that have made *being Jewish* a magnificent mode of humanity. Zionism, on the contrary, supplies Jewry with still another set of experiences, another set of insights into what it means to be human. Only those who repudiate the unity of Israel, the Jewish people, in favor of either of its segments can see things otherwise. But viscerally American Jews know better, and I think they are right in refusing to resolve the tensions of their several commitments. Zionism creates problems for Judaism only when Zionists think that all that being Jewish means is 'enlandisement' and, thereby, redemption. But Zionists *cannot* think so when they contemplate the range of human needs and experiences they as men must face. Zionism is a part of Judaism. It cannot be made the whole, because Jews are more than people who need either a place to live or a place on which to focus fantasies. The profound existential necessities of Jews—both those they share with every man and those they have to themselves—are not met by Zionism or 'enlandisement' alone. Zionism provides much of the vigor and excitement of contemporary Jewish affairs, but so far as Jews live and suffer, are born and die, reflect and doubt, raise children and worry over them, love and work —so far as Jews are human, they require Judaism.

A STRANGER AT HOME:
AN AMERICAN JEW VISITS IN ISRAEL

JACOB NEUSNER

I HAVE VISITED the State of Israel three times: during the summer of 1954 on the Jewish Agency's Summer Institute; during the academic year 1957-1958 as a Fulbright Scholar at the Hebrew University; and this past summer on the Agency's Seminar for Educators. I have travelled the length and breadth of the country, from Eliat to Metullah, from Jerusalem to Safed, from Haifa to the Dead Sea. I have been obsessed with the land and the State, both as a believing Jew and as an American Zionist.

The more I know about Israel, the less I feel I understand. The more I meet Israelis, the less I comprehend them. The reality of the State and its people overwhelms me, perplexes me, troubles and disturbs me.

The astonishing fact about Israel is that it is what it claims to be, a Jewish State built by Jewish people on Jewish soil and by Jewish labor; a state in which the Hebrew language and the Jewish creative genius form the foundation of national culture; a state in which the Jew is at home, no longer challenged by the Gentile to explain who

---

Dr. Neusner, a frequent contributor to scholarly journals on Jewish history and religion, was ordained at the Jewish Theological Seminary of America. He is currently chairman of the Department of Hebrew Studies at the University of Wisconsin, Milwaukee.

he is and why he persists in history, no longer faced with the task of mediating between his Jewishness and another culture.

These are facts, no longer hopes, and hence are easy to forget. Perhaps the only time one really faces them is in the first few days in Israel. Afterward, the reality of Israel fades away, because it is commonplace, and one pays more attention to the superficialities of daily life. Each visit to Israel I have faced these facts, and asked myself the question too many Israelis ask, Why do I not settle here? Too much troubled by the question, I seek, and find, the answers in daily life, both at home and in Israel.

At home, one is most aware that he is a Jew, because that is how he is distinguished from other Americans, with whom he has so much in common. In Israel, one is mostly an American, or, less appropriately, an "Anglo-Saxon" (I think certain exclusive hotels and country clubs would find *that* interesting). Even though I want to feel at home, more often than not I am treated as a foreigner and a tourist: I am an American. In the end, I find myself affirming just that: I am an American, both sentimentally and culturally, and my deepest loyalties are to America.

How then may I, as a Jew, take into account the astonishing facts that the

State of Israel realizes? If it is all true, as it is, then how am I to respond?

Anyone might find numerous answers, in the superficialities of daily life there and in the profundities of civilization here. Here I find much that I like, admire, accept, and want to transmit to the future. I do not believe any society has been so open or free, so fundamentally decent, as American society. I do not believe daily life anywhere else can be so easy and relaxed. I do not find any national culture developing with such vigor, variety, or soundness, the proof of which is the eagerness of other nations to appropriate elements of American culture. Here, furthermore, I find an ideal, a "way of life," unique in human affairs today, and I want to share in the defense of that ideal, which is, quite simply, democracy in political, cultural, social, and religious life. Just as the Israeli easily forgets the astonishing facts represented by Israel, so we regard the unique achievements of American democracy as commonplace, and are more aware of contradictions of the democratic ideal within American society than of its realizations.

Israelis do not understand the nationalism and patriotism of Jewish Americans, for in no European country was a Jew able to feel that he was part of the "majority" culture; the exceptions, in Western Europe, were few in number, and generally entered the majority by relinquishing ties to their own religious and cultural minority. Israelis generally regard the loyalty of American Jews to America as similar to the loyalty of "Egyptian" Jews to the fleshpots of Pharoah, and similarly reprehensible. It is difficult for the Israelis I met to refrain from warning me of historical facts I know full well, that no other Diaspora community ever was entirely spared, at some points in its history, the rigors of anti-Semitism. I often replied that security is not available to a people that persists too long in history. No matter where one lives, if he stays there for long enough, times are likely to change, and earlier certainties vanish. I ask only the uninterrupted and generally happy tenure of the Jews in Babylon, longer, in fact, than that of the Jews in Palestine. The Jews in Palestine trace a history, during the First Commonwealth, of about six hundred years, and during the second, of about eight hundred years (measuring from the return under Cyrus to the beginning of the fourth century of the Common Era), while (so far as we can tell) the Jews in Babylon lived under reasonably secure conditions, by comparison to those affecting other peoples in Mesopotamia, from the time of Jeremiah at least until the decline of the Sassanian Empire in the sixth century of the Common Era, eleven hundred years, or even further, until 1948. In truth, security could hardly be the criterion to measure the value of settling among forty million hostile Arabs. Finally, the experience of German Jewry, which felt analagously toward Germany, is hardly decisive, first, because America is not Germany, and has no such black hatred of Jews as part of its nationalism, and second, because if Rommel had won at El Alamein in 1942, Palestinian Jewry would, alas, have had no better fate than Dutch, German, or Italian Jewries. In fact, history proves nothing about the truth of ideas, but renders them, without reference to their rightness, either real or tragic.

DAILY LIFE IN ISRAEL seemed to me unnecessarily difficult, not only because of the difficulty of making a living, but because of different attitudes toward the conduct of life and standards of right action. It would be discourteous of a visitor to become specific, but on more than one occasion, I felt "Israel for the Israelis."

At times I felt that the xenophobia of Israelis, and, in particular, their disdain for American Jewry, expresses less a considered judgment than a response to the question, What are *we* doing here? One well-educated young Israeli told me that he would find a certain satisfaction in forced emigration of American Jewry; and, in general, I can see *shelilat hagolah* as little more than a very specific form of xenopohia, expressed also in ridicule of the pronounced American accent in speaking Hebrew, of American ways of dress, of Americans' insistence even on clean kitchens and sanitary facilities. We, for our part, ought not to feel we must criticize the conditions of Israeli life and social intercourse in order to justify our "remaining" in America. I do not think we need to exalt the situation of *Golah*, its cultural and social benefits, in order to defend our status quo. I was born in America, as a part of the third generation of American Jews and an educator of the fourth; I do not feel the necessity to affirm reality, or to promise, even, to write a Babylonian Talmud in order to justify life in our modern Babylon. "Blessed is he who inspires the inhabitants of a place with love for it." I neither affirm nor deny destiny, but, only, accept it.

I think that a far more significant problem than American *aliyah* or Israeli *yeridah* (since 1948, more Israelis have settled in the Western hemisphere than have Americans, both north and south of the border, immigrated to Israel) is the problem of future relationships between the State and the Diaspora, particularly the American Diaspora. The tragic necessities of the past decades, of saving a remnant and helping them to build a homeland, have demanded an awful price in blood. They have, however, only begun to manifest the price to be paid by the living. The American Jewish community has generously responded to Israel's legitimate financial requirements, and will, I hope, continue to do so for decades. It has received in exchange a great and welcome return: the State itself, its extraordinary achievements, its successful refutation of any and every anti-Semitic canard against the Jewish people. In truth, whatever factual basis anti-Semitism ever had in economic, social, political, or cultural life has been swept away. The Jew can no longer be accused of economic parasitism, for he has drained swamps and planted deserts; of social or cultural parasitism, for he has recovered and enhanced his own heritage; of political impotence, for he has reentered the drama of history. All this has been achieved by the State of Israel. The State has, moreover, ended the corroding fear of Jewish homelessness, and however secure the Jew is in America, he has shared that fear if he has read either history or the daily newspaper. Israel owes absolutely nothing to American Jewry, and can never be properly repaid for the blood and iron it has lavished to create and sustain itself. I think a great part of American Jewish consensus has to do with the pride and affirmation of American Jewry toward the State and the Zionist cause. In this sense, Israel has served to unify American Jewry, to give its disparate elements a common cause and a common purpose. Finally, the cultural benefits of the State have only begun to reach and fructify our community life.

ISRAELIS, on the other hand, have too little awareness of how much they have given American Jews, and have a sense of obligation that is neither appropriate nor affirmative. They see themselves as takers, not givers, and such a self-image does not lead to pride or love. I think another part of Israeli xenophobia may be therefore explained by the Israeli's need to show his independence of his "rich American" guests. "We may be dependent on your money," I was told, "but we will not therefore kowtow to you." (Alas, not a few tourists expect just that.) Nonetheless, the interest most Israelis seem to have in the *Golah* communities is apparently limited by Israeli needs for money and man-power. "Be kind to tourists, they bring hard currency," a poster for children reads; and another, "Every tourist is a potential immigrant." I found very little curiosity about the development of American Jewish life, except as related to Israeli affairs; very little interest in non-Zionist activities in general; and none whatever in our hopes for American Jewry's future. Furthermore, I regretted to find that Israelis are far less prepared to support voluntary communal activities than American Jews are.

When a perfectly legitimate social welfare institution, or cultural activity requires support, the first and primary source of financial support is either the Government—or the *Golah*. It is certainly true that Israelis have much, much less to give. Giving, however, is measured not only by the size of the gift, but by the benefit to the giver. For example, a certain synagogue in Jerusalem was built mainly by American Jews. When two women who had shared in the project asked the president of the congregation why no landscaping had been done for the building (now standing for more than a decade on one of Jerusalem's main streets), he replied that they ought to ask their husbands to raise the funds. (Indeed, the synagogues pay their rabbis abysmal salaries, most of which come from government funds.)

Seeing themselves, however inaccurately, as takers and not givers, Israelis apparently see the need to defend whatever they do against moderate and intelligent criticism. They appeal all too often to clichés in order to explain deficiencies. An old story, out of the 1930's, tells about an American who is shown through the new subway system in Moscow. He is impressed by the marbled halls, the immaculate floors, the displays of fine art on the walls, and asks, "This is all very lovely, but where are the subway trains themselves?" "And what about the Negroes in the South?" his guide exclaimed. In Israel, I found two stock replies to the most gentle criticism: first, an appeal to "two thousand years of *Golah*," or alternatively, to "the first Jewish State after two thousand years"; or, secondly, to the relative youth of the country, and its obviously formidable achievements in so few years. Israel is, however, not a great deal younger than the organized American Jewish community, which for all practical purposes may be dated at about 1880 (Reform and Conservative institutions) or 1900 (Orthodox institutions). In any case, how long does it take to clean the garbage that litters the streets in so many cities? I once asked why the newest and most modern apartment houses invariably have obvious and malodorous garbage cans in the front entry, instead of at the back door, and was accused of being a Jewish anti-Semite or an assimilationist. Indeed, one of the costliest charges of building the State has been paid by the Jew's ancient, resourceful capacity to to laugh at himself.

AS I SAID, the problem that troubles me most is the future relationship between the State and the American *Golah*. It is fashionable in Israel to ridicule the Jewish Agency, but what I know of its work impresses me. It is actively interested in bringing *Golah* Jews to Israel, and I think its interest is not only *aliyah* or potential leadership in pro-Israeli activity, but also in a cultural and national renaissance, based on the foundation of Israeli realities and Hebrew culture, throughout the Jewish world. I heard a speech by an Agency official, on the importance of Jewish education everywhere, in which the attraction of Castro for South American Jewish youth was described as a great calamity. That official, and his colleagues, voiced concern for the future of South American Jewry not on account of specific Israeli interests, but on account of the interest of the Jewish nation everywhere. The Agency's work has only just begun. If, as I believe, a Jew who has visited Israel for any substantial period is fundamentally changed in his attitude toward himself as a Jew and toward the potentialities of Jewishness and Judaism, then the importance of the Jewish Agency's program is greatly enhanced. A Jew who has seen the State, the land, and the people must be utterly different from a Jew who has not. The Agency, for all its imperfections, is one effective means of bringing Israel and its benefits into the lives of Jews everywhere.

I do not understand the State of Israel yet, but I understand the fact of its existence, and find myself compelled to rethink the meaning of the Jewish faith and of Jewish destiny because of that fact. That is why I shall return, I hope, to Israel many times, perhaps to stay, not because of what I could ever hope to give to the Jewish State, but because of what the Jewish State has already given me.

Zionism and "The Jewish Problem"

By JACOB NEUSNER

I

WHEN HERZL proposed Zionism as the solution to the Jewish problem, the "Zionism" of which he spoke and the "Jewish problem" which he proposed to solve constituted chiefly political realities. But, as Arthur Hertzberg trenchantly argues in *The Zionist Idea,* Zionism actually represented not a merely secular and political ideology, but the transvaluation of Jewish values. If so, the same must be said of the "Jewish problem" to which it addresses itself. Zionism as an external force faced the world, but what shall we say of its inner spirit? The inwardness of Zionism—its "piety" and spirituality—is not to be comprehended by the world, only by the Jew, for, like the Judaism it transformed and transcended, to the world it was worldly and political, stiff-necked and stubborn (in Christian theological terms), but to the Jew it was something other, not to be comprehended by the gentile.

In his celebrated correspondence with Eugen Rosenstock-Huessy, Franz Rosenzweig wrote (in *Judaism Despite Christianity, The "Letters on Christianity and Judaism" Between Eugen Rosenstock-Huessy and Franz Rosenzweig,* edited by Eugen Rosenstockzweig-Huessy, [University of Alabama Press, 1969], p. 133):

> ... I find that everything that I want to write is something I can't express to you. For now I would have to show you Judaism from within, that is, to be able to show it to you in a hymn, just as you are able to show me, the outsider, Christianity. And for the very reason that you can do it, I cannot. Christianity has its soul in its externals; Judaism, on the outside, has only its hard protecting shell, and one can speak of its soul only from within ...

Following Hertzberg, one can hardly see Zionism except as a New Judaism, a completely new view of all that had gone before and an utterly different conception of what should come hereafter. But this Zionism—neither spiritual nor political, but in a measure a unique amalgam of the spirit and the *polis*—is hidden by its hard protecting shell. What then can we say of its soul from within?

The Zionism of which I speak is the effort to realize through political means the hope supposed to have been lost in the time of Ezekiel, proclaimed imperishable in the time of Imber, the continuous hope of restoration and renaissance first of the land of Israel, then of the people of Israel through the land, finally, since 1948, of the people and the land together, wherever the people should be found. This Zionism did not come about at Basel, for its roots go back to the point in the ages at which Jewry first recognized, then rejected, its separation from the land. Zionism is the old-new Judaism, a Judaism transformed through old-new values. It is a set of paradoxes through which the secular and the religious, separated in the nineteenth century, were again fused—re-fused—in the twentieth. Zionism to be sure is a complex phenomenon; within it are tendencies which are apt to cancel each other. But all forms of Zionism are subsumed under the definition offered here, which represents, I think, the lowest common denominator for all Zionist phenomena.

The Jewish problems which Zionism successfully solved were the consequence of the disintegration of what had been whole, the identity, consciousness, and the culture of the Jew. It was, as I said, Zionism which reconstructed the whole and reshaped the tradition in a wholly new heuristic framework.

II

In former times it was conventional to speak of the "Jewish problem." Most people understood that problem in political and economic terms. What shall we do about the vast Jewish populations of Eastern and Central Europe, which live a marginal economic life and have no place in the political structures of the several nations? Herzl proposed the Zionist solution to the "Jewish problem." Dubnow wished to solve the "Jewish problem" by the creation of Jewish autonomous units in Europe. The Socialists and Communists proposed to solve the "Jewish problem" by the integration of Jewry into the movement of the international proletariat and to complete the solution of the problems of the smaller group within those of the working classes.

Today we hear less talk about the "Jewish problem" because Hitler brought it to a final solution: by exterminating the masses of European Jews, he left unsolved no social, economic, or political problems. The Western Jewries are more or less well-integrated into the democratic societies. The State of Israel has no "Jewish problem" in the classic sense. The oppressed communities remaining in the Arab countries are relatively small, and the solution of their problems is to be found in migration to the West and to the State of Israel. The "Jewish problem" to be sure continues to confront Soviet Russia, and there the classic Marxist formulation of the problem still persuades people. But, for the rest, the "Jewish problem" does not describe reality or evoke a recognized, real-life perplexity. (That does not mean Jews do not have problems, or that gentiles do not have problems in relating to and understanding both Jews and Judaism.)

I shall concentrate on three aspects of the contemporary Jewish situation, all closely related, and all the result of secularism. The first is the crisis of identity, the second, the liberal dilemma, the third, the problem of self-hatred. The Jewish identity-crisis may be simply stated: There is no consensus shared by most Jews about what a Jew is, how Judaism should be defined, what "being Jewish" and "Judaism" are supposed to mean for individuals and the community. The liberal dilemma is this: How can I espouse universal principles and yet remain part of a particular community? The problem of self-hatred needs little definition, but provokes much illustration, for many of the phenomena of contemporary Jewish life reflect the low self-esteem attached to being Jewish.

III

For Jews the secular revolution is not new. From the Haskalah, the Jewish Enlightenment in the eighteenth century onward, Jews have come forward to propose a non-religious interpretation of "being Jewish," an interpretation divorced from the classic mythic structure of Judaism. The God-Is-Dead movement evoked little response among Jewish theologians and ideologists because they found nothing new in it. If the issue was naturalistic, instead of supernatural, theology, Jewish theologians had heard Mordecai Kaplan for half-a-century or more. If the issue was atheism, it had been formulated by Jewish secularists, socialists, and assimilationists in various ways from the mid-nineteenth-century forward. If the secular revolution means that large numbers of people cease to look to religion, or to religious institutions, for the meaning of their lives and cease to practice religious traditions and to affirm religious beliefs, then this is neither news nor a revolution. Jews have participated in that sort of "revolution" for two centuries. They have done so without ceasing to regard themselves, and to be regarded by others, as Jews. That does not mean the Jews have found antidotes to the secular fever, but it does mean that they by now have a considerable heritage of experience, a substantial corpus of cases and precedents, for what Christians find to be new and revolutionary: the loosing of the world from all religious and supernatural interpretations.

IV

The secular revolution has imposed upon Jews a profound crisis of identity. In former times everyone knew who who was a Jew and what being a Jew meant. A Jew was a member of a religious nation, living among other nations by its own laws, believing in *Torah* revealed at Sinai and in one God who had chosen Israel, and hoping for the coming of the Messiah. The gentile world shared the philosophical presuppositions of Jewish beliefs. Everyone believed in God. Everyone believed in prophecy, in revelation, in the Jews' holy book. Everyone believed in the coming of the Messiah. Above all, everyone interpreted reality by supernaturalist principles. To be sure groups differed on the nature of God, the particular prophets to be regarded as true, the book God had revealed. But these differences took place within a vast range of agreement.

When religious understandings of the world lost their hold on masses of Western men, "being Jewish" became as problematical as any other aspect of archaic reality. If to be Jewish meant to be part of a Jewish religious community, then when men ceased to believe in religious propositions, they ought to have ceased being Jewish. Yet that is not what happened. For several generations Jewish atheists and agnostics have continued to take an active role in the Jewish community—indeed, functionally to constitute the majority in it—and to have seen nothing unusual either in their participation in Jewish life or in their lack of religious commitment. Indeed today the American Jewish community is nearly unique in interpreting "being Jewish" primarily in religious, or at least rhetorically-religious, terms. Other Jewish communities see themselves as a community, a nation, a people, whether or not religion plays a role in defining what is particular about that community. The secular revolution immensely complicated the definition of Jewish identity, not only by breaking down the uniform classical definition, but also by supplying a variety of new, complex definitions in its place.

Today, therefore, if we ask ourselves, "What are the components of 'Jewishness'?" we are hard put to find an answer. What are the attitudes, associations, rituals both secular and religious, psychology and culture, which both Jews and others conceive to be Jewish? The truth is, today there is no such thing as a single Jewish identity, as there assuredly was in times past an identity one could define in meaningful terms. Jewishness now is a function of various social and cultural settings, and is meaningful in those settings only.

The Jews obviously are not a nation in the accepted sense; but they also are hardly a people in the sense that an outsider can investigate or understand the components of that peoplehood. There is no "Jewish way" of organizing experience and interpreting reality, although there was and is a Judaic way. There is no single Jewish ideology, indeed no single, unitary Jewish history, although there once was a cogent Judaic theology and a Judaic view of a unitary and meaningful progression of events to be called "Jewish history." Only if we impose upon discrete events of scarcely related groups in widely separated places and ages the concept of a single unitary history can we speak of "Jewish history." Jewish peoplehood in a concrete, secular, this-worldly historical sense is largely a matter of faith, that is, the construction of historians acting as do theologians in other settings. There once was a single Jewish ideological system, a coherent body of shared images, ideas and ideals, which provided for participants a coherent over-all orientation in space and time, in means and ends. There once was such a system, but in the secular revolution it has collapsed.

It is indeed, the secular revolution that has imposed on Jewry a lingering crisis of identity. Jews today may find in common a set of emotions and responses. These do not constitute an "identity," but rather, a set of common characteristics based upon differing verbal explanations and experiences. That does not mean no one knows what a Jew is. In particular settings Jews *can* be defined and understood in terms applicable to those settings. But as an abstraction the "Jewish people" is a theological or ideological construct not to be imposed upon the disparate, discrete data known as Jews or even as Jewish communities in various times and places. Lacking a common language and culture, even a common religion, the Jews do not have what they once had. Today Jewish identity so greatly varies that we need to reconsider the viability of the very concept of "Jewishness" as a universal attribute, for today Jewishness cannot be defined in neutral, cultural terms.

If there are no inherent and essential Jewish qualities in the world, then nothing about "being Jewish" is natural, to be taken for granted. Being Jewish becomes something one must achieve, define, strive for. It is today liberated from the forms and content of the recent past, from the "culture-Judaism" of the American and Canadian Jewish communities. If the artifacts of that "culture-Judaism"—matters of cuisine, or philanthropy, or cliquishness—are not part of some immutable and universal Jewish identity, then they may well be criticized from within, not merely abandoned and left behind in disgust. One can freely repudiate them in favor of other ways.

Omissions in contemporary Jewish "identity" are as striking as the inclusions. Among the things taken for granted are a sense of group-loyalty, a desire to transmit "pride in Judaism" to the next generation, in all a desire to survive. But the identity of large numbers of Jews, whether they regard themselves as secular or not, does not include a concept of God, of the meaning of life, of the direction and purpose of history. The uncriticized, but widely accepted Jewish-identity syndrome is formed of the remnants of the piety of the recent past, a piety one may best call residual, cultural, and habitual, rather than self-conscious, critical, and theological (or ideological). That identity is not even ethnic, but rather a conglomeration of traits picked up in particular historical and social experiences. It is certainly flat and one-dimensional, leaving Jews to wander in strange paths in search of the answers to the most fundamental human perplexities.

V

Why are Jews in the forefront of universal causes, to the exclusion of their own interest and identity? Charles Liebman, writing in *The Religious Situation 1969*, examines the reasons given for this phenomenon. He rejects the notion that Jewish liberalism, cosmopolitanism, and internationalism rest on "traditional" Jewish values, for, he points out, it is the secular, not the religious, Jew who espouses cosmopolitanism. Jewish religious values in fact are folk-oriented rather than universalistic.

Liebman likewise rejects the view that the Jews' social status, far below what they might anticipate from their economic attainments, accounts for their attraction to the fringes of politics. This theory accounts, Liebman says, for Jewish radicalism rather than Jewish liberalism, that is, for only a small element of the community. Further, Jewish radicals normally abandon Jewish community life; the liberals dominate it.

A third explanation derives from the facts of history. Liberal parties supported the emancipation of the Jews; conservative ones opposed it. But for the U.S.A. this was not the case. Indeed, until the New Deal, Jews tended to be Republican, not Democratic or Socialist. Liebman posits that the appeal of liberalism is among Jews estranged from the religious tradition. This appeal, he says, "lies in the search for a universalistic ethic to which a Jew can adhere *but* which is seemingly irrelevant to specific Jewish concerns and, unlike radical socialism, does not demand total commitment at the expense of all other values."

Since the Emancipation, Jews have constantly driven to free themselves from the condition which Judaism thrusts on them. This Liebman calls estrangement: "The impetus for intellectual and religious reform among Jews, the adoption of new ideologies and life styles, but above all else the changing self-perception by the Jew of himself and his condition was not simply a desire to find amelioration from the physical oppression of the ghetto. It was rather a desire for emancipation from the very essence of the Jewish condition. . . . The Jew's problem was his alienation from the roots and the traditions of the society."

Here is the point at which the phenomenon of secularization becomes important. Jews earlier knew they were different, estranged. But with the collapse of religious evaluations of difference, the Jews ceased to affirm that difference. Secularization changed the nature of the Jew's perception of his condition, transferred the estrangement from theology to the realm of contemporary culture and civilization.

Jews supported universal humanism and cosmopolitanism with a vengeance. They brought these ideals home to the community so that Jewish difference was played down. Look, for example, at the Union Prayerbook, and count the number of times the congregation prays for "all mankind." The New Liberal Prayerbook in England so emphasizes the universal to the exclusion of the particular that one might write to the English liberal rabbi responsible for the liturgy: "Warm and affectionate regards to your wife and children, and to all mankind." Liebman concludes, "The Jew wished to be accepted as an equal in society *not* because he was a Jew, but because his Jewishness was *irrelevant*. Yet at the same time, the Jew refused to make his own Jewishness irrelevant.... He made ... contradictory demands on society. He wants to be accepted into the tradition of society without adapting to the society's dominant tradition." This constitutes the liberal dilemma: how to affirm universalism and remain particular.

VI

Complex though the liberal identity of secular Jews, it is still more complicated by the phenomena of anti-Semitism and consequent self-hatred. The "Jewish problem" is most commonly phrased by young Jews as "Why should I be Jewish? I believe in universal ideals—who needs particular ones as well?"

Minorities feel themselves "particular," see their traditions as "ritual," and distinguish between the private, unique, and personal and the public, universal, and commonplace. Majorities do not. Standing at the center, not on the fringe, they accept the given. Marginal men such as the Jews regard the given as something to be criticized, elevated, in any event as distinguished from their own essential being.

Jews who ask, "Why be Jewish," testify that "being Jewish" somehow repels, separates a person from the things he wants. American society, though it is opening, still is not so open that men who are different from the majority can serenely and happily accept that difference. True, they frequently affirm it —but the affirmation contains such excessive protest that it is not much different from denial. The quintessential datum of American Jewish existence is anti-Semitism, along with uncertainty of status, denial of normality, and self-doubt. The results are many, but two stand out. Some over-emphasize their Jewishness, respond to it not naturally but excessively, to the exclusion of other parts of their being. Others question and implicitly deny it. The one compensates too much; the other finds no reward at all.

As Kurt Lewin pointed out (in *Resolving Social Conflicts. Selected Papers on Group Dynamics* [N.Y., 1948: Harper & Bros.], p. 164), ".... every underprivileged minority group is kept together not only by cohesive forces among its members but also by the boundary which the majority erects against the crossing of an individual from the minority to the majority group." An underprivileged group-member will try to gain in social status by joining the majority—to pass, to assimilate. The basic fact of life is this wish to cross the boundary, and hence, as Lewin says, "he [the minority-group member] lives almost perpetually in a state of conflict and tension. He dislikes ... his own group because it is nothing but a burden to him. ... A Jew of this type will dislike everything specifically Jewish, for he will see in it that which keeps him away from the majority for which he is longing." Such a Jew is the one who will constantly ask, "Why be Jewish?" who will see, or at least fantasize about, a common religion of humanity, universalism or universal values that transcend, and incidentally obliterate, denominational and sectarian boundaries. It is no accident that the universal language, Esperanto, the universal movement, Communism, the universal psychology, Freudianism, all were in large measure attractive to marginal Jews.

True, Jews may find a place in social groups indifferent to their particularity as Jews. But a closer look shows that these groups are formed chiefly by deracinated, deJudaised Jews, along with a few exceptionally liberal non-Jews standing in a similar relationship to their own origins. Jews do assimilate. They do try to blot out the marks of their particularity, in ways more sophisticated, to be sure, than the ancient Hellenist-Jews who submitted to painful operations to wipe away the marks of circumcision. But in doing so, they become not something else entirely, but another type of Jew. The real issue is never, to be or not to be a Jew, any more than it is, to be or not to be my father's son.

Lewin makes this wholly clear: "It is not similarity or dissimilarity of individuals that constitutes a group, but interdependence of fate." Jews brought up to suppose being Jewish is chiefly, or only, a matter of religion think that through atheism they cease to be Jews, only to discover that disbelieving in God helps not at all. They still are Jews. They still are obsessed by that fact and compelled to confront it, whether under the name of Warren or of Weinstein, whether within the society of Jews or elsewhere.

Indeed, outside of that society Jewish consciousness becomes most intense. Among Jews one is a human being, with peculiarities and virtues of one's own. Among gentiles he is a Jew, with traits common to the group he rejects. That is probably why Jews still live in mostly Jewish neighborhoods and associate, outside of economic life, mostly with other Jews, whether or not these associations exhibit traits supposed to be Jewish. And when crisis comes, as it frequently does, then no one doubts that he shares a common cause, a common fate, with other Jews. Then it is hardest to isolate oneself from Jews, because only among Jewry are these intense concerns shared.

The Jewish community has yet to face up to the self-hatred endemic in its life. Jews are subtle enough to explain they are too busy with non-Jewish activities to associate with Jews. Students coming to college do not say to themselves or others, "I do not want to be a Jew, and now that I have the chance not to be, I shall take it." They say, "I do not like the Hillel rabbi; I am not religious so won't go to services; I am too busy with studies, dates, or political and social programs to participate in Jewish life." From here it is a short step to the affirmation of transcendent, universal values, and the denial of particular "religious" identity. That those who take that step do so mostly with other Jews is, as I said, proof of the real intent.

The organized Jewish community differs not at all from the assimilationist sector of this student generation. Indeed, it shows the way. Leadership in Jewry is sought by talented and able people, particularly those whose talents and abilities do not produce commensurate results in the non-Jewish world. Status denied elsewhere is readily available, for the right reasons, in Jewry, but in Jewry status is measured by the values of the gentile establishment.

Lewin says, "In any group, those sections are apt to gain leadership which are more generally successful. In a minority group, individual members who are economically successful . . . usually gain a higher degree of acceptance by the majority group. This places them culturally on the periphery of the underprivileged group and makes them more likely to be 'marginal' persons. . . . Nevertheless, they are frequently called for leadership by the underprivileged group because of their status and power. They themselves are usually eager to accept the leading role in the minority, partly as a substitute for gaining status in the majority. As a result, we find the rather paradoxical phenomenon of what one might call 'the leader from the periphery.' Instead of having a group led by people who are proud of the group, who wish to stay in it and to promote it, we see minority leaders who are lukewarm toward the group..." This, I think, is very much true of U.S. Jewry.

American Jews want to be Jewish, but not too much so, not so much that they cannot be just "people," part of the imaginary undifferentiated majority. And herein lies their pathology: they suppose one can distinguish between one's Jewishness, humanity, personality, individuality, and religion. A human being, however, does not begin as part of an undifferentiated mass. Once he leaves the maternity ward, he goes to a home of real people with a history, a home that comes from somewhere and that was made by some specific people. He inherits the psychic, not to mention social and cultural, legacy of many generations.

VII

What has Zionism to do with these Jewish problems? It is, after all, supposedly a secular movement, called "secular messianism," and the problems I have described are the consequences of secularity. How then has an allegedly secular movement posited solutions to the challenges of secularity faced by the formerly religious community?

Zionism provides a reconstruction of Jewish identity, for it reaffirms the nationhood of Israel in the face of the disintegration of the religious bases of Jewish peoplehood. If in times past the Jews saw themselves as a people because they were the children of the promise, the children of Abraham, Isaac, and Jacob, called together at Sinai, instructed by God through prophets, led by rabbis guided by the "whole Torah"—written and oral—of Sinai, then with the end of a singularly religious self-consciousness, the people lost its understanding of itself. The fact is that the people remained a community of fate, but, until the flourishing of Zionism, the facts of its continued existence were deprived of a heuristic foundation. Jews continued as a group, but could not persuasively say why or what this meant. Zionism provided the explanation: The Jews indeed remain a people, but the foundation of their peoplehood lies in the unity of their concern for Zion, devotion to rebuilding the land and establishing Jewish sovereignty in it. The realities of continuing emotional and social commitment to Jewish "grouphood" or separateness thus made sense. Mere secular difference, once seen to be destiny— "who has not made us like the nations" —once again stood forth as destiny.

Herein lies the ambiguity of Zionism. It was supposedly a secular movement, yet in reinterpreting the classic mythic structures of Judaism, it compromised its secularity and exposed its fundamental unity with the classic mythic being of Judaism. If, as I suggested, groups with like attributes do not necessarily represent "peoples" or "nations," and if the common attributes, in the Jewish case, are neither intrinsically Jewish (whatever that might mean) nor widely present to begin with, then the primary conviction of Zionism constitutes an extraordinary reaffirmation of the primary element in the classical mythic structure: salvation. What has happened in Zionism is that the old has been in one instant destroyed and resurrected. The holy people are no more, the nation-people take their place. How much has changed in the religious tradition, when the allegedly secular successor-continuator has preserved not only the essential perspective of the tradition, but done so pretty much in the tradition's own symbols and language?

Nor should it be supposed that the Zionist solution to the Jews' crisis of identity is a merely theological or ideological one. We cannot ignore the practical result of Zionist success in conquering the Jewish community. For the middle and older generations, as everyone knows, the Zionist enterprise provided the primary vehicle for Jewish identity. The Reform solution to the identity-problem—we are Americans by nationality, Jews by religion—was hardly congruent to the profound Jewish passion of the immigrant generations and their children. The former generations were *not* merely Jewish by religion. Religion was the least important aspect of their Jewishness. They deeply felt themselves Jewish in their bone and marrow and did not feel sufficiently marginal as Jews to *need* to affirm their Americanness/Judaism at all. Rather they participated in a reality; they were in a situation so real and intimate as to make unnecessary such an uncomfortable, defensive affirmation. They did not doubt they were Americans. They did not need to explain what being Jewish had to do with it. Zionism was congruent to these realities, and because of that fact, being Jewish and being Zionist were inextricably joined together.

But how different is the newer generation? True, extreme aberrant Jewish elements in the New Left are prepared to turn against the State of Israel. But what, more than anything else, has weakened the New Left and caused its split into numerous bickering factions, if not the defection of considerable numbers of Jewish radicals, unable to stomach both the crude anti-Semitism and the mindless pro-Nasserism of the Communist-line New Left groups? If so, we can only conclude that the younger generation is as viscerally Zionist as the older generations. The rock on which the New Left split was none other than 1967 Zion. I cannot think of more striking evidence of the persistence of the Zionist conception of Jewish identity among the younger generation.

The Zionist critique of the Jews' liberal dilemma is no less apt. Zionism has not stood against liberal causes and issues. On the contrary, Zionist Socialists have stood at the forefront of the liberal cause, have struggled for the working-class ideals, have identified the working class cause with their own. The record of Israeli and American Zionist thought on liberal issues is unambiguous and consistent. The liberalism of which Liebman writes is of a different order. It is a liberalism not born in Jewish nationhood but despite and against it. The liberal cosmopolitan Jew, devoted to internationalist and universal causes to the exclusion of "parochial" Jewish concerns, is no Zionist, but the opposite. He is a Jew acting out the consequences of deracination in the political arena. His universal liberalism takes the place of a profound commitment to the Jews and their welfare. Indeed, it is a liberalism that would like to deny that Jews have special, particular interests and needs to begin with. "Struggling humanity" in all its forms but one claim his sympathy: when Jews suffer, they *have* to do so as part of undifferentiated humanity.

So far as this Jewish liberalism was non-sectarian and hostile to the things that concern Jews as Jews—as in those Jewish welfare federations which articulately state their purpose as humanitarian to the exclusion of Judaism—Zionism has rejected that liberalism. It has done so because of its critical view of the Emancipation. Unlike the Jewish liberals, the Zionist saw the Emancipation as a problem, not a solution. He was dubious of its promises and aware of its hypocrisies. He saw Emancipation as a threat to Jewry and in slight measure a benefit for

Jews. The Jews' problem was that Emancipation represented de-Judaization. The price of admission to the roots and traditions of "society" was the surrender of the roots and traditions of the Jew, so said Zionist thought.

At the same time the Zionist stood between the religious party, which utterly rejected Emancipation and its works, and the secular-reform-liberal party, which wholly affirmed them. He faced the reality of Emancipation without claiming in its behalf a messianic valence. Emancipation is here, he thought, therefore to be criticized, but coped with; not utterly rejected, like the Orthodox, nor wholeheartedly affirmed, like the secular, reform and liberal groups. Zionism therefore demanded that the Jew be accepted as an equal in society because he was a Jew, *not* because his Jewishness was irrelevant. Its suspicion of the liberal stance was based, correctly in my opinion, on the Jews' ambivalence toward Jewishness. Zionism clearly recognized that the Jewishness of the Jew could never be irrelevant, not to the gentile, not to the Jew. It therefore saw more clearly than the liberals the failures of the European Emancipation and the dangers of American liberalism to Jewish self-respect and Jewish interests. Zionists were quick to perceive the readiness of non-Jewish allies of Jewish liberals to take the Jewish liberals at their word: We Jews have no special interests, nothing to fight for in our own behalf. Zionists saw Jews had considerable interests, just like other groups, and exposed the self-deceit (or hypocrisy) of those who said otherwise. The liberal Jew wanted to be accepted into the traditions of society without complete assimilation, on the one side, but also without much Jewishness, on the other. The Zionist assessment of the situation differed, as I said, for it saw that Jews could achieve a place in the common life *only* as Jews; and, rightly for Europe, it held this was impossible.

In its gloomy assessment of the European Emancipation, Zionism found itself in a position to cope with the third component in the Jewish problem, the immense, deep-rooted, and wide-ranging self-hatred of Jews. The Zionist affirmation of Jewish peoplehood, of Jewish-being, stood in stark contrast to the inability of marginal and liberal Jews to cope with anti-Semitism. Cases too numerous to list demonstrate the therapeutic impact of Zionism on the faltering psychological health of European Jews, particularly of more sensitive and intellectual individuals.

The American situation is different in degree, for here anti-Semitism in recent times has made its impact in more subtle ways, but its presence is best attested by the Jews themselves. Yet if a single factor in the self-respect American Jewry does possess can be isolated, it is its pride in the State of Israel and its achievements. Zionism lies at the foundation of American Jewry's capacity to affirm its Jewishness. Without Zionism religious conviction, forced to bear the whole burden by itself, would prove a slender reed. To be a Jew "by religion" and to make much of that fact in an increasingly secular environment, would not represent an attractive option to many. The contributions to Jewry's psychological health by the State of Israel and the Zionist presence in the diaspora cannot be over-estimated. It is striking, for example, that Kurt Lewin, Milton Steinberg, and other students of the phenomena of Jewish self-hatred invariably reached the single conclusion that only through Zionism would self-hatred be mitigated, even overcome.

The role of Zionism as a therapy for self-hatred cannot be described only in terms of the public opinion of U.S. Jewry. That would tell us much about the impact of mass communications, but little about the specific value of the Zionist idea for healing the Jewish pathology. In my view, the Israelis' claim "to live a full Jewish life" is a valid one. In Zionist conception and Israeli reality, the Jew is indeed a thoroughly integrated, whole human being. Here, in conception and reality, the Jew who believes in justice, truth, and peace, in universal brotherhood and dignity, does so not despite his peculiarity as a Jew, but through it. He makes no distinction between his Jewishness, his humanity, his individuality, his way of living, and his ultimate values. They constitute a single, undivided and fully integrated existential reality.

Part of the reason is the condition of life: The State of Israel is the largest Jewish neighborhood in the world. But part of the reason is ideological, and not merely circumstantial: Zionists always have rejected the possibility of Jews' "humanity" without Jewishness, just as they denied the reality of distinctions between Jewishness, nationality, and faith. They were not only *not* Germans of the Mosaic persuasions, but also *not* human beings of the Jewish genus. The several sort of bifurcations attempted by non-Zionists to account for their Jewishness along with other sorts of putatively non-Jewish commitments and loyalties were rejected by Zionists. It was not that Zionists did not comprehend the dilemmas faced by other sorts of Jews, but rather that they supposed through Zionism they had found the solution. They correctly held that through Zionist ideology and activity they had overcome the disintegrating Jewish identity-crisis of others.

VIII

At the outset I suggested that, like Judaism, Zionism can be understood from within, from its soul. My claim is that Zionism is to be understood as a solution to Jewish problems best perceived by the Jews who face those problems. The "Jewish problem" imposed by the effects of secularism took the form of a severe and complex crisis of identity, a partial commitment to universalism and cosmopolitan liberalism while claiming the right to be a little different, and a severe psychopathological epidemic of self-hatred. But the way Zionism actually solved those problems is more difficult to explain. If, as I suppose, because of Zionism contemporary Jewries have a clearer perception of who they are, what their interests consist of, and of their value as human beings, then Zionism and the State of Israel are in substantial measure the source of the saving knowledge. But *how* has Zionism worked its salvation on the Jews? Here I think we come to realities only Jews can understand. They understand them *not* because of rational reflection but because of experience and unreflective, natural response.

Zionism, and Zionism alone, proved capable of interpreting to contemporary Jews the meaning of felt-history, *and* of doing so in terms congruent to what the Jews derived from their tradition. It was Zionism which properly assessed the limitations of the Emancipation and proposed sound and practical programs to cope with those limitations. It was Zionism which gave Jews strength to affirm themselves when faced with the anti-Semitism of European and American life in the first-half of the twentieth century. It was Zionism and that alone which showed a way forward from the nihilism and despair of the DP camps. It was Zionism and that alone which provided a basis for unity in U.S. Jewry in the fifties and sixties of this century, a ground for common action among otherwise utterly divided groups.

These achievements of Zionism were based not on their practicality, though Zionism time and again was proved "right" by history. The Jews were moved and responded to Zionism before, not after the fact. And they were moved because of the capacity of Zionism to resurrect the single most powerful force in the history of Judaism: Messianism. Zionism did so in ways too numerous to list, but the central fact is that it represented, as Hertzberg perceptively showed, not "secular Messianism" but a profound restatement in new ways of classical Messianism. Zionism recovered the old, still evocative messianic symbolism and imagery and filled them with new meaning. And *this* meaning was taken for granted by vast numbers of Jews because it accurately described not what they believed or hoped for—not faith—but rather what they took to be mundane reality. Zionism took within its heuristic framework each and every important event in twentieth century Jewish history and gave to all a single, comprehensive, and sensible interpretation. Events were no longer random or unrelated, but all were part of a single pattern, pointing toward an attainable messianic result. It was not the random degradation of individuals in Germany and Poland, not the meaningless murder of unfortunates, not the creation of another state in the Middle East. All of these events were related to one another. It was Holocaust and rebirth, and the state was the State of *Israel.*

In so stating the meaning of contemporary events, Zionism made it possible for Jews not only to understand what they witnessed, but to draw meaning from it. And even more, Zionism breathed new life into ancient Scriptures, by providing a contemporary interpretation—subtle and not fundamentalist to be sure—for the prophets. "Our hope is lost," Ezekiel denied in the name of God. "Our hope is not lost," was the response of Zionism. These things were no accident, still less the result of an exceptionally clever publicist's imagination. They demonstrate the center and core of Zionist spirituality and piety: the old-new myth of peoplehood, land, redemption above all. The astonishing achievements of Zionism are the result of the capacity of Zionism to reintegrate the tradition with contemporary reality, to do so in an entirely factual, matter-of-fact framework, thus to eschew faith and to elicit credence. Zionism speaks in terms of Judaic myth, indeed so profoundly that myth and reality coincide.

JACOB NEUSNER is Professor of Religious Studies at Brown University. This is his first appearance in Midstream.

DIASPORA JUDAISM—AN ABNORMALITY? THE TESTIMONY OF HISTORY

JAKOB J. PETUCHOWSKI

The creation of the State of Israel in 1948 brought in its train a number of problems which Jews have not been facing for almost two millenia. Soon after the establishment of the State it became obvious that large numbers of Jews—with all their devotion to the cause of Zion, and with all their readiness to help Israel—had no intention of availing themselves of the provisions of the Israeli "Law of the Return," and of being "gathered in." Henceforth, therefore, one would have to reckon with two major Jewish entities: the State of Israel *and* the Diaspora.

What will be the relations between them? There are those who argue that the Diaspora will exist as long as the State of Israel needs it for financial support. Then it will disappear. The disappearance is inevitable, according to the more pessimistic view, because what has happened in Germany can, and is likely to, happen also in the United States. According to a somewhat less pessimistic view, the disappearance of Diaspora Jewry will be due to large-scale assimilation. In other words, the *raison d'être* of the Diaspora, now that the State of Israel has been established, is its usefulness to the Jewish State. The moment that usefulness comes to an end, the Diaspora is doomed.

Few Diaspora Jews assent to this description of their existence. The question, therefore, arises: How are the two entities of modern Jewish life to look upon each other? Three possible solutions present themselves, and are, at this moment, being championed by various factions in Jewry.

First of all, it is possible to regard the State of Israel as *the* center of Jewish life, with the Jews of the Diaspora being cast in the rôle of mere recipients. Diaspora Jews would henceforth be nourished and sustained by a Judaism "made in Israel" and exported for Diaspora consumption. This view can be held by the religionist as well as by the secularist. The former would be prepared to submit to a Sanhedrin convened in Israel, or at least to a "central religious authority" located there. The latter, feeling that Israeli dances have already helped to revive Jewish life in America, would wish to be de-

---

To the on-going discussion of the relationship, possible and desirable, between Israel and the Diaspora, Jakob Petuchowski, Assistant Professor of Rabbinics at Hebrew Union College-Jewish Institute of Religion, adds historical perspective in the form of this present essay. It is based on a lecture delivered by him at the "Annual Homecoming" on the Cincinnati campus of that institution in March, 1959. The author dedicates this essay to the memory of his "Rabbi and Teacher," the late Prof. Samuel S. Cohon.

pendent upon further cultural importations.

The second view which is possible is that which conceives of Israel-Diaspora relations in terms of a mutual give-and-take. Judaism in Israel will flourish because of Diaspora contributions, and Diaspora Judaism will maintain itself because of its contact with the State of Israel.

The third view would have us take note of the existence of the State of Israel, as that of a country largely inhabited by Jews, and then proceed with the business in hand. It might recognize the State of Israel as Judaism's "show case" to the world at large. But it would also maintain that Judaism has become sufficiently independent of geography, so that the Jewish religious problems of New York and of London can be, and have to be, settled in New York and in London—and not in Tel-Aviv or Jerusalem.

All three views, however, assume a continued Diaspora existence. Curiously enough, though, champions of all the three views often create the impression as if the problems with which they are dealing were altogether unprecedented problems which came into being with the establishment of the modern State of Israel. But it so happens that similar problems were faced before. The days of the Second Temple and the period of the Tannaim saw both a Jewish center in the Holy Land and a far-flung Diaspora.

This is not to suggest that present-day conditions and the conditions of two thousand years ago are absolutely congruent. History does not work that way. The external political situation is different, and what is known as "Judaism" has itself undergone a considerable development and transformation between the time of Hillel and of Philo and the present day. But it might well be instructive for us today to take into account the views of our predecessors of long ago, both about the viability of Judaism beyond the confines of Palestine, and about the nature and character of Diaspora existence itself.

Anyone even vaguely familiar with the basic works of Derenbourg and Juster[1] knows that the Diaspora was *not* the result of the year 70, and that, though the presence of many Jews outside of Palestine was due to their ancestors' deportation from that country—and that would apply particularly to the Babylonian Jewish community—many a Diaspora community originated through *voluntary* emigration, at a time when a Jewish State, of more or less independence, still existed. Even those Jews who left Palestine as captives and as slaves very soon obtained their release, because, as Reinach claims,[2] their unswerving attachment to their customs made them inefficient servants, and because, on account of Jewish solidarity, they never had much trouble finding co-religionists who were willing to pay their ransom.

But, above all, the Diaspora was due to economic factors. The Jewish "colonies" are the exact counterparts of the "colonies" of Egyptians, Syrians, and Phoenicians, in Greece, in Rome, and in the important commercial centers of Italy.[3]

---

[1] Joseph Derenbourg, *Essai sur l'histoire et la Géographie de la Palestine*. Paris, 1867; and Jean Juster, *Les Juifs dans l'Empire Romain*. Paris, 1914, 2 vols.

[2] Theodere Reinach, art., "Diaspora," in J. E., Vol. IV, pp. 559–574.

[3] Reinach, *op. cit.*, p. 561.

The extent of the Diaspora is impressive. Juster, whose investigation, however, takes in the whole period of the Empire—thus extending the scope beyond the period under discussion here—knows of some 120 Jewish communities in Europe, of 90 in Asia Minor, of 95 in Africa, and of 35 in the area of Mesopotamia, Babylonia, and Arabia.[4] No wonder, then, that the Jewish *Sybil* can speak of the Jews as "filling every land and every sea,"[5] or that Strabo, writing in the first century B.C.E., can speak of the Jews as "already gotten into all cities; and it is hard to find a place in the habitable earth that has not admitted this tribe of men, and is not prospered by them."[6]

Justin Martyr, in the second century C.E., accuses the Jews of sending "selected men from Jerusalem *into all the earth*" to agitate against the Christian sect;[7] and the *Book of Acts*, describing the experience of Pentecost, speaks of "there dwelling in Jerusalem Jews, devout men from every nation under heaven,"[8]—which it then proceeds to identify as Parthians and Medes and Elamites and residents of Mesopotamia, Judaea and Cappadocia, Pontus and Asia, Phrygia and Pamphylia, Egypt and the parts of Lybia belonging to Cyrene, and visitors from Rome, both Jews and proselytes, Cretans and Arabians.[9]

In terms of Roman Law, all these Jews had judicial autonomy, even where (and if) they lived as Greek and Roman citizens. Such, at any rate, was the situation before the year 70, and there does not seem to have been any modification thereafter.[10] Such rights were granted by Caesar to Hyrcanus II, who was also accorded the title of *Ethnarch;* and, while we do not know whether the rights were invariably maintained by all of Caesar's successors, we do know that, on several occasions, the successors of Hyrcanus intervened with the Roman authorities on behalf of Diaspora Jewry.[11] Philo describes the Jews in the Diaspora as "colonies" of the Jewish population in Judaea; and these colonial Jews, while "holding the Holy City where stands the sacred Temple of the Most High God to be their mother city (*metropolis*)," still account each city in which they have been born and brought up as their native city (*patris*), just as Jerusalem is the *patris* of the Jews born therein.[12] The Jews of Palestine and of all these colonies constitute, according to Philo, one whole nation *(hapan ethnos)*, of which the Jews in each locality are a part. That whole nation of the Jews forms a polity which, in comparison with the local polities of each individual Jewish locality, is described as the more universal polity, which bears the general name of the nation, "Israel," and which depends for its existence upon the existence of the Temple.[13]

In Alexandria the Jews are said to

---

[4] Juster, *op. cit.*, Vol. I, pp. 180–209.
[5] *The Sibylline Books*, Bk. III, Line 271; in *The Apocrypha and Pseudepigrapha of the Old Testament* (ed. Charles), Vol. II, p. 385.
[6] Quoted by Josephus, *Antt.* Bk. XIV, ch. vii, 2.
[7] *Dialogue with Trypho* 17:1, and 108:2.
[8] *Acts* 2:5.
[9] *Acts* 2:9–11.

[10] Juster, *op. cit.*, Vol. II, pp. 110ff.
[11] Juster, *op. cit.*, Vol. I, p. 391f; and cf. *op. cit.*, Vol. I, p. 233f about the universal application of the legislation granting privileges to the Jews.
[12] Harry A. Wolfson, *Philo* (rev. ed.). Cambridge, Harvard University Press, 1948, Vol. II, p. 397, quoting *In Flaccum*, 7, 46; *De Legatione ad Gaium* 36, 278 & 281.
[13] Ibid., quoting *De Legatione ad Gaium* 29, 184 & 194.

have had a polity which entitled them to the pursuit of "ancestral customs and the enjoyment of political rights." The term "ancestral customs" quite clearly describes the Jewish *politeia* in Alexandria as a religious organization. The second term, "the enjoyment of political rights," is not so clear, but, according to Wolfson, it is quite certain, on the evidence of the Claudine letters to the Alexandrines, that the Jews were not full citizens of Alexandria. The term seems to be used in the sense of the Jews being members of the Jewish *politeia*.[14] But, whether they were full citizens or not, we know from Strabo[15] that a large part of the city of Alexandria was alloted to the Jews, and the literary remnants of Hellenistic Judaism leave us in no doubt that the Jews of Alexandria and of other parts of the Hellenistic world were quite *au courant* with the culture and thought of that world. It should be noted, however, that, as Lieberman has demonstrated in detail, the Palestinian Jewish community did not escape these cultural influences either.[16]

We shall have occasion to see that Reinach has somewhat overstated his case when he attributed the facility with which Jews emigrated from Palestine to the fact that the Jewish creed "is linked to a book, not to a place."[17] But this much is true: that the basis of Jewish life in all places of the Dispersion was the Bible. Yet the Bible, to remain alive, has to be interpreted; and interpretation inevitably takes into consideration local circumstances, and is influenced by local trends of thought. Hence the existence of the Septuagint, and hence, too, the existence of a Hellenistic Jewish exegesis, parts of which would hardly have been recognized by contemporary Pharisaic Jews in Palestine. That is why scholars like Goodenough and Sandmel stress the fact that Hellenistic Judaism had its own doctrines and emphases, which distinguished it from Palestinian Judaism.[18]

Just how independent a Diaspora community could feel *vis a vis* the religious authorities in Palestine is evidenced by the Onias Temple in Leontopolis, in the district of Heliopolis, of Egypt. According to Krauss,[19] the establishment of that sanctuary was not due to the disorders in Palestine under Antiochus Epiphanes, nor to the supplanting of the legitimate family of priests by the installation of Alkimos in Jerusalem, nor again to the personal ambition of Onias IV, but simply to "the vast extent of the Jewish Diaspora in Egypt itself."

Onias IV, a mere youth at the time of his father's murder, had fled to the court of Alexandria, and had obtained permission from Ptolemy VI and Cleopatra to build a sanctuary in Egypt "similar to the one in Jerusalem, where he would employ Levites and priests of his own race." The Temple was closed by the Roman governor of Egypt about three years after the destruction of the

---

[14] Wolfson, *op. cit.*, Vol. II, p. 398.
[15] Quoted by Josephus, *Antt.* Bk. XIV, ch. vii, 2.
[16] Cf. Saul Lieberman, *Greek in Jewish Palestine*. N.Y., JTS, 1942; and idem, *Hellenism in Jewish Palestine*. N.Y., JTS, 1950.
[17] Reinach, *op. cit.*, p. 561.

[18] Cf. Erwin R. Goodenough, *By Light, Light*. New Haven, Yale University Press, 1935; and Samuel Sandmel, "Philo's Place in Judaism," in HUCA, Vol. XXV (1954) and Vol. XXVI (1955).
[19] Samuel Krauss, art. "Leontopolis," in J. E., Vol. VIII, pp. 7-8.

Jerusalem Temple—after it had been in existence for 243 years! The Onias Temple, though not an exact replica of the Jerusalem sanctuary, did center around sacrificial worship. Here, then, in the second century B.C.E., we find Jewish sacrificial service on Egyptian soil—in blatant violation of the Deuteronomic law! If ever there was a clear assertion of Diaspora independence, this was it. What is more, according to Josephus,[20] Onias even had a Scripture verse to "justify" his innovation. He quoted *Isaiah* 19:19:

"In that day there will be an altar to the Lord in the midst of the land of Egypt, and a pillar to the Lord at its border."

Verse 18 of the same chapter in *Isaiah* may have some connection with our topic as well. It reads:

"In that day there will be five cities in the land of Egypt which speak the language of Canaan and swear allegiance to the Lord of Hosts. One of there will be called *ir haheres*."

Now, *ir haheres* means "City of Destruction," and it is either a corruption of, or a malicious pun on, *ir hacheres*, "City of the Sun,"—which is Heliopolis. But, amazingly enough, the Septuagint reads *polis asedek*, which is clearly *Cir hatzedek*, "City of Righteousness," and this might easily reflect the sentiments evoked by that locality in the hearts of the supporters of the Onias Temple.

How influential that Temple must have been becomes evident once we note that even rabbinic literature had to reckon with it—and was unable to reject it completely. According to the *Tosefta*, if a man vows to bring a burnt-offering in Jerusalem, but brings it in the Onias Temple (*beth chonyo*), he has not fulfilled his obligation, and he incurs the punishment of *kareth* (premature death). The same applies to the Nazirite vow.[21] The *Mishnah*, however, distinguishes between making the vow in relation to the Jerusalem Temple and making it in relation to the Onias Temple. In the latter case, its valid fulfillment is possible there.[22] Though Rabbi Simeon demurs, the *halakhah* is not according to him.[23]

Both the *Mishnah* and the *Tosefta* contain references to the priests of the Onias Temple,[24] and, although their legitimacy is rejected, as late as in Amoraic times we find R. Isaac reporting: "I have heard that legitimate sacrifices can be brought in the Onias Temple *bazeman hazeh* (i.e. after the destruction of the Jerusalem Temple),"[25]—which view, according to the *Gemara*, would imply that the Onias Temple is *not* a place of idolatry, and that the choice of Jerusalem as the single central sanctuary was not a permanent one. Naturally, the Talmud rejects this view. But that it should have been voiced in the first place is nothing less than remarkable, and testifies to the tremendous hold which the Onias Temple must have had on certain circles of Diaspora Jewry.

Equally remarkable, under the circumstances, is the fact that a Jew as "assimilated" as Philo *makes no mention of the Onias Temple*, and that, when he wanted to worship God by

---

20 Josephus, *Wars*, Bk. VII, ch. x, 3.

21 *Tosefta Menachoth* 13:12-13 (ed. Zuckermandel, p. 533).
22 *Mishnah Menachoth* 13:10.
23 Cf. Bertinoro's commentary ad loc.
24 *Mishnah Menachoth* loc. cit.; *Tosefta Menachoth* 13:14 (ed. Zuckermandel, p. 533).
25 b. *Megillah* 10a.

means of sacrifices as prescribed by the Law, he made a pilgrimage to the Temple in Jerusalem.[26] Apparently, then, the Onias Temple was not even favored by all the Jews living in Egypt. After all, the Jerusalem Temple was still in existence, and many Jews of the Diaspora, including those of Alexandria, "participated in the sacrificial rites, not only vicariously through their annual contribution of the Temple tax, which was used for the purchase of the public sacrifice, but also personally through their pilgrimages to Jerusalem during the holidays."[27]

As Goodenough says, it is difficult for non-Jews "or for modern Jews to imagine how intense must have been the emotional association of the Jews of antiquity with the secret Ark of the Covenant. . . . It was the abode, the presence, of God in a sense completely unique."[28] Perhaps that is the main reason why Philo, with all of his stress on the long Jewish residence in the Diaspora, going back to "fathers, grandfathers, and ancestors even farther back," can speak of Jerusalem, "where stands the sacred Temple of the Most High God," as the *metropolis*, the "mother city," of all Jews.[29]

This—and something else. Philo, as a student of Scripture, could not help looking upon the Dispersion of the Jews as a divine punishment. The Jewish polity in Alexandria, despite its external semblance of a self-government, still represented to him what Scripture calls "captivity."[30] He, therefore, considered the Diaspora only as a temporary stage in Jewish history—a stage which was to be terminated with the coming of the Messianic Age when all the exiles would be reunited under one government of their own.[31]

We would indeed be wrong were we to associate the rise of the doctrine of the "Ingathering of the Exiles" with the destruction of the year 70. No doubt, it became highly intensified then, but it seems to have been a permanent part of Judaism ever since it was proclaimed by the Biblical Prophets. "The Lord doth build up Jerusalem, He gathereth together the dispersed of Israel," sang the Psalmist (*Psalm* 147:2); and, as long as there were "dispersed of Israel," living under circumstances however prosperous, it must have been felt that the ideal future would see their "ingathering." Thus Sirach prays:

"Give thanks unto the Redeemer of Israel; For His mercy endureth forever.
Give thanks unto Him that gathereth the outcasts of Israel; etc.
Give thanks unto Him that buildeth His city and His Sanctuary; etc."[32]

Note that this was written when there *was* a Temple in Zion, and at a time when Jews *voluntarily* left Palestine to seek their fortunes elsewhere. Similarly, in the *Psalms of Solomon*, probably dating from the middle of the first century B.C.E., we read:

"Turn, O God, Thy tender mercy upon us, and have pity upon us;

---

26 Cf. Wolfson, *op. cit.*, Vol. II, p. 395f.
27 Wolfson, *op. cit.*, Vol. II, p. 241f.
28 Goodenough, *By Light, Light*, p. 23.
29 *In Flaccum* VII, 45–46; quoted by Salo W. Baron in *A Social and Religious History of the Jews*. Vol. I, Pt. I, Philadelphia, JPS, 1952, p. 200.

30 Wolfson, *op. cit.*, Vol. II, p. 403.
31 Wolfson, *op. sit.*, Vol. II, p. 401f.
32 Sirach 51:2, v–vii, extant in the Hebrew version only. Cf. *Apocrypha and Pseudepigrapha of the Old Testament*, ed. Charles, Vol. I, p. 514.

Gather together the dispersed of Israel, with mercy and goodness; For Thy faithfulness is with us."[33]

What might be questioned, though, is the *urgency* with which the granting of such prayers was desired. We have to remind ourselves, as Robert Gordis put it so well, that by the year 70 C.E., "there were more Jews living outside of Palestine than within its borders, with Alexandria probably possessing a larger Jewish population than Jerusalem. These Jews, during the centuries preceding the destruction of the Temple, and in the decades following, were physically free to return to the land of Israel, but there was no call for a mass emigration from the Diaspora by Jewish leaders in Palestine. . . . The bulk of Diaspora Jews . . . did not migrate to Palestine, undoubtedly being deterred by social, economic, or political considerations."[34]

Under the circumstances, it might even be legitimate to assume that the prayers for the "Ingathering" acquired a spiritual, rather than a concrete meaning. This is perhaps best illustrated by the liturgy of the early Christian Church. Thus, while *Matthew* 24:31 ("And he shall send his angels with a great sound of trumpet, and they shall gather together his elect from the four winds, from one end of Heaven to the other.") may contain a genuine piece of Jewish apocalyptic, meant to be taken literally,—this can hardly be the case in the *Didache*, where the Christian prays: ". . . so let Thy Church be gathered from the ends of the earth into Thy kingdom."[35] And again: "Remember, Lord, Thy Church, to deliver her from all evil, and to perfect her in Thy love; and gather together from the four winds her that is sanctified into Thy kingdom which Thou didst prepare for her."[36] The "Ingathering" here seems to be a call for a *spiritual* "show of strength," —very much along the lines of what must have been in the minds of the Jewish Reformers in Germany, when, in their *Einheitsgebetbuch*, they emended the text of the 10th benediction of the daily *Amidah* to read: ". . .and raise the banner to gather all that fear Thee *in* (sic) all the four corners of the earth."

But even without an emendation of the liturgy, the American Orthodox Jew today manages to implore God for a speedy "Ingathering of the Exiles,"— when all he has to do is to pack his bag, buy a ticket, and move to Israel! Those who really understand their prayers, and still do not move to Israel, undoubtedly invest their prayers with a *messianic-spiritual* significance—which is probably very much the same thing that was done with the "Ingathering" prayers of the second and first centuries B.C.E.

And yet, the messianic prophecy about the Torah's "going forth from Zion" was fulfilled, at least partially, in the religious supervision of the Diaspora which was exercised by the Jerusalem authorities. According to Juster, we do not know what means of communication were used between Palestine and the Diaspora before the year 70, although, after 70, we find the institution

---

[33] *The Psalms of Solomon* 8:33–35, in Charles, *op. cit.*, Vol. II, p. 641.

[34] Robert Gordis, *Judaism for the Modern Age*. N.Y., Farrar, Straus & Cudahy, 1955, p. 110f.

[35] *Didache* 9:4, in *An English Translation of the Teachings of the Twelve Apostles*. London, S.P.C.K., 1922, p. 11.

[36] *Didache* 10:5, *op. cit.*, p. 12.

of the *apostoli* whose function it was to supervise the magistrates of the communities, to interpret the Law in the Diaspora, and, if necessary, to preach in the synagogues. In addition, of course, they also had the more mundane function of collecting money.[37] But, according to Vogelstein, the Jewish apostolate—the prototype of the later Christian institution—goes back to a date even earlier than that of the Biblical Books of Chronicles![38]

Without going into the question of "origins," we shall confine ourselves to some of the actual reports about Palestine-Diaspora relations as we encounter them in Tannaitic Literature. We hear, for example, that, when Alexander Jannaeus was persecuting the Pharisees, R. Jehoshua ben Perachyah (accompanied, in disregard of chronolgy, by Jesus!) fled to Alexandria in Egypt. When peace was restored, Shimeon ben Shettach sent word from Jerusalem: "From me, Jerusalem the Holy City, to you Alexandria of Egypt, my sister. My husband is dwelling in your midst, while I am sitting desolate."[39] (When we today use the term "sister-congregation," we do not often realize that we are speaking in terms used by Shimeon ben Shettach to describe the relationship of Jerusalem and Alexandria.)

Two centuries later we find "the men of Alexandria" addressing questions—both of a *halakhic* and an *aggadic* nature—to Rabbi Joshua ben Hananiah.[40] This may not have involved any correspondence, for, in his various travels, Rabbi Joshua also made his appearance in Alexandria.[41]

It is even more instructive to see how the Palestinian authorities were concerned with the detailed goings-on in the far-away city of Rome. One Theudas, or Theodosius, (our sources call him *Thodos*) in Rome, probably a second-century C.E. figure, introduced the custom in the Roman Jewish community of preparing the Passover lamb in the manner appropriate to the actual Paschal sacrifice as brought in the Jerusalem Temple. Whereupon the Palestinian authorities let him know: "If you were not Theudas, we would have excommunicated you; for you are causing Israel to eat sacrificial meat outside (sc. of the legitimate sanctuary)."[42] The

---

[37] Juster, *op. cit.*, Vol. I, p. 388f.

[38] Hermann Vogelstein shows the Jewish origin of the Christian apostolate in MGWJ 1905. He develops his theme in HUCA II (1925), pp. 99-123, where he also attempts to prove that the institution of *shelichim* antedates the Biblical Books of Chronicles.

[39] b. *Sanhedrin* 107b, and parallel in b. *Sotah* 47a,—to be read in conjunction with the *Chesronoth haShas* ad loc.

[40] Cf. *Mishnah Nega'im* 14:13, and *baraitha* in b. *Niddah* 69b.

[41] Cf. Z. Frankel, *Darkhé HaMishnah*. Leipzig, 1859, p. 84.

[42] This is reported in *Tosefta Yom Tobh* 2:15 (ed. Zuckermandel, p. 204); j. *Pesachim* VII, 1 (p. 34a); b. *Pesachim* 53a; b. *Betzah* 23a; and b. *Berakhoth* 19a. In all passages but the last named this occurrence is reported by the Tanna Rabbi Yosé, and the Palestinian condemnation is introduced either by *ameru lo* or *shalechu lo*. Only in the b. *Berakhoth* passage is the story reported by the Amora Rabh Joseph, and it is here that we are told that *Simeon ben Shettach* sent the message to Theudas. Apparently ignoring the other passages, and taking the b. *Berakhoth* passage at face value, A. Berliner places Theudas at the time of Simeon ben Shettach. Cf. his *Geschichte der Juden in Rom*. Frankfurt, 1893, Vol. I, p. 30. W. Bacher, however, taking all the other passages into consideration as well, concludes that the b. *Berakhoth* passage is an anachronism. Cf. his *Agada der Tannaiten*, Vol. II (1890), p. 560f. Schulim Ochser, in J. E., Vol. XII, p. 140, describes Theudas as "flourishing in Rome during the Hadrianic persecutions."

early *Christian* community in Rome also seems to have maintained close relations with their headquarters in Jerusalem; for, when Paul appears in Rome, they tell him: "We have received no letters from Judaea about you, and none of the brethren coming here has reported or spoken evil about you."[43]

Indicative of the *type* of community with which the Palestinian authorities kept in touch is the following report of the *Tosefta*:[44] "It once happened that Rabbi Meir went to *Asia* (probably a place in Asia Minor)[45] to intercalate the year; and he did not find there a *Megillah* written in Hebrew. So he wrote one from memory, and read from it." This passage is intriguing—not so much on account of R. Meir's feat of memory —which, no doubt, could have been paralleled many a time in succeeding centuries— but because it sets us guessing as to the nature of the community. Note that the *Tosefta* does not really say that they had no Scroll of Esther at all, but only that they did not have one "written in Hebrew." This still leaves open the possibility that they had one *in Greek*, which, according to the *Mishnah*, would have been quite permissible.[46] In this case, we would find Rabbi Meir in contact with a typical outpost of *Hellenistic Judaism*!

If, however, the *Tosefta* passage be understood in the sense of there being no Scroll of Esther at all, the passage would be no less intriguing. We know that the inclusion of *Esther* in the canon was long debated,[47] and it has also been noted that no *Esther* fragments have been found among the Qumran Scrolls. In either case, therefore, Rabbi Meir is seen to be engaged in an important religious mission to a community not completely identified with what some would call "normative" Judaism.[48]

Our *Tosefta* passage is interesting also in another respect. Together with similar reports—like the one about Rabbi Akiba's going to Nehardea to interca-

---

[43] Acts 28:21.
[44] *Tosefta Megillah* 2:5 (ed. Zuckermandel, p. 223).
[45] I. H. Weiss, *Dor Dor weDorshaw* (6th ed.), Vol. II, p. 132n, insists that neither the *Asia* in which R. Meir is said to have died, nor the *Asia* of our passage, is to be identified with Asia Minor. Similarly, Gedalyahu Allon, *Toledoth haYehudim be-Eretz Yisrael bithequfath haMishnah wehaTalmud*, 3rd ed. (1958), Vol. I, p. 152f, rejects the identification of the *Asia* of our passage with Asia Minor. He takes *Asia* to be a name for Ezion-Geber, which, though not a part of Palestine in the tannaitic period, was regarded as being "a little like Palestine," and, having been promised to Abraham, as ultimately to become part of Palestine again. But the instructions Rabbi Meir gave prior to his death in *Asia*, cf. j. *Kil-ayim* IX, 4, p. 32c (viz. that he wants his corpse transferred to Palestine, and that, in the meantime, his coffin is to be placed by the sea-shore so that he comes to rest by the water which also washes the shore of Palestine), make it very doubtful to us that the *Asia* where he died could possibly have been Ezion-Geber. Note the location of the latter in Wright and Filson, *The Westminster Historical Atlas of the Bible* (1946), p. 31, and note also the Mediterranean as the sea which washes the shores of both Palestine and Asia Minor. Cf. also Kohut, *Aruch Completum*, Vol. I, p. 178, for the identification of *Asia* with Asia Minor. We see no compelling reason why the *Asia* of our *Tosefta* passage could not also have been Asia Minor—particularly in view of the fact that, as has already been noted, Juster was able to enumerate some 90 Jewish communities in that area.
[46] *Mishnah Megillah* 1:8, and 2:1.
[47] Cf. George Foot Moore, *Judaism*, Vol. I, pp. 244–246.
[48] Cf. now my Hebrew article, *HaMegillah She-enennah*, in *HADOAR* of June 19, 1959, p. 549.

late the year[49]—it indicates, as Allon has pointed out,[50] that the Palestinian Patriarchate occasionally permitted the intercalation of years outside of Palestine. Now, such a procedure was contrary to the *theoretical* Halakhah, but the latter was set aside to take into account the needs of the Diaspora, and also to give the Diaspora leaders a feeling of importance and participation.

All this, of course, is merely an indication of the fact that the Palestinian authorities tried to lay down the law for the far-flung Diaspora. No doubt, they were aided in this by the Roman recognition, even after the year 70, of a "head of all the Jews in the Empire," who held this position even though he could not be a territorial sovereign,[51] and by the Roman permission, until the fourth century, for the collection of a tax to support the Patriarchate—a tax collected by the *apostoli* who where sent out from Palestine.[52] But how far was Palestinian *religious* guidance really accepted by the Diaspora communities?

We receive an answer from a most unexpected quarter. The *Apostolic Constitutions* contain a number of early Christian prayers—some of them reprinted with notes in Goodenough's *By Light, Light*[53]—which are really Jewish prayers with Christian glosses. As Goodenough puts it, the liturgy was "unmistakably Jewish, though obviously from a Judaism strongly Hellenized."[54] Yet, as Marcel Simon points out, there are Bible quotations in these *Hellenistic* prayers which do not come from the Septuagint, but from the translation of Aquila![55] Aquila the Proselyte prepared a Greek version of the Bible under rabbinic auspices, including those of Rabbi Akiba.[56] The Christian use of the Septuagint in anti-Jewish polemics had made it discredited in Jewish circles, and the Rabbis were substituting for it the Aquila version.[57] No doubt, the Greek-speaking Jews were none too happy about giving up their Septuagint, which in their circles played a role comparable to that of the Luther Bible in German Protestantism. But apparently even the authors of the Hellenistic prayers under discussion must have done so. Says Simon: "That a Judaism so Philonic in spirit as that of our prayers should have given up the Septuagint in favor of Aquila is proof of the fact that it entertained close relations with, and a respectful subordination to, the Palestinian authorities."[58]

What we see here in the religious sphere is seen—and *criticized*—by Baron in the *political* sphere as well. Baron criticizes Diaspora Jewry for having "abdicated its part in shaping policies affecting world Jewry."[59] "There neither existed any regular forum for the exchange of ideas and the airing of mutually adventageous proposals, nor any permanent agency whereby Diaspora Jewry could make its weight felt before

---

[49] *Mishnah Yebamoth* 16:7.
[50] Allon, *op. cit.*, Vol. I, pp. 149–156.
[51] Juster, *op. cit.*, Vol. I, p. 393.
[52] Cf. the edict of Julian the Apostate prohibiting the further levy of this tax in Jacob R. Marcus, *The Jew in the Medieval World*. Cincinnati, U.A.H.C., 1938, p. 9.
[53] Cf. Goodenough, *op. cit.*, pp. 306ff.
[54] Goodenough, *op. cit.*, p 306.

[55] Cf. Marcel Simon, *Verus Israel*. (French) Paris, Boccard, 1948, p. 76f.
[56] Cf. j. *Kiddushin*, I, 1, end (p. 59a), and j. *Megillah* I, 11 (p. 71c); and cf. Frankel, *op. cit.*, pp. 88 and 100f.
[57] Cf. M. Joël, *Blicke in die Religionsgeschichte*, Pt. I, Breslau, 1880, pp. 43–67.
[58] Marcel Simon, *op. cit.*, p. 81f.
[59] Salo W. Baron, *op. cit.*, Vol. I, Pt. I, p. 247f.

decisions affecting all Jews were reached in Jerusalem."⁶⁰

We may doubt Baron's assumption that, if Palestine and the Diaspora had acted in political concert, it would have made very much of a difference to the fate of first-century Jewry. But, at any rate, the survival of *Judaism* was assured—and not least because of a *halakhic* consideration propounded on Palestinian soil itself. The *Tosefta*⁶¹ records the distinction made by Rabbi Eleazar bar Simeon between the commandments which the Israelites were obligated to observe even before they entered the Land, and the commandments which they were obligated to observe only *after* they had entered the Land. The observance of the latter, with but two exceptions, was confined to Palestine, whereas the former were to be observed both in Palestine and abroad.

Rabbi Eleazar, the son of the fanatical Simeon bar Yochai, was a realist—as may also be seen from the fact that he worked for the Roman administration, for which he was severely censored by Joshua ben Karecha.⁶² He was a realist in that he made it possible for the Jew, even after the fall of Temple and State, to feel that the Judaism he is *able* to practice in the Diaspora is all that he is *required* to practice. And this was not Rabbi Eleazar's view alone. The *Mishnah* gives this distinction between the commandments as an anonymous *halakhah*,⁶³ while the *Sifré* derives it from the text of *Deuteronomy* 12:11⁶⁴

There is a direct line which stretches from this basic distinction to the Amora Samuel's dictum that the Jews are religiously bound to abide by the civil law of the country of their residence (*dina demalkhutha dina*),⁶⁵ and from there to Judah bar Ezekiel's insistence that his students stay with him in Babylonia, for they have nothing to learn in Palestine;⁶⁶ and from there to Samuel Holdheim and modern Reform Judaism. When Holdheim differentiated between the *religious* and the *political* elements in Judaism, claiming permanency only for the former, and associating the latter with the temporary existence of the theocratic state in Palestine, he did no more than restate in modern terms the old tannaitic distinction between "commandments depending for their observance upon the Land" (*mitzwoth hateluyoth ba-aretz*) and "commandments not depending upon the Land" (*mitzwoth she-enan teluyoth ba-aretz*). When Holdheim went further than this, when he relegated every provision of Jewish Law he did not care for (including Sabbath observance on Saturday) to the realm of the "political," he became vulnerable to criticism. But the fact remains that he helped to lay the theoretical groundwork which made it possible for Reform Judaism to believe in the viability of a full-blooded Judaism which is in no need to hope and to pray for a messianic return to Palestine.

That this latter-day Reform position is really related to the tannaitic distinction between commandments which are

---

⁶⁰ Ibid.
⁶¹ *Tosefta Kiddushin* 1:12 (ed. Zuckermandel, p. 336).
da der Tannaiten, Vol. II, pp. 309 and 400.
⁶² b. *Baba Metzi'a* 83b; and cf. Bacher, *Aga-*
⁶³ *Mishnah Kiddushin* 1:9.
⁶⁴ *Sifré RE-ÉH*, Pisqa 59 (d. Friedmann, p.

87a). As examples of *mitzwoth ha-guph*, i.e. of commandments not dependent upon the Land, we hear of *tephillin* and *Talmud torah*. Cf. *Sifré EGEBH*, Pisqa 44 (p. 82b).
⁶⁵ b. *Gittin* 10b, and parallels.
⁶⁶ Cf. b. *Kethuboth* 111a.

"dependent upon the Land" and those which are not, becomes evident from the reaction which this distinction called forth in Rabbinic Judaism itself. Not only does Rabbi Simlai explain the wish of Moses to enter the Promised Land in terms of his desire to observe the many commandments which can only be observed in the Land of Israel,[67] but also the tannaitic teaching prohibiting emigration from Palestine except under the most dire conditions (coupled with the condemnation of Elimelech and his sons for leaving the Land in time of distress),[68] seems to be predicated upon the assumption that residence in the Land of Israel is meritorious on account of the many commandments which can be observed only there.

But those were rear-guard actions. When the Karaites—for example, Al-Qumissi in the 9th century—attacked the Rabbanites for their lack of the love of Zion, and for having come to terms with *galuth* existence, we have clear evidence that out of the Tannaitic Period—which began with a Palestine-dominated Diaspora—there evolved a Judaism viable in any locality, and ultimately independent of any central authority in the Land of Israel or anywhere else.

---

[67] b. *Sotah* 14a.
[68] Cf. *Tosefta Abodah Zarah* 4:4 (ed. Zuckermandel, p. 466); *baraitha* in b. *Baba Bathra* 91a; and *Ruth rabbah* 1:4 (Vilna ed.).

ZIONIST POLEMICS IN A POST-ZIONIST AGE

A Reply by JAKOB J. PETUCHOWSKI

MICHAEL ROSENAK'S REVIEW-ESSAY, "THE OLD-NEW ANTI-ZIONISM," IN WHICH he attacks my book, *Zion Reconsidered*, is a masterpiece of satire and irony, and gives evidence of much erudition. Though it is directed against me, I was able to appreciate it and even to enjoy it—to enjoy it from the literary and scholastic point of view, and to appreciate it as a contribution to a much needed discussion. In fact, it had been my stated intention to give impetus to such a discussion, which, as I expressed it in *Zion Reconsidered* (page 13), might contribute "to the laying of the foundations of a healthier relationship between the Jewish citizens of the State of Israel and the wider brotherhood of Jews in the so-called Diaspora."

I do not even resent the implied *ad hominem* attacks. As the Israelis would say, *zeh magi'a li* ("I had it coming to me"). I am willing to admit that *Zion Reconsidered* was not altogether written with the necessary scholarly detachment. The book was begun in Jerusalem itself, at a time when I had to labor under the following "disadvantages": (a) I was a *yekkeh* (a Jew of German origin); (b) I was an American who made no bones about the fact that he intended to return to the United States after his year in the State of Israel; (c) I was a Reform Jew; and (d), worse still, I was a Reform *rabbi* who made an attempt to contribute something to the spiritual rebirth of the Jewish State. What I experienced in any of those capacities was enough to add a note of frustration and polemics to anything I might have had to say.

Being guilty of this, I cannot very well resent Mr. Rosenak's own personal bias which colors his review of my book. After all, he is a lecturer at the Institute for Youth Leaders from Abroad, and, I suppose, it is his function to indoctrinate young people from the Diaspora with the vision that "only in Israel" can the full Jewish life be lived. If my

33. *Ibid.*, p. 107.
34. *Ibid.*, p. 132.

major thesis should be correct, then what Mr. Rosenak is doing professionally is entirely wrong. He is certainly entitled to hit back by way of self-defense. And he has done so beautifully.

But Mr. Rosenak is wrong in regarding my book as an attack on the State of Israel. Nor did he have a right to expect of me that I would offer ready-made solutions to the various problems which beset the young state. Such solutions should more appropriately come from the nation that dwells in Zion, and particularly from those in Zion who train youth leaders for the Diaspora, youth leaders whose task it will be to induce Diaspora Jewish youth to settle in the State of Israel. Besides, could Mr. Rosenak really assure me that any advice offered from the "outside" would be heeded in the State of Israel?

Mr. Rosenak is wrong in saying that I raise the questions of integration, culture, politics and philanthropy in order to "libel" the State of Israel. I wrote, on page 47 of my book, "One can view all this with a certain amount of sympathy, with a benign understanding of the growing pains of a young nation. All countries have had their initial problems; and Israel is a young country." This hardly sounds like libel. But it does sound like saying that the messianic age has not yet arrived—not even for the State of Israel. And that was indeed the reason for my discussing those problems in the first place. If the State of Israel claims that it, and it alone, is the venue of messianic fulfillment, then a Jew has the right to apply the same criteria in judging this claim as he has, in the past, applied to the messianic claims of Jesus and of Sabbatai Zevi. Has the Messiah come, or has he not? I answer that he has not come; and I offer the various problems which beset the State of Israel as evidence for my contention. Mr. Rosenak does not deny the evidence. He only resents my bringing it into court.

HIS RESENTMENT, ONCE AROUSED, knows no bounds. He not only accuses me of "crimes" I have committed, but he also holds me responsible for "crimes" I did not commit. Thus, throughout Mr. Rosenak's polemic, I figure not only as an opponent of Zionism's claims to messianic fulfilment (which I am), but also as the false prophet of Emancipation messianism (which I am not). In the very paragraph in which I cast doubts on Herzl's messiahship, I also do not spare those as whose spokesman Mr. Rosenak chooses to regard me. To set the record straight, the passage should be quoted in full.

> On the other hand, the followers of Jesus of Nazareth in the first century, the followers of Sabbatai Zevi in the seventeenth century, *and some of the Jewish Reformers in the nineteenth century,* all committed the same mistake. They did not allow enough time to elapse in order to gain perspective. They read the signs of history too soon, and suffered from illusions of messianic fulfilment when, in fact, the world was as yet unredeemed. The lesson they bequeath to us is the danger of jumping to conclusions on the basis of historical events while they are as yet in progress. *The Messiah did not answer to the name of Napoleon or of Bismarck.* We know that now. They might not have been able to know it then. But it does not follow from their mistaken identification that the Messiah answered to the name of Theodor Herzl. This, too, could turn out to be a case of mistaken identification. (*Zion Reconsidered,* pp. 16 ff. Emphasis added.)

While it may be flattering to have *Deuteronomy* 18:22 invoked against oneself, and to be considered a "prophet [who] hath spoken presumptuously," I can, alas, lay no claim to that distinction. Moreover, Mr. Rosenak can bestow that distinction on me only because he has totally ignored the bulk of my fourth chapter, in which I am as critical of what is presently going on in American Judaism (and not least in its Reform wing) as I am of anything that I felt called upon to criticize in the State of Israel. But, then, Mr. Rosenak is in the habit of ignoring things which do not fit into his neat scheme. (But *Zion Reconsidered* is in good company here. The Hebrew Prophets, as seen in the light of modern scholarship, and the Mission of Israel fare no better at his hands.) If he had not ignored the last chapter of *Zion Reconsidered*, with its stress on the "family of Abraham," and with its assertion (page 119) that "the categories of race, nation, *and religion* are utterly useless when it comes to defining the Jew" (emphasis added for purpose of quotation), he could not have attributed to me much of what he accuses me of advocating, nor could he have ascribed to me the view that "the 'Prophetic faith' of Judaism is best served by dissolving the Jewish people."

Readers of JUDAISM might also have been surprised to learn from Mr. Rosenak that I—of all people!—regard the "commandments" of Judaism *only* as "spiritual truths." But, then, Mr. Rosenak is no fan of mine; and I shall not hold it against him if he has not read any of my other writings. But, frankly, I would have expected him to read *Zion Reconsidered* more carefully before telling the world what the book is all about.

And yet, I have the feeling that the one paragraph which really provoked Mr. Rosenak's whole diatribe is a paragraph he does not even care to discuss. It reads:

> No doubt, the State of Israel is one possibility which some heirs of the old Jewish way of life may choose for their self-fulfilment. But it is only one possibility, not the sole one. Its relationship to the past Jewish heritage is no more direct, and no more complete, and even no more authentic, than that of those Jews who, living as citizens of other sovereign states, elect to relegate the "national" aspects of Jewish existence to the historical past, preferring, instead, to single out the religious side of Jewish experience as the only meaningful criterion of their Jewish self-identification. Both the Israeli citizen and the American of the Jewish faith are modern types, made possible by the fall of the Ghetto walls. Neither is completely identical with the Jewish type of the pre-Emancipation era. And both are unable to put back the clock of historical development. (*Zion Reconsidered*, pp. 47 ff.)

This is the theme of *Zion Reconsidered* in a nut-shell, this and the groping for a meaningful link between those two types of the modern Jew. I affirm both of them, recognizing their common origin in the age of Emancipation. Mr. Rosenak, too, shows himself fully aware of that common origin, and of the role played by the Emancipation. He goes on to indicate that the Zionists have made the right choice, and the non-Zionists the wrong one. Then, reversing the plus and minus signs, he attributes a similar attitude to me. This is where he is making his mistake. I do not resent the Israeli nearly as much as Mr. Rosenak resents the Jew who has decided to live his Jewish life in the Diaspora. I only resent that Israeli who claims to be in possession of the sole key to Jewish living and Jewish survival. Apparently, Mr. Rosenak is such an Israeli; and that is why he felt the need to mount his attack.

In doing so, Mr. Rosenak has accomplished something which was probably the last thing on earth he intended. I must admit that, after the Six-Day War, I had become somewhat doubtful about certain aspects of *Zion Reconsidered*. The geopolitical references had, of course, become out of date. Some of the minor irritations I experienced in Israel, irritations which may have been responsible for a number of things I said without charity, were receding into the background. Absence makes the heart grow fonder, and three years had passed since my return to the United States from Israel. The spontaneous reaction of world Jewry to the danger which faced the State of Israel in May 1967, and the enthusiastic participation of world Jewry in Israel's joy of victory—a reaction and a participation in which I fully shared—had made me realize that the emotional significance which Zion and Jerusalem hold for the "family of Abraham" was considerably underestimated in *Zion Reconsidered*. There is nothing like a crisis to bring out the underlying interrelatedness of the "family of Abraham"—particularly if it is a crisis brought about by the threat of destruction facing one of its branches. And if the locale of that crisis should be the Land of the Prophets, then atavistic overtones come into play which, perhaps, have, after all, not been completely drowned out by the rarefied theology which was the theme song of Western Jews—and to which Mr. Rosenak himself has listened, as is evidenced by his mode of reasoning. I had, in fact, come to the conclusion that, after June 1967, old-style debate between Zionism and anti-Zionism had become obsolete, and that a new era was dawning in Israel-Diaspora relations.

I was strengthened in that conclusion by reading the words of Dr. Amnon Rubinstein, a leading spokesman of the younger generation in Israel, in *Haaretz* of August 25th, 1967:

> Let us remember . . . how a firm band of partnership at once united us with the Jews beyond the seas. We shall have to accept that this partnership is no longer Zionist in the traditional sense. . . . Israel will not preoccupy the Jews of the world every day of the year, but at times of crisis it will be uppermost in their hearts. They will not live with us, but will look at us from across the seas with pleasure, and sometimes they will visit us. We shall continue to consider our life here superior, but we shall have no choice but to agree that a Jew can feel a community of fate with Israel, as the War has proved, even without living here. We shall have to draw conclusions from this strange partnership, and to give up our arrogant attitude towards them. . . . They will go on being different, yet similar; distant, and yet so close.

I felt that, with such sentiments voiced by Israelis, a new phase had, indeed, set in, and I began to question the continued usefulness of *Zion Reconsidered*.

But Mr. Rosenak's review-article has convinced me that a book like that is still needed—now, perhaps, more than ever. Naturally, were I to write the book today, a number of things would be re-formulated. Yet Mr. Rosenak's position, were it to be shared by the majority of Israelis and by the youth leaders Mr. Rosenak is training, is a position which the Diaspora Jew is entitled to criticize, and that most emphatically.

AT THE END OF HIS ATTACK ON *Zion Reconsidered*, Mr. Rosenak grudgingly admits that I concede the possibility that Israel might well become the "testing ground of Israel's Prophetic faith in action, with the Jews as the sole bearers of responsibility." But, having made this grudging admission, Mr. Rosenak continues:

> But, alas, even after having caught a glimpse of the Zionist idea, the solution that he offers to our national problem is—the dissolution of our nation. (The Jewish State may remain, if it promises to become a more "enlightened" member of the emancipated Jewish religion.)

I suppose that what Mr. Rosenak calls my "advocacy of the dissolution of our nation" is his paraphrase of the concluding remarks of my book. The actual words of *Zion Reconsidered* read as follows:

> Members of the family of Abraham have been called upon to witness to their faith in all sorts of conditions and under all kinds of circumstances. It may well be that some of them, in our own day, have been called upon to witness through their own state. The witness of the Jew in America will be different from the witness of the Jew in the State of Israel. But who is to say which form of the testimony is more vital to the divine economy? Both of them may be equally needed. (Page 131)

> Only the renewed dedication to this family tradition—a tradition which, as we have seen, transcends all national and cultural definitions—both in the Diaspora and in the State of Israel will bring us closer to God's Kingdom. And only the mutual recognition by members of Abraham's family of their respective rights to live and to labor where they choose to do so, and to flourish and to succeed where they desire, will integrate the State of Israel into the millennial pattern of our family tradition. (Pp. 132 ff.)

This, then, is the "dissolution of our nation," which, according to Mr. Rosenak, I am advocating. Some dissolution! Yet Mr. Rosenak's interpretation—or misinterpretation—of my words is highly significant. It means that he is rejecting any or all of the following:

(a) That American Jewry and Israeli Jewry may be equally vital to the divine economy.

(b) That our Jewish tradition transcends all national and cultural definitions.

(c) That Jews, both in Israel and in the Diaspora, are entitled to live and to flourish where they are.

(d) That the State of Israel needs to be integrated into the millennial pattern of our family tradition—a tradition which, by implication, is of greater significance than the State of Israel itself.

As to (a), Mr. Rosenak is doing to American Jewry precisely what he is (wrongly!) accusing me of doing to Israeli Jewry. He is denying our right to exist, or, at the very least, he is questioning our Jewish authenticity. His own Israeli existence is, of course, authentically Jewish; and he can quote Prophets and philosophers to prove it to be so. Yes, there has always been the centrality of the Land of Israel in traditional Jewish thought; but, until modern Zionism arose, those who wanted to do more than *think* that centrality, those, that is to say, who actually came to *live* in the Land of Israel, looked and behaved pretty much like the Neturei Karta do today. Now, it seems that Mr. Rosenak does not have too much use for the Neturei Karta; but I can assure him that, in their eyes, his own brand of Israeli triumphalism looks every bit as suspicious as my affirmation of American Judaism looks in his. Why, then, not be honest enough to admit that neither he nor I can afford to be literalists when it comes to the "fulfilment" of Biblical prophecies? To justify the modern State of Israel, in terms of Biblical prophecy, may take quite as much "stretching" of Ezekiel on Mr. Rosenak's part as my interpretation of the Mission of Israel may require a non-literalist understanding of Prophetic literature. In other words, we are back at the point where we have to recognize that both of us are modern types, made possible by the fall of the Ghetto walls, and that neither of us is identical with the Jewish type of the pre-Emancipation era. Why cannot Mr. Rosenak leave off playing the game of "I-am-more-authentically-Jewish-than-you-are"?

Instead of reiterating the whole content of *Zion Reconsidered*, let me merely suggest that Mr. Rosenak read something else for a change. Since he does not seem to care for Reform and/or non-Zionist authors, I would refer him to an essay written by a rabbi who is both Conservative and Zionist. It is entitled, "Israel and the Diaspora in History and Reality," and it is included in the book by Robert Gordis, *Judaism for the Modern Age* (New York, 1955, pp. 103-125). Let him come to terms with Gordis' thesis which, in spite of some differences in emphasis and nuance, is not so different from my own. Unfortunately for Mr. Rosenak, his learned ammunition against classical Reform Judaism will not help him much in this case.

Concerning (b), Mr. Rosenak has made it abundantly clear that Judaism is not a "religion" in the conventional sense. (I did so, too, in my book!) But is "nation" (in the conventional sense) any better? Is the "holy nation" of *Exodus* 19:6, to which Mr. Rosenak refers, to be construed in terms of modern nationalism? What about the pre-modern use of that word? Many of the early classical Reformers, who were striving for Emancipation and for assimilation, spoke in terms of their membership of the "Jewish nation." (It was only after the rise of modern Jewish nationalism, with its secularist emphases, that the Pittsburgh Reformers found it necessary to explain that they considered themselves "no longer a nation, but a religious community.") I would submit that the *goy kadosh* of *Exodus* 19:6 transcends both the nineteenth-century and the twentieth-century meanings of the word "nation." And what about "culture"? Is there really some culture which *all* Jews have in common, apart from their common religious heritage? But if "nation" and "culture" do not adequately describe the phenomenon of Judaism, then Mr. Rosenak cannot really disagree with my assertion that our Jewish tradition transcends all national and cultural definitions.

In part, I have already dealt with (c) when discussing (a). But (c) is even more inclusive. At issue here is not only American Judaism, but Diaspora Judaism as such—in space and in time. It is actually only an anti-Semite who could deny my statement that "Jews, both in Israel and in the Diaspora, are entitled to live and to flourish where they are." I would hate to think of Mr. Rosenak as an anti-Semite. He just chooses, as he does in other contexts, to ignore some relevant facts.

Of the roughly four thousand years of Jewish history, how much of a "national Jewish life" has there actually been on the soil of the Land of Israel? There were approximately 700 years between the Conquest of Canaan and the destruction of the Kingdom of Judah. There were, roughly, another 600 years during the Second Commonwealth, of which, however, only some 150 years marked the duration of an independent Jewish kingdom. (And, towards the end of that period, more Jews were actually living in the Diaspora than in the Land of Israel itself.) In addition, we have thus far had twenty years of the modern State of Israel. In other words, out of four thousand years, Jews have spent no more than—at the very most—one thousand years as an independent national entity on Palestinian soil.

One might almost be tempted to say that the "normal" form of Jewish existence is Diaspora existence—were it not for the fact that Mr. Rosenak would then point to the repeated persecutions to which Diaspora Jews have been subjected. Is that *normal*?, he might well ask. Has not the God of History shown by these repeated persecutions, and not least by the recent Holocaust, that He does not care for the Diaspora existence of Jewry? Yet the Jew who affirms Diaspora existence will be no more deterred from his affirmation by the Crusades, by Chmielnicki, and by Auschwitz, than the Jew who affirms national sovereignty on the soil of the Land of Israel will let himself be dissuaded by the cruel and bloody destructions of such national sovereignty in 722 B.C.E., in 586 B.C.E., and in 70 C.E.

Who, under such circumstances, can have the temerity to assert that Jews are entitled to live and to flourish *only* in the Land of Israel, or *only* in the Diaspora? I, hopefully and prayerfully, wish to see a flourishing Jewish existence wherever Jews live. By what right does Mr. Rosenak desire to restrict that existence?

As for (d), I suppose that Mr. Rosenak would argue that our tradition is so intimately bound up with the Land of Israel that one cannot really say that the tradition is greater than the Land. (Incidentally, in *Zion Reconsidered*, pp. 120 ff., we have defined that tradition in terms of "the unique relationship to the Sovereign of the Universe" in which this "family," unlike other "families," knows itself to be standing.) But the Land also provided a foothold for the prophets of Baal, and for the Hellenists of Hasmonean days. It was only in the light of the tradition that the idolaters could be, and were, rejected. (Lest Mr. Rosenak now accuse me of regarding all residents of the Land of Israel as "prophets" of Baal" and as "Hellenists," I hasten to add that, of course, the Land also contained both types. It was not, therefore, the Land in and by itself which guaranteed the survival of Judaism.) And it was the tradition which set up certain standards by which life on the Land was to be judged, standards which had to be met "lest the Land spew out its inhabitants" (*Leviticus* 18:25). To accomplish that, the tradition had to be greater than the Land—just as it had to be in order to sustain Jewish life and creativity through two millennia of Diaspora existence.

Not only Diaspora Jews, but also the more thoughtful Israelis, are very much afraid of certain tendencies that would make the tradition subservient to the Land, instead of having the Land serve the tradition. To say, as we have done, that the State of Israel needs to be integrated into the millennial pattern of our family tradition means to be committed to the future of that state and to its Jewish significance.

I HAD HOPED THAT, after June 1967, this type of argumentation would no longer be necessary. With the unity of the People of Israel so clearly recognized and demonstrated, both in the State of Israel and in the Diaspora, I had imagined that we were now definitely living in a post-Zionist age, when the slogans and shibboleths of yesteryear could be quietly and unceremoniously interred. I was evidently wrong. Mr. Rosenak has shown that there can still be Zionist polemics in this post-Zionist age. It is one thing for the State of Israel to appeal for the moral and financial support of Diaspora Jewry. Only the callous would be able to ignore such an appeal. But it is quite another thing to preach an ideology which fails to comprehend the coexistence of Israeli and Diaspora Judaism and their potential for equal worth. Yet it is precisely such an ideology which is responsible for Mr. Rosenak's numerous misreadings, and for his attributing to me of positions which I do not maintain—but which, for the last seven decades or so, have indeed been components of the classical Zionist stereotype of the "anti-Zionist assimilationist."

As long as this ideology continues to be preached, Mr. Rosenak must not take it amiss if, from time to time, books like *Zion Reconsidered* make their appearance in order to speak up on behalf of a form of Jewish existence which is beyond his intellectual horizon, even as it seems to be beyond the width of his heart.

The Tasks of Israel And Galut

DAVID POLISH

FOR THE DIASPORA JEW, A CRISIS CAME WITH the power of a black revelation during May and June, 1967. He was no longer the easy dweller in the dual Zion of the Diaspora and the vicarious homeland in Israel. Suddenly he found himself confronted with a challenge that he had never envisioned—to be passionately fearful for Israel in places where his generations-old roots suddenly seemed to shrivel.

Let us not waste time on berating ourselves for having expected too much of the new Diaspora. And let us not be diverted by a debate as to whether the lands of Diaspora had let us down in the moment of Israel's peril. What is significant for this discussion is that suddenly we felt alone and abandoned, and, whether the psychological experience of bereftness in a silent world was justified or not, the pain and the fear were there, and these were true enough to compel many of us to ask whether our prior assumptions about our Jewish being in a benevolent non-Jewish world were valid. Suddenly we found ourselves emotionally and spiritually uprooted, and our entire beings, which until then we were capable of sharing with generous capacity both with Israel and with our own Western society, were violently torn from their moorings. During those days a *midrash* kept recurring to me, of the Babylonian Diaspora going forth to meet the victims of the Judean conquest. Like their fellow Babylonians, the Jews celebrated the triumph over the Judean state. But beneath their festive garments they wore black, and Jews furtively addressed captives: "How is father? How is brother?"

To understand the depth of the paroxysm that seized many of us, it must be realized that American Jews were not merely integrated into their society or even wholly engaged in its economic and political life, but many were also fully committed in the critical issues that have been besetting our nation. We had entered unreservedly into the struggle over America's Vietnamese war. We had taken unequivocal positions on the issue of race. I am speaking now of Jews who had entered into these causes as Jews, convinced that there was a Jewish mandate to speak and to act, and who at the same time felt bound by covenantal ties to the sur-

---

DAVID POLISH *is rabbi of Beth Emet the Free Synagogue in Evanston, Ill. He is the author of* The Eternal Dissent, The Higher Freedom, *and co-author of* A Guide for Reform Jews. *The present essay was originally presented as a paper to the Biennial Convention of the World Union for Progressive Judaism, Jerusalem, July, 1968.*

vival of the Jewish people. Even after the first shock waves of our desolation in the face of the threat to Israel in its solitude had subsided, we continued to be beset by the pull of loyalties which had never before challenged us. They were of a piece. Being Jewish meant waging a battle for Jewish existence and justifying that existence by concern for the world in which we lived. But after June, 1967 we were not so sure. Could we in fact sustain the multiple burdens of defending not only Israel but the Jewish people and at the same time spend ourselves on the issues of peace and race and poverty? What for the better part of our lives had appeared to be a multiple yet homogeneous agenda for religious existence suddenly turned into divisive and irreconcilable demands upon our time and our loyalties. Then, as the months passed, it was America's turn to become convulsed and to see the abyss opening at its feet. The terrors of Vietnam proliferated, and the apocalypse of the racial struggle grew wilder. Once again many of us were driven to the other end of the spectrum by the wildly gyrating events which took possession of us. Not as citizens but as Jews, Jews of the Diaspora, we found ourselves driven by the events themselves to make our commitment. It was impossible to stand aside, and our response to the death of Martin Luther King symbolized our impassioned immersion in the moral struggle which will determine America's fate.

ISRAELIS MAY NOT FULLY UNDERSTAND our schizoid state. We are fiercely bound up with Israel. We are fiercely committed to the social struggle in America. This alone does not make for the schizoid state. It is that we swing so wildly from one to another, swept up by the violence of the events which tear us from one orbit to the next. To an Israeli, whose existence appears to be of one piece, this is incomprehensible. At the inception of the civil-rights struggle in the United States, a prominent and highly informed Israeli friend asked me: "Why must Jews be involved? Why can't the Negroes practice auto-emancipation as the Zionists did?"

We must not dismiss those Jews, not only in Israel but in growing numbers also in the United States, who argue that it is not the function of Jews as Jews to enter so deeply into the issues that beset Diaspora Jewry. They may take whatever positions they wish as private citizens, but to enter into the fullness of Jewish commitment is not only inexpedient and tactically unsound, but Jewishly inauthentic. They say: "Let us walk our Jewish path alone."

The weight of Jewish precedent is on their side. This has always been the way of the *Galut*. When, at any time of our history until the Emancipation, have Jews expended themselves in universal causes? Our history both in the land of Israel and in *Galut* has been concerned with the preservation of the people and its Torah. Our conception of our history was that it was deviant and contemptuous of the history of the nations. We had learned from disastrous experience that our entrance into history in the form of intimate relationships with empire and world affairs proved costly again and again to our vulnerable people. When the Hasmonean dynasty courted imperial Rome, Pharisaic Judaism rejected this course, because it felt that we had no business being diverted from our isolate and sacred way in the world back into the gravitational pull of temporal history. What did we, the people of the covenant, have to do with power which could never right the wrongs of existence as long as it stood outside the sovereignty of the God of Israel?

It will be argued that this is a distortion of the prophetic and universal conception of Judaism which informs our sacred literature. But we should be careful about placing a false construction upon prophecy. Prophecy was, in the first place, primarily concerned with God's justice within the community of Israel, and, second, it saw the ultimate hopes of a redeemed humanity in eschatological terms. The prophetic vision did not contemplate the transformation of mankind by human endeavor or within the historical process, but rather by divine intervention and only "in the end of days." We may properly invoke the eternal and passionate prophetic hopes for a transformed world, but we cannot impose upon them our own conception of a human strategy for transforming society. The prophets spoke for God and within the context of God's time, not for Immanuel Kant or for Karl Marx within the schedule of revolutionary time. While our tradition was fully committed to the rights of the stranger, it must be understood that it referred to the stranger who was under our jurisdiction and not to the oppressed of other nations. Our expectations were universal; our existence was particular, especially when we entered upon the long night of the *Galut*. Our unfulfilled hopes for the world were concentrated inwardly upon our own morality, our own sense of justice, our own piety. This, too, is prophetic.

With this construction, Jews who follow a single track of exclusive concern with Jewish existence and survival can certainly appeal to an authentic tradition. In this context, those who found themselves standing alone a year ago can validate their separation from the world and can find precedent for their withdrawal into the struggle for Jewish preservation. After all, who demonstrates for Soviet Jewry? Who is appalled by the recrudescence of Polish anti-Semitism? Who is contrite for the Western world's moral, if not physical, complicity in the murder of our martyrs? When nations were silent in May, 1967, when Negro leaders proclaimed an anti-Jewish, pro-Arab line, why should Jews feel summoned to risk so much? Jews hear the bitter disappointment of a poet in the Psalms:

6 : *Judaism*

> *For it was not an enemy that taunted me,*
> *Then I could have borne it;*
> *Neither was it mine adversary that did magnify himself against me,*
> *Then I would have hid myself from him.*
> *But it was thou, a man mine equal,*
> *My companion, and my familiar friend;*
> *We took sweet counsel together,*
> *In the house of God we walked with the throng.*

WE MUST CONFESS THAT WHATEVER THE MERITS or inadequacies of this position, it has the value of two strong conditions. One is that there is no lack of a sense of Jewish identity. The Jewish ego is strong. The crisis of existence is intensely severe, but there is no identity crisis here. At its best, it is the crisis of the Warsaw Ghetto fighters who were illusionless not only about their fate, not only about the stony indifference of the world, but also about the cause for which they were dying. They were dying not to quicken world conscience, not to redeem humanity, not to be suffering servants, but to perform a despairing act for the Jewish people. The second authentic quality of this point of view is that it is a product of *Galut*. Even within the beleaguered borders of the Jewish commonwealth, we experienced a foretaste of *Galut* in the omnipresence of threat. And certainly until the Emancipation, *Galut* was pervasive.

As a consequence of May-June, 1967, I believe that we must abandon an illusion about Jewish existence which we have embraced like a mother clinging to a dead infant. *Galut* is still with us. When we confront the Jewries of the Soviet Union and of Poland, we automatically reject the possibility that we, too, might be living in *Galut*. I think that we would see our situation in a more correct perspective if we realized that *those* Jewries live in captivity, while our status of *Galut*, Exile, remains unchanged. The term *Golah*, Diaspora, is an evasion of our true condition, which is now, as it has always been, contingent. The uncertainty of existence is what characterizes *Galut*, and no polls, no scientific studies—which, after all, objectify only what they can presently sample—can project the unexpected shift of winds and currents to which Jewish life is subject. This is precisely what the Jew alone, not the social scientist, felt in May, 1967, when our world turned cold overnight. This is why I consider Norman Podhoretz's *Making It* so fraudulent: it is predicated on the naive assumption that the American Jew, in attaining success, has at last entered upon his inheritance. Podhoretz may have heard of Peretz Smolenskin who, toward the end of the nineteenth century, had a different interpretation of Jewish success:

> It is true that Israel has a strong hand in Germany and finds shelter in the shadow of the law. . . . But who knows what may happen? Hatred

will increase and will send forth its shoots in secret and pass from land to land. . . . Our short-sighted brethren refuse to see, and they imagine that all will be well with them . . . but it is a vain dream. . . . Whereas at one time those who hated them despised the faith of Israel or else paid usury to a single Jew and blamed all Israel, now the enemies increase who [hate us] both because of the faith and because of the usury, and even because of a prominent seat in the theater which the Jew can afford to buy. . . . When the government will have need for such a rabble, . . . then will come a time of trouble for Jacob.

In addition *Galut* has psychological dimensions, existential dimensions, as well as historical. To *feel* contingency, or to apprehend it when it is not yet a reality, is itself *Galut*. And this the Jew of the West possesses in great abundance. This is perhaps one of his greatest contributions to the culture and spirit of the West, the ability to transmit the intuition that the atmosphere of the world is charged with ominous storms, the sensitivity which led a Zalman Shneour to write in 1913:

*Again the Dark Ages draw nigh! Do you harken,
O man, do you sense it,
The whirling and swirling of dust and the
sulphurous scent in the distance?
The air is with omens impregnate, with omens
grim evil foreboding.*

Friedmann caught this existential *Galut* of the Western Jew, when he wrote of his "consciousness of the precariousness of life" as his "essential dignity." It has been suggested by him and by Hazaz that the *Galut*-Jew does not really want to abandon the anxiety of his insecurity.

HAVING GRANTED ALL THIS, I must nevertheless depart from the conclusions toward which this analysis would seem to drive us. The assumptions implicit in the argument I have developed are theologically based in two interrelated principles: God alone governs history, and He alone will change history by destroying the *Galut*. These assumptions made life possible for the Jew, but if we read some of the current reconsiderations of Jewish history, we will discover that even this was not good enough for great numbers of Jews who preferred instant apostasy to deferred redemption. What has happened to us is not that our history has undergone a real transformation. The twentieth century reduced the Emancipation to a fleeting interlude, just as Hitler demolished the interlude of the Weimar Republic. What has changed is our attitude toward history, and in this respect Zionism has played a mighty role in changing our theology from one of waiting for God to one of acting for God. At the same time, the realities of Zionist history have revealed to the Jewish people that, for good or ill, *Galut* has become an inescapable and ineradicable part of Jewish existence, and no Jewish

8 : *Judaism*

State will alter that reality. We can take Jews out of *Galut*, but we cannot take *Galut* out of Jewish life. Out of the historical process has emerged a people which is altogether different from any other people and perhaps may be a forerunner of other communities of man. By the recreation of Israel the State we are again a people of both space and eternity. We are again an amphibian people, capable of existence on the land, without which our existence is imperiled, and on the many seas of contingency where the currents of history bear us.

The Zionist contribution to Jewish theology—the mandate to the Jew to assume his responsibility for redemption—has further implications —that the Jew must also now unlock the prophetic hopes, once deferred to messianic time, which are part of the moral treasure of the Jewish people. If *Galut* is to have redemptive meaning for the Jew, if it is to transcend "making it" alone, or anxiety about our fate or our destiny, then as Jews, not as citizens merely, we are called upon to bring prophetic visions down from heaven into earthly endeavor.

To those to whom this is an impudent tampering with the will of God or of Jewish history, it should be pointed out that Zionism, predicated on similar assumptions, was also a tampering with the will of God. Only the loyalty of the *Neturei Karta* to the eschatological hope could permit the Jews of the *Galut* now to withdraw from the human struggle. But this will require of us an unprecedented expansion of spiritual and moral capacities. Being inhabitants of land and sea, we will have to learn to encompass both our commitment to Israel and our concern for the world.

To us is given, for perhaps the first time in history, to yoke the national and the universal, not only theoretically but dynamically. To us is given to repudiate the course of self-rejection by some Jews in the interests of a spurious liberalism and to avoid the counsel of isolation by others in defense against the assimilating influences of a more honest liberalism. To us is given what a Moses Hess taught—that Judaism requires a union of our intensest social concerns with our love for the Jewish people. But we must try to apply this lesson to Rome as well as to Jerusalem.

The *Galut*-Jew can rediscover identity not by swinging erratically from loyalty to loyalty, from Israel to the social crisis and back, but by integrating them both into his being and making them an organic aspect of his Jewish existence. Even here, however, there is a scale of priorities, and I will deal with them later. Only when *Galut* becomes more than an historical accident or a deliberate choice for the entrenchment of success and power, only when it becomes a value, however painful and deceptive, a value by which the Jewish ethic can be released into the world, can we justify Jewish existence outside of Israel. I do not suggest that the intrinsic values of Judaism are not cardinal, such as learning, *mitzvot*, the community and the synagogue. But unless the urge "to perfect the world" is taken seriously, these very ingredients of Jewish life can become subverted in symbols of Jewish banality and exhibitionism. A Jewry existing only for the sake of glorifying its own success will quickly become corrupt and decrepit.

If we see Israel as an expression of the messianic impulse in Judaism (and all of us are aware of the needs for self-preservation and viability, which cannot help but obscure the messianic impulse in these difficult days), then there is another front on which this Jewish task must be carried out—and that is the *Galut*. It is precisely because it is *Galut*, and not a more assuring Diaspora, that this task devolves upon us.

THERE ARE THOSE WHO WILL SAY that this is too great a risk, that in Jewish involvement in issues of peace and race are imbedded the seeds of anti-Semitism. Our response should be that the risks lie not in what we say but in who we are, not in our action but in our identity. The centuries should have taught us that there is no tactical escape from the nature of our confrontation with the world, and the hard events that the State of Israel indicate that this is as true of a sovereign Jewish State as it is of the Jewish people wherever it may be dispersed. Our risk is in being Jews, not in pursuing the paths of justice and freedom.

Yet we must always be aware that there is the gravest difference between the *Galut* of the West and the Captivity of the East. It is only in *Galut* that the Jew may take risks. In the Captivity no one would be fool enough to call upon him to assume his prophetic role. It is risk enough if he stands and waits. And this should be a lesson to us that only if the *Galut* remain *Galut* may we summon the courage required for these days.

Therefore, realism demands that a further qualification be made. Our universal commitment cannot be unconditional. If the world closes in upon us too much, we will be too embattled for any concern except for our survival. The Jews of every generation who would march to Utopia on the trampled bodies of the Jewish people expose the lie of their cause, since, in the name of a new life, they would deny life to this people; in the name of freedom, would enslave this people; in the name of redemption of every group, would thwart the redemption of this group. Even now we stand on the narrow ledge of Western society. This has been our historical posture. Nevertheless, despite the sorry record of the twentieth century, we must cling from that ledge to our identification with the ethical impulses of Judaism. If we abandon them, where can we turn? But this is conditional upon the stability of the *Galut*. If it falters, we have no choice but to turn inward. We will be prophetic if we can; defensive if we must. Those of us who are engaged in the issues of the world have cherished eternal hopes. Those of us who are detached have ancient memories. From a coldly scientific view, their memories have more substance than our hopes. If it comes to that, the Jewish people's courage to be in a hostile world is also a prophetic act. In the revolution in which the United States is now convulsed, on what shores can we yet be swept up? If our hopes are dashed, it could be for always. If we are driven in upon ourselves, it will not be for primitive self-preservation alone. It will be because we believe that locked within this people are possibilities for itself and the world which, in God's time, are yet to be released, as similar possibilities were released again and again for three thousand years. Ultimately—and I hope that we must not be driven to this ultimacy—the endurance of the Jewish people is paramount. Why? Because the faith of the Jewish people is the most authentic test yet devised of the world's integrity. The truth of every cause is validated or found fraudulent in the way in which it confronts the Jewish people. Thus, if the *Galut* should fail us, as it did in May, 1967, then not only are we in jeopardy but so is Israel, and in this lies the ultimate truth of our identity. In *this* world, the Jewish State and the *Galut* are one, and if the domino theory applies anywhere, it applies with grimmest realism here.

AS FOR ISRAEL, IT IS NOT WITHOUT ITS OWN crisis of identity. Agnon understands it well, and his work reflects a special kind of schizoid gyration to which sensitive spirits in Israel are victim. His *Oreah Natah Lalun* evokes the tragedy of the Jew who is torn by the conflicting pulls of Jewish existence in *Galut* and *Eretz Yisrael*, and *Tmol Shilshom* reveals the even more radical tension between the secular Zionist world and the sacred religious world struggling for the soul of the Jewish pioneer in *Eretz Yisrael*. The identity crisis in the Jewish State is the crisis of Jewishness as against Israeliness. I do not believe that the Six-Day War resolved it, touching episodes reflecting sudden Jewish awareness notwithstanding. I hope I am wrong, but I see the Jewish consciousness that emerged among many as a sudden conversion-experience, with all the defects of this kind of phenomenon. Like fox-hole religion, it rarely survives the moment of intensest crisis. The breach in the soul of the *Galut*-Jew is matched by a schism in the Israeli spirit. There is the fateful danger that we and they may become separated brethren because they, like us, are separated and disjointed personalities. The depths of this condition are apparent to American Jews who experience great difficulty in coming to know Israelis studying in our country. Repeated efforts by my congregation to open the doors of our Jewish community to them have met with rebuff, though we have had no difficulty in bringing many hundreds of foreign students from other lands into our midst. The sense of kinship is becoming more and more jaded as older-brother generations yield to younger-cousin generations. If Israeliness will ultimately supersede Jewishness, then, of course, a new identity will emerge in this land; and, while it would be foolish to predict, we have reason to fear that the *Galut* will become exceedingly lonely. Israel has brightened our lives, but, whatever Israel may become, it could (except for a stubborn enclave here and there) become lost to the Jewish people. Having lost most of European Jewry by annihilation, Soviet Jewry (possibly) by spiritual strangulation, how could we endure if an entity called Israel, on which we had staked our greatest hopes, were to cease to be Israel?

It is against the background of these fears that many of us hope that Israelis will understand our motivation in seeking to contribute toward the restoration of Jewish identity in this land. It is well known in Israel that the bonds with the *Galut* cannot long be sustained by financial ties alone. Outright or quasi-contributions to Israel are symbols, vital as they are, of concern for Israel. But the outpouring of May-June, 1967 notwithstanding, there is a statute of limitation on this kind of response, particularly because of the methods, conceived and contrived in Israel and in the *Galut,* for eliciting the response. (The present generation tolerates the vulgarity and the debasing of personality which accompany certain fund-raising efforts, but a new and perhaps more sensitive generation, which faults the synagogue for its crassness, will be no less critical of fund-raising for Israel.) Jewish community life is being reduced to the cynically manipulated adulation of Jews, some unsavory, whose claim to manhood of the year is wealth alone. This is symptomatic of a malaise within Jewish life and a deterioration of the Jewish community. It is reminiscent of a Hebrew story of my childhood, in which a Jewish community was swept by a wave of suicides by despondent people. To counteract this, it was decreed that every Jew in town should be made an honoree at one of a series of public functions. Jewish culture has become a massive bash, at which those who pay the price of admission are treated to performances by the giants of TV inanity in honor of Israel's independence. The Jewish community and Jewish fund-raising agencies are becoming synonomous, and, while the gifts may for a while increase, identity as well as sensitivity will shrivel, and Jewish life will be in peril for want of a *Yiddish vort.*

THE SEARCH FOR IDENTITY MUST ULTIMATELY drive us to ultimate questions: Who am I? What is the meaning of my existence? What is my task in the world? How can I bridge the abyss between myself and the universe? How shall I submit to death?

Our times are mistakenly regarded as irreligious or anti-religious, because the sounds of destruction of the old forms and old institutions possess our consciousness. But beyond the clamor one can hear less

12 : *Judaism*

strident voices, not only of theologians and scholars, but of simple people, asking those questions with mounting urgency in a world where the foundations are crumbling, and apocalypse hangs like a deadly missile in orbit. It is no accident that among the thinkers, the writers, the cultural leaders, Jews are frontiersmen in the desperate search for meaning. This is not a time for answers. It is a time of questing, which is in itself a great religious experience. It is no accident that in circles outside of Jewish life, people are again turning to the teachings of Judaism, from the Bible to Hasidism to this very day, for insights and directions in finding a way for man. Thus, what we seek in this land is not a cheap device for linking Israel to the *Galut*. What we seek is the restoration for us all—*Galut* and Israel alike—of those spiritual and moral impulses which make us one people, pursuing our solitary way in a world that learned again and again to follow in our wake.

This should not be novel or revolutionary for Israelis, and, in particular, it should not be novel for Israelis who still find satisfaction in the formulative influence of the labor movement and its gifted spiritual leaders upon the land. Aaron David Gordon was such a religious spirit. He spoke to his generation of man in the universe. He spoke to his generation of the problem of the *ani*, the I: ". . . When you perform your work . . . you will feel that you absorb something hidden . . . something you do not understand . . . but which will add light and life to your spirit. Moments will come to you when you will melt into the Infinite." Aaron David Gordon spoke to his generation of the cosmic significance of human existence:

> On an evil day, when suffering comes upon you, your suffering shall be sacred. You will know trouble, which will shed upon you a spirit of transcendent holiness and transcendent love for all who live and suffer. You will know neither ordinary life nor pettiness nor empty existence. . . . Then all of nature will be close to your heart. . . . Then you will see eternity in a moment—for man will be a brother to man and to the stars of the heavens, for there will be enough heaven in the soul of every man . . . and no man will fall upon his neighbor. . . . On that day your wisdom in science will not be a cold and terrible light, but a living light, pouring out from all the worlds.

When the absorption in anti-religion or non-religion will become a weariness, when men will no longer be content to live by national slogans alone, they will turn again to the sources of our being for assurance that their life is not a deception. This eagerness is to be found here. We seek to help to awaken it, not for the sake of this brand of Judaism or that, but for the sake of *am olam*, the Eternal People. In the Ben Zvi Library of the Hebrew University, I found this extract of a letter from a young soldier from Ein Harod, writing from a North African battlefield during World War II to his father:

> Yesterday we celebrated the First of May. . . . If Marx said that the workers will ultimately triumph and establish absolute equality, our prophets said this thousands of years before he did. . . . They proclaimed fifty-two First of Mays—the *Shabbat*. . . . The prophetic aspiration for justice serves as spiritual food. . . . I have hardly spoken of this holiday, and, to my sorow, neither I nor the youth in general know enough about it. If we are to be reproached for this, then our shame must be turned against you, our parents.

Young American Jews who return from Israel enthralled and inspired are nevertheless puzzled by the religious indifference they encounter, and hurt by the official religion which is so alien to them. They are impressed by the national diversity which a pioneer land has encouraged, a diversity flowing from variant ethnic, cultural, social, political, economic, racial sources, but a diversity which stops short at the gateway of religion. Israel, in its appeal for *aliyah*, says to the Jewish youth of the world: "Whoever you are, come to us." Yet, while I recognize that there are factors beyond religion involved in this issue, *aliyah* will not be stimulated when young Jews from all lands, where the essence of religion is freedom, are told, in effect: "You will have to comply with the demands of the religious party when you come here." The State of Israel has gone a long way in encouraging capital, industry and investment from other lands. It has made concessions and accommodations in order to encourage, not to thwart, the flow of economic strength to the State. When will the government of Israel come to recognize that it will have to make accommodation and adjustment to fulfill the spiritual needs of our young people, many of whom represent some of the greatest wealth of mind and spirit that could be invested in the country? I reject the notion that this subject must not be pressed now, during a time of difficulty for the State. This is a counsel of delay which can be invoked indefinitely in a world where we live constantly with crisis. The United States is going through a crisis more shattering than a cultural struggle, and, if it is to be redeemed, it will be because young people, clergymen, university professors, have refused to accept the argument that "now is not the time." "If not now, when?"

NEVERTHELESS, I BELIEVE THAT THE SECRET of Jewish survival is imbedded chiefly in the State of Israel. This has been true historically. The expectation of redemption alone, wrapped up with the faith in the redeeming God of Israel, made existence possible for the otherwise hopelessly entrapped people. This is also true currently. How else can we account for the primal upsurge of Jewish energies and creativity as well as instinctive identity, if not through the redemptive forces released by the State of Israel? We like to think that the creation of the State and everything consequent to it are the products of certain forces generated within the Jewish people and within the world. Just the reverse. It is Zionism and Israel which have set loose mighty moral and spiritual currents in the modern world. It is not humanity's contrition for the Holocaust, but the Jewish people's determination to redeem the Holocaust that triggered a measure of expiation on the part of the nations. Elsewhere, I have pointed out that within a couple of years after the Holocaust the World Council of Churches could say nothing about either the martyrdom or about the newly created State except to issue a call to conversion. How much more urgent would have been the call, not to atonement by the world but to apostasy by Jewry, if we had been left without a State, only with the torn limbs of a beaten and demoralized people! As for us, we need only look about to see how the dynamics of the State and the community within the State have sent waves of moral power and influence coursing throughout our lives. We, who properly wish to bring the message of religion to Israel, must be mindful of the enormous motivation for our work, for the new lease on life, which Israel has given to our movement. And I might add that Jewish theology, which is rapidly reasserting itself in our midst, will immeasurably benefit from once again joining itself, as it always has, to the historic experiences of our people as the ground of Jewish thought about man, God and eternity. The ingredients for Jewish survival are here—from the reminders of our origins at Hazor and Qumran, to the kibbutz movement which has already moved beyond Israel's borders, to the doctrine of a Buber, to the proliferating universities, to the rebirth of the Hebrew language, to the mysticism which may yet again enrapture the world, to the literary, scholarly explosion of creativity as nowhere else.

Most of all, Israel contains the secret of survival for us all because through it the Jewish people has demonstrated the historically unprecedented capacity to undergo resurrection. Ezekiel's vision about the valley of the dry bones has been fulfilled before our eyes. What people, once destroyed and exiled for nearly two millennia, has ever been born again? What do the wise men say who measure the life and death of every civilization, who predict the decline and fall of every living society—what do they say of Israel?

To have crawled out of the sewers of Warsaw, the barracks of Auschwitz, the forests of Poland, and to give birth to a people again is a marvel that no deterministic interpretation of history, no economic dialectics can possibly cope with. *This* is the moment from which Jewish theology and a theology of consolation for men everywhere arises. And this is the saving event which rescues the Jewish people from ultimate terror and despair. No one should dare to speculate about the meaning of Auschwitz, least of all those who reject all meaning and who deny its victims the title of martyrs. But this can be said— the State of Israel and the people within it represent a measure of vindication of Auschwitz. The capacity of a people to face the demonic in man and to overwhelm its own fate is a vindication not only of this people, Israel, but of the spirit of man, flickering desperately in the dark night of human anguish. If there is no meaning in Auschwitz, there is transcendent meaning in remembering Auschwitz from the midst of a people reborn to be a witness to the world.

In the words of Sh. Shalom:

Wherever I go I hear footsteps
—My brothers on the road, in the swamps, in the forests,
Swept along in darkness, trembling from cold,
Fugitives from flames, plagues and terrors.

Wherever I stand I hear rattling
—My brothers in chains, in chambers of the stricken—
They pierce the walls and burst the silence.
Through the generations their echoes cry out
In torture camps, in pits of the dead.

Wherever I lie I hear voices
—My brothers herded to slaughter—
Out of the burning embers, out of the ruins,
Out of cities and villages, altars for burnt offerings;
The groaning in their destruction haunts my nights.

My eyes will never stop seeing them
And my heart will never stop crying "outrage";
Every man will be called to account for their death.
The heavens will descend to mourn for them.
The world and all that is therein will be a monument on their grave.

If there is no meaning in Auschwitz, there is meaning in the surge of hope released by the reality of Israel. As Yehuda Karni put it:

Seal me into the Wall with Jerusalem stones.
Set me in mortar, and from
The midst of the stones my bones shall call,
Proclaiming the Messiah.

This is the miracle—not military victory, not the defeat of the many by the few, but Jewish existence itself, the return, the rebirth, the renewal. God wants Israel to endure. This wish is a paradigm for God's wish that man endure. This is why the Jewish State is called to higher statehood. This is why the wisdom of the Pharisees was greater than the statecraft of the Hasmoneans. Even in the midst of a world caught in nationalist frenzy, the possibilities of community beyond national idolatry are beginning to emerge. Can it be that this people, rooted in soil and drifting in the world at the same time, can show a new way—a love of land and a kinship with mankind, an attachment to home modified by an openness to the world? The *Galut* says to the State: "Remember, you were born for prophecy and for messianism." The State says to the *Galut*: "Remember, you have gone forth into the world to live and not to die." Let the world, which is also in *Galut*, learn this lesson of the two-fold existence. For this reason, we want Israel to be exemplary of our people's moral and spiritual, yes, and pious genius, imbedded within it. In learning this lesson, we may begin to find the path back to our true identity.

Israel: The Ever-Dying People
SIMON RAWIDOWICZ

I

THE WORLD MAKES MANY IMAGES OF ISRAEL, but Israel makes only image of itself—that of a being constantly on the verge of ceasing to be, of disappearing.

The threat of doom, of an end which forecloses any new beginning, hung over Israel even before it gained its nationhood, while it was taking its first steps on the stage of history. Indeed, it would often seem as if Israel's end preceded its very beginning. Almost from the first meeting in the desert between Moses and Israel, when the prince of prophets uttered the dread admonitions of *Deuteronomy*, to the pseudo-prophetic outbursts of Bialik in the twentieth century, seers and mentors in Israel have time and again pronounced the dire warning: "Israel, thou art going to be wiped off from the face of the earth; the end is near—unless and if . . ." There were many "ifs," and yet they were always the same.

On the soil of ancient Palestine, when there were still priests and Levites and the Israelites enjoyed a happy life, the merry drunkards of Ephraim and the fashionable daughters of Zion (who today would be beauty queens sent abroad on fund-raising campaigns) aroused the wrath of Isaiah. When the worshipers of Baal sang their song of earth and nature alongside humble, pious servants of God searching for a new and deeper way of life and thought—in those remote and happy days, the best men of Judea and Samaria would sally forth in Israel's towns and villages, warning their careless inhabitants of the national and individual disasters that were imminent. This vision was not confined to a few prophetic fanatics. It was flesh of the flesh of the people,

---

This article constitutes an abridged, popularized and updated lecture version of the Hebrew chapter, "Am Holech Va-met," published in Metzudah V-VI (1948), which the late PROF. SIMON RAWIDOWICZ, *chairman, until his death in 1957, of the Department of Near Eastern and Judaic Studies at Brandeis University, designated as part of his philosophy of history, a work which his untimely passing prevented him from writing. (An appreciation of Prof. Rawidowicz, by Nahum N. Glatzer, appeared in our summer 1967 issue.) Other fragments of this unwritten work include the article "On Interpretation," Proceedings of the American Academy for Jewish Research XXVI (1957), and the Hebrew "Sha'ar Ha-Bayit: Al Parashat Batim," published in Babylon and Jerusalem (1957). The Hebrew original of this article and the chapter "Sha'ar Ha-Bayit" will be included in Volume I of the collected Hebrew philosophical studies of Prof. Rawidowicz, currently being published in Jerusalem. The present English text, preserved among Prof. Rawidowicz's literary remains, has been prepared for publication by his son, Benjamin Rawidowicz, who has incorporated marginal notes and additions made by Prof. Rawidowicz in the last years of his life.*

their daily fare—"the bread of affliction that our fathers ate" all over the land.

Often our seers craved for the new heaven and new earth which would come into being after the approaching destruction, as if they hoped for a second creation, for the rebirth of the world—as if they visualized a cycle of appearance, disappearance, and reappearance. Yet their message of the impending end imposed itself on their audience, as well as on themselves, as that of an end that is not final but also irrevocable.

After the destruction of the Temples and the two Hebrew states, which shook the souls of the Judeans to the very depth and thus prepared the ground for a great spiritual metamorphosis, this feeling of the approaching end attained an especially high degree of predominance in the mind of the nation. It gained in intensity during the past 2,000 years of our history, years of greatest heroism and disappointing weakness, years of triumph and defeat, glory and disgrace in all the four corners of the earth, wherever history has given us a chance to make a stand and to try again.

He who studies Jewish history will readily discover that there was hardly a generation in the Diaspora period which did not consider itself the final link in Israel's chain. Each always saw before it the abyss ready to swallow it up. There was scarcely a generation which, while toiling, falling and rising, again being uprooted and striking new roots, was not filled with the deepest anxiety lest it be fated to stand at the grave of the nation, to be buried in it. Each generation grieved not only for itself but also for the great past which was going to disappear forever, as well as for the future of unborn generations who would never see the light of day.

The leading spirits of past generations felt this impending doom not only as a collective but also as an individual fate. In the centuries following the destruction of the Second Temple, almost every leading poet and scholar in Israel considered himself the last—the last poet, the last scholar. *His* Torah was the end of Torah; *he* had written the concluding page in the great book of learning of the nation; when *he* will have recited the *Shema* for the last time, the Torah will either return to Sinai or be discarded as a useless object in the corner in which it has apparently lain so often since its beginning. And, in truth, the Torah was forgotten in Israel again and again; its memory was almost obliterated in ancient Palestine, where, according to tradition, three great Babylonians had to restore it to life—Ezra, Hillel and Rabbi Hiyya.

This was even truer in the Diaspora, where there was scarcely a moment when the Torah did not lie neglected, while at the same time it flourished, becoming a sea of Leviathan Talmud-swimmers who would be a credit to any racing team in the world. As to the corner where the Torah reposes, is it not as if every sage in Israel finds the Torah therein, forsaken and forgotten, picks it up, dusts it, lives with it, and on leaving this world returns it with an almost traditional feeling of the final end? That corner—what students of Jewish history do not see it before their eyes, day and night, as a monument to the despair of generations, a testimony of sadness and despondency, unspeakable and inexpressible?

This feeling of frustration, waste and hopelessness has persistently harassed the minds of the many generations of the "last Jews"—and most of the Diaspora-generations were of this kind: last Jews. It has depressed the best and greatest in Israel, darkened the light of their lives, poisoned the well of their creativeness. What reward can the son of a generation that is the last expect? What good, what meaning, what value can there be in the efforts of him who is the last? "Rabbi, to whom do you entrust us?"—every generation of pupils would ask every dying sage in Israel. For he was the last in his eyes and in theirs. Hence the deep and incessant lamentation which fills our literature of the past 2,000 years. In every grave of a sage wisdom was buried; learning departed, and the world was left void.

The last generation of the Tannaim summed up, in the *Mishnah*, that feeling in a very concise way. So we read at the end of Tractate *Sotah*:

> When R. Meir died, there were no more makers of parables. When R. Azzai died, there were no more expounders. When R. Joshua died, goodness departed from this world. When Rabban Simeon B. Gamliel died, the locusts came and troubles grew many. When R. Eleazar b. Azariah died, wealth departed from the Sages. When R. Akiba died, the glory of the Law ceased. When R. Hanina b. Dosa died, men of good deeds ceased. When R. Jose Katnuta (or of Ketanit) died, there were no more saintly ones. When Rabbenu Yohanan b. Zakkai died, the splendor of wisdom ceased. When R. Gamliel the Elder died, the glory of the Law ceased and purity and abstinence died. When R. Ishmael b. Piabi died, the splendor of the priesthood ceased. When Rabbi [Judah Hanassi, the compiler of the *Mishnah*] died, humility and the shunning of sin ceased.

It was Maimonides who seems to have been somewhat puzzled at the fact that Rabbi Judah Hanassi should say of himself in his own *Mishnah*: "When Rabbi died, humility and the shunning of sin ceased." He suggests that the phrase, "when Rabbi died" is a later addition. He is certainly right. As the famous anecdote has it: "I, too, agree with the words of the Tosafists."

Of far greater interest are the two remarks by the Amoraim of the third generation, R. Joseph and R. Nahman. R. Joseph said: "One should not say 'humility died,' for I am still here." R. Nahman said: "One should not say, 'the shunning of sin ceased,' for I am still here (*d'ika ana*)." It is incredible that the modest R. Joseph should boast so immodestly of his modesty. It reminds one of that benefactor for many good causes who, after hearing the citation read at his testimonial dinner, observed: "They omitted to mention my modesty." Does a man who shuns sin advertise it in such a way as did R. Nahman? Still more amazing is the fact that these two statements are the concluding words of the *Gemara* of *Sota*. Is one perhaps entitled to interpret this as an outspoken intention on the part of the two Amoraim and of the collator of the Babylonian *Gemara* to record their protest against the Palestinian *Mishnah* and against the Tannaim for their tendency to consider themselves the last sages of Israel? Did the Babylonians mean to proclaim thereby that Torah was still alive as long as they kept the torch of learning burning in their native land? Is this *d'ika ana*—"for I am still here"—a challenge to those who were inclined to minimize the work done by the Amoraim, to those who interpreted the verse, "He hath made me to dwell in dark places" as referring to the Babylonian Talmud—an attitude known in the days of the Haskalah and even in some quarters in our own day?

I am not a "Hadranist"—a specialist in reciting a *hadran* ("concluding section") at the completion of a tractate, a well-known custom among Talmudists. Let those specialty it is explain this double *d'ika ana* of *Sota*. I return to my theme: the particular *Mishnah* demonstrated again how every generation of sages considered itself the last, and how, with the death of their leading figures, would be buried one of the foundations, one of the cardinal virtues on which the House of Israel was built.

II

THE POIGNANT REFRAIN OF OUR MISHNAH'S *mi-she-met*—"with the death of so-and-so died this or that cardinal virtue—echoes throughout post Mishnaic literature, throughout the Middle Ages up to recent times. Almost every Leviathan in the sea of Talmudic lore lived all his life under the stress of thinking himself to be the last giant in that great deep: with his passing, he feared, no Leviathan would ever swim in it again. It is of interest to quote Maimonides' letter to the scholars of Lunel, Southern France. After the "Spanish eagle" had lived to finish his last major opus, the *Moreh Nevuchim* (*Guide for the Perplexed*), he wrote to them—this is not a literal translation—as follows: "This I have to tell you, that in our difficult times there are none left in Israel who care for the Torah and Talmud except for you and your neighbors. All other places are either dead or dying (as far as the Torah is concerned). There are three or four decaying centers in Palestine, one in Syria, a few in Babylonia. Little is studied in the Yemen and other Arab countries, although they have acquired three copies of the *Mishneh Torah*. The Jews in India do not know even the Written Law. Thus all that is left to us is you, in Southern France. Be strong and fortify yourselves for the benefit of our people, for the matter depends on you—that is, the survival of Israel and the Torah depends on you alone." This was the picture of the end of the glorious Golden Age as painted by one of the greatest and most creative Jews of the Middle Ages.

Maimonides did not realize, could not have realized, that, while he was lamenting the end of the Torah almost all over the world, new Jewish settlements were striking roots on both sides of the Rhine, that would soon spread as far as the borders of the Vistula, Nieman, Dniester, Dnieper, Bug and other famous rivers, on the shores of which there would sit for hundred of years tens of thousands of scholars who would study the Torah, and that many of them would specialize in Maimonides to such an extent that they would think that they understood him better than he understood himself. These Rambam-specialists would consider the solving of a Rambam problem or contradiction, which is often based on a copyist's or printer's error, as the greatest test, privilege and joy of a Jewish scholar. It is told of one of these specialists, a Lithuanian Talmudist, that, when questioned by the angel in charge of the gates of the Garden of Eden about his work and learning on earth, he replied proudly: "I specialized in solving difficult Rambam-problems." The examining angel said: "This suits us very well; Maimonides himself is here with us; let him come and judge for himself as to the merits of your work." Maimonides came, was very pleased to hear about his student, then asked him to give some illustration of his special learning. The Lithuanian Rambam-specialist demonstrated an almost insoluble contradiction in Maimonides' *Mishneh Torah* and proceeded to expound his solution. Maimonides was amazed and said to his admirer: "But I do not see any contradiction; there is no *kashya* here, for I never wrote in my *Mishneh Torah* what you quote; I said such-and-such; your text must have been corrupted by some of your copyists." The Lithuanian Rambam-specialist looked with contempt at the great master and said: "What a facile solution of a Rambam problem!"

It could not have occurred to Maimonides what he would mean for so many centuries to great masses of Jews in countries like Poland, Lithuania, Hungary and many others—may I add America—of which he knew nothing. Likewise, the last sage of Sippori and Yavneh, Sura and Pumbeditha could not have foreseen the great centers of Jewish learning in so many parts of Europe, nor that the Jews of the Rhineland, void of any Jewish knowledge in the days of the flourishing of the *Gemara* in Babylonia, would after some time build up a great reservoir of Talmudic lore for themselves and other Jewries in the world at large.

In turn, many of these Rhineland sages, like Maimonides, often perceived the admonishing finger of the approaching end. They, too, feared that they were the last. Take, for instance, our older *Musar-*

literature: how full it is of this fear of the approaching end! I am fully aware of the fact that this type of literature of castigation and admonition is bound to exaggerate when it describes prevailing conditions which it deplores and rejects. Those who consider *Musar*-literature as authentic and truthful sources of historical reality, a kind of mirror of their times, are very far from gasping the true nature of that passionate and tendentious outburst of reformers and visionaries of all kinds. It is, after all, propaganda literature—and we, in our own days, have too much of it. The question of how far it is justified to regard any prophetic literature as an authentic source of history is not our concern here. But even after every allowance has been made for the purpose of *Musar*-literature and a great deal of its descriptions discounted there still remains much that is valid in its prognosis of the approaching total annihilation of Israel, of the deep anxiety about the end of the nation.

The same fear is revealed in many other documents of our literature, in letters, casual remarks in prefaces to older books, as well as in *obiter dicta* in the responsa literature. One often gets the impression that many, if not most, of the spiritual leaders and spokesmen of traditional Israel in the last centuries saw before them the imminent disappearance of the Sabbath, the end of *tefillin*, piety, *yirat shamaim* (fear of heaven), and faith in general. These centuries are today considered by us as a kind of flowering of Jewish thought and life. These great Jews, whom we regard as important inaugurators of Jewish values and ideas, veritable *Rishonim*, saw themselves as the last guardians of a treasure that would soon disappear forever. The fear of the fast approaching end was also a great stimulus to Jewish Messianic movements, but this is another chapter in itself. Of course, there always lived in Israel the faith that *netzach yisrael lo yeshaker* ("The Eternal of Israel will not be belied")—but the consuming fear of the end, of the *acharit ketz*, should not be overlooked.

When we probe more deeply along these lines, we see that not only traditional Judaism, the Judaism of Torah and *mitzvot*, but also so-called modern or secular Judaism tended from its very beginning to consider itself the end of Israel—to regard its efforts in various fields of life and thought as those of the last Jews, edging toward the precipice from which there is no return, no second chance for a new struggle.

When the so-called New Israel began, after the French Revolution, to unburden itself of many traditions of the past, it did not relinquish the old tradition of the fear of the end, of the conviction of being the last. Not only the great Jewish sons of Western Europe, like Heinrich Heine (who slammed the door behind him and yet to a certain extent remained at home), or Leopold Zunz (the father of *Wissenschaft des Judentums*), or Steinschneider considered themselves the last Jews, last scholars in Israel, *Totengraeber* (gravediggers), last custodians and collators of a vast tradition which was dying out—not only they, but also Jews in Eastern Europe who, in the 19th century, fought to establish a new literature in the language of the Jewish past, often felt as if they were standing at the grave of their people, its history and language.

Y. L. Gordon (Yalag), the leading poet of the Haskalah, gave the most outspoken expression to this great dread, when he burst out in his famous lamentation: "For whom do I labor? Who will tell me the future, will tell me that I am not the last poet of Zion, and you my last readers?" "The last poet—the last readers." Yalag carried this gloom to his grave. After his death, most of his contemporaries felt that, with his passing, Hebrew poetry had ceased to be. Had they written their *Mishnah*, they would have said: "When Yalag died, poetry ceased in Israel." I have met many *Maskilim* who took this *mi-she-met Yalag* very seriously.

Yalag, who lived in St. Petersburg, had no idea that in his own country a young, shy man was growing up, first in Zhitomir, then in the Yeshiva of Volozhin, who would one day overshadow him, while, of course, benefiting from his troubles and efforts—Chaim Nachman Bialik. Gordon, obsessed by deep despair, did not know that another young lion was making his way to the forefront of Hebrew poetry—Saul Tchernichovsky, a pupil of a Russian secondary school in Odessa. Still less could that "last Hebrew poet" foresee the advent of the many younger Hebrew poets who would soon rise, inspired by his great followers, Bialik and Tchernichovsky.

And Bialik—did he not himself often surrender to the fear of being the last? Did he not speak of himself in his poem, "Before the Bookcase," as the *acharon ha-acharonim*, "the last of the last"? Did he not see himself as the prophet of the end, and was he not so considered by many of his contemporaries? This fear of the impending end, of some ultimate catastrophe, was much in his mind. It was this, too, which drove him to try to save the past, to recreate and refashion it. Whoever has not grasped this psychological background of Bialik's effort—his fear of the end and his struggle between end and beginning—cannot really understand his life, his conflicts and achievements.

If these were the optimist Bialik's fears, how much more were they shared by M. J. Berdichevski, who, during the whole of his life, saw the end of Israel nearing, and became the poet and thinker of the last Jews! And Berdichevski was far from being alone. Joseph Chaim Brenner felt for the greater part of his life, which ended so tragically, that he was one of the last Jews. In *Me-ever Le-gvulin*, for instance, he describes Hebrew literature as the pouring out of the soul of the last Jews, the disappearance of last Jews who will be unknown to succeeding generations. He was the last Jew, writing in the language of the last Jews—writing for and to these last survivors, who will soon disappear without leaving a trace.

III

FROM THE PATRIARCH ABRAHAM, who lamented that "I go hence childless, and he that shall be possessor of my house is Eliezer of Damascus," through the compilers of the *Mishnah* and the *Gemara*, and from Maimonides in the 12th century to Brenner in the 20th, we encounter the same theme of *mi-she-met*, the last Jews! Rabbi Akiba was the last representative of Torah; Brenner and Berdichevski, the last Jews.

When Brenner wrote about being the last, there were several million Jews in his country of origin, Russia, and another three millions or so in the other European lands. Now, after our great European tragedy—"tragedy" is too weak a word for this third great disaster in our history—the traditional dread of being the last naturally assumes dimensions of great magnitude in the minds of our European brethren —but not only with them. Every effort to revitalize Jewish life and learning is stamped—and handicapped—by the fear of being the last. Every Jewish teacher, community worker who toils for the sake of Israel, "for the sake of heaven in truthfulness," every Jewish scholar and thinker who dares to continue the great tradition of Jewish scholarship in the face of growing assimilation and adjustment to the outside world—each considers himself the last of his kind, and is so considered by those around him. They know he is the last—for they feel it in their very bones that they, too, are the last. How often do we feel—not only in the present-day Diaspora—seeing a great creative Jew, watching a gathering of "good Jews" to preserve their identity by all means and whatever cost, that they are the last, that we all are the last; and how often are we full of doubt as to whether the future will give rise to further teachers, scholars and even plain ordinary Jews. Often it seems as if the overwhelming majority of our people go about driven by the panic of being the last. It hardly needs emphasizing that this sense of fear is naturally bound to exercise a most paralyzing effect on our conscious and subconscious life, on our emotions and thoughts.

When we analyze somewhat more deeply this constant dread of the end, we discover that one of its decisive psychological elements is the general, not particularly Jewish, sense of fear of losing ground, of being deprived of possessions and acquisitions—or, still deeper, the sense of fear which came over man when he first saw the sunset in the west, not knowing that every sunset is followed by a sunrise, as the *Midrash* so beautifully described Adam's first great shock.

Is Israel alone a dying nation? Numerous civilizations have disappeared before there emerged the one in which we live so happily and unhappily at the same time. Each dying civilization was confident that earth and heaven would disappear with it. How often did man feel he was finished forever! When ancient Rome began to crumble, Romans and others felt sure that the end of the universe was at hand. St. Augustine thought that the "anti-Christ" would appear after the destruction of Rome and man would be called to his last day of judgment. In various aspects, this fear of being the last was also manifest in Christianity and Islam. In addition, the lamentation of *mi-she-met* has its psychological origin in man's great admiration for his living masters, in his fear lest the miracle will not occur again, lest there will be no second set of masters—as if genius rises only once, never again to re-appear.

Yet, making all allowances for the general motives in this dread of the end, it has nowhere been at home so incessantly, with such an acuteness and intensity, as in the House of Israel. The world may be constantly dying, but no nation was ever so incessantly dying as Israel.

Going deeper into the problem—and here I have to confine myself to a hint—I am often tempted to think that this fear of cessation in Israel was fundamentally a kind of protective individual and collective emotion. Israel has indulged so much in the fear of its end, that its constant vision of the end helped it to overcome every crisis, to emerge from every threatening end as a living unit, though much wounded and reduced. In anticipating the end, it became its master. Thus no catastrophe could ever take this end-fearing people by surprise, so as to put it off its balance, still less to obliterate it—as if Israel's incessant preparation for the end made this very end absolutely impossible.

Philosophers like Hegel and Schopenhauer have spoken of the guile of Nature, of the guile of History. Is not this peculiar sense of the end also the guile of a nation *sui generis*, a nation that would use every device for its survival, even that of incessant anticipation of its disappearance, in order to rule it out forever? This aspect of national psychology deserves special attention.

As far as historical reality is concerned, we are confronted here with a phenomenon which has almost no parallel in mankind's story: a nation that has been disappearing constantly for the last 2,000 years, exterminated in dozens of lands all over the globe, reduced to half or third of its population by tyrants ancient and modern—and yet it still exists, falls and rises, loses all its possessions and re-equips itself for a new start, a second, a third chance—always fearing the end, never afraid to make a new beginning, to snatch triumph from the jaws of defeat, whenever and wherever possible. There is no nation more dying than Israel, yet none better equipped to resist disaster, to fight alone, always alone.

As far as our foreign relations, if I may so call them, are concerned, there is much comfort in our thorny path in the world. The first ancient non-Jewish document which mentions Israel by name is, symbolically apt, a message of total annihilation. It is the monument —in possession of the British Museum—on which Mercuptoch, the 13th century B.C.E. Egyptian forerunner of Nasser, boasts of his great deeds and triumphs over nations, and, among other things, states succintly: "Israel is desolated; its seed is no more." Since 1215 B.C.E. how often did prophets at home and abroad prophesy Israel's desolation! How often did nations try to translate this prophecy into practice, and in the most cruel ways! About 3,150 years after that boastful Egyptian conqueror, there arose Satan in the heart of Europe and began to predict Israel's total annihilation—and to prepare the most modern technical devices to make his prophecy come true. And after it was given to him—to our greatest sorrow and the world's the greatest shame—to reduce Israel by one-third, Israel is still alive—weakened, to be sure, robbed of its best resources for recuperation, of its reservoir, its fountains of life and learning, yet still standing on its feet, numbering four times as many souls as in the days of the French Revolution, rebuilding its national life in the State of Israel, in the face of so many obstacles! Though not perfect, its spiritual creativity continues. Filled with fear of its end, it seeks to make a new beginning in the Diaspora and in Israel.

If so, many will say, what is all the lamenting about? Many nations have suffered, and, if we suffered a little more, we should not exaggerate or carry on hysterically. No need to worry, no need of superhuman efforts—wait and see—nothing will happen; and if it should happen—surely it has happened before. As it is said in the *Sidur*: *Maftirin k'detmol*—"we continue as of yesterday."

Such easy comfort, such exaggerated optimism is no less dangerous than the pessimism of Israel's end. Neither is justified, neither is helpful.

In the beginning, Israel's message was that of a universal optimism —salvation, happiness and perfection for all peoples. "The mountain of the Lord's house will be established in the top of the mountains" means: the peoples of the world will also share alike, with Israel, in the blessing of the Messianic age. Many well-known and understandable factors compelled post-Exilic and medieval Messianism to become more one-sided and directed exclusively toward the redemption of Israel; optimistic toward Israel, pessimistic toward the world. In more recent times, most Jewish ideologies and political movements were dualistic inasmuch as they saw a world divided, Israel and world torn apart— nay, still more: Israel itself was to them no more. Thus, to give one illustration, Jewish Reform on both sides of the Rhine, 19th-century liberalism, was optimistic as far as the world's future was concerned, pessimistic for the survival of Israel as a nation with all national attributes. This same dualistic attitude was taken up by all kinds of assimilated Jewish revolutionaries in Eastern and Western Europe. Later, two Jewish ideologies fought each other in Europe: one was most optimistic for the remnant of Israel in Zion and pessimistic as far as the Jewish people in the Diaspora was concerned, while the other reversed this dichotomy, maintaining that only Diaspora Jewry had a future in some liberal or socialistic order.

Both made the fundamental mistake of dividing Israel into two parts. Israel must always be considered one and indivisible—*yisrael echad*. As long as one part of Israel lives in a hell, the other cannot live in Paradise.

I therefore say: we may not split up Israel into two spheres of reality. Israel is one. Neither may we approach the Jewish problem from an optimistic or pessimistic angle. Optimism and pessimism are only expressions or indications of our fears, doubts, hopes and desires. Hopes and desires we must have; fears and doubts we cannot escape. Yet, what we need most at present is a dynamic Jewish realism which will see our reality, the reality of the world, our problem, the problem of the world, in their entirety, without any dualism—hell-paradise or whatever.

Such a Jewish realism will also show us the real meaning of that fear of the end which is so inherent in us. A nation dying for thousands of years means a living nation. Our incessant dying means uninterrupted living, rising, standing up, beginning anew. We, the last Jews! Yes, in many respects it seems to us as if we are the last links in a particular chain of tradition and development. But if we are the last—let us be the last as our fathers and forefathers were. Let us prepare the ground for the last Jews who will come after us, and for the last Jews who will rise after them, and so on until the end of days.

If it has been decreed for Israel that it go on being a dying nation —let it be a nation that is constantly dying, which is to say: incessantly living and creating—one nation from Dan to Beersheba, from the sunny heights of Judea to the shadowy valleys of Europe and America.

To prepare the ground for this great oneness, for a Jewish realism built on it, is a task which requires the effort of Jewish scholarship and statesmanship alike. One nation, one in beginning and end, one in survival and extinction! May it be survival rather than extinction, a beginning rather than an ignominious end—one Israel, *yisrael echad*.

Can There be a Revival of Zionist Ideology?

NATHAN ROTENSTREICH

The point of departure of the following analysis is that there is no Zionist ideology today. In seeking to explain this condition, we cannot make use of the well-known claim that we live in a post-ideological era. Our task is to ask about more specific questions related to the Jewish situation as we experience it. This situation is characterized by two elements: the existence of the State of Israel and the shift of world Jewry to the American continent. These two elements must be seen not as dependent upon each other, but as coexistent.

The existence of the State of Israel can explain the disappearance of the Zionist ideology insofar as any realization of a broad social-political goal may make the guiding ideology obsolete. Obviously the emergence of the State of Israel has been grounded in the Zionist ideology. Hence, the question of the connection between the ideology and its realization, is bound to be a central issue in present day Jewish awareness. Zionist ideology has a special character which makes it different from the ideologies of other national movements. Zionist ideology aiming to establish an independent Jewish entity has not been part of an existing society. It has belonged to the Jewish people living in the diaspora, outside the boundaries of the projected political entity. Hence, it is a national movement of return, not one aiming to establish a correlation between a given infrastructure and a political structure. Zionisn has not been based on the desire to achieve continuity between the social existence of a people and its manifestation in statehood. It has been based on an attempt to create both the social groundwork and its political expression.

The aspirations for independence have been related to a central issue in the classical Zionist ideology, namely the analysis of the situation of the Jewish people in the diaspora particularly since the 19th-century. To identify the essence of that classical ideology, it is appropriate to follow some of the distinctions made in the formulation of that ideology. We observe the distinction between what has been called the question of the Jews and the question of Judaism. We adhere to these distinctions

NATHAN ROTENSTREICH is professor of philosophy at Hebrew University in Jerusalem and the author of Essays on Zionism and The Contemporary Jewish Condition (Herzl Press, 1980).

not because of nostalgia but because they contain some relevant points which may direct us in dealing with the situation of the Jews today.

Concern with the condition of the Jews began because Jews lived among and depended on the peoples of the world. This dependence found its concrete expression in persecution, rejection, and, generally speaking, the failure of even the modern, legally constituted state, to absorb the Jews without distinguishing between them and their environment. It is appropriate to mention that Herzl, who so sharply analyzed the facts of the Jewish situation, clung to Lessing's idea of the education of mankind, that is to say, he adhered to the historical aim or hope of the progress of the human race while trying to show that reality as it is fell far to short of that goal.

Empirical, that is to say historical, reality leads to disappointment in emancipation, or to the loss of hope that emancipation will achieve its goal in the foreseeable future. Hence against the background of persecutions, and the tensions that go with them, the solution has been proposed, that Jews withdraw from day-to-day social and political relations and move toward independence. Jews in that framework of independence will be released from the continuous tension between them and their environment. Thus, independence and its political expression is a solution based on the withdrawal of the Jews from the network of relations with their environment. Independence is by definition the opposite of encroachment on the life of the Jews.

Against this view, Ahad Ha'am formulated a position which he himself called an analysis of the problem of Judaism and which we can perhaps now call the problem of Jewishness. Ahad Ha'am distinguished between the question of the Jews and the question of Judaism. He argued, among other things, that the question of the Jews cannot be solved, because they are bound always to live among the gentiles of the world and suffer the difficulties of that existence. Hence he emphasized the question of Judaism that was tantamount to the contraction of the national ego, i.e. the collective Jewish existence which, among other things, is also a cultural entity, is the creativity of the Jewish people in pursuing its own tradition, beliefs, orientations.

In the modern era that creativity is exposed to a persistent limitation, since the Jews cannot maintain what we would now call their cultural identity. This is so because they are so influenced by the surrounding world that their own creativity is progressively diminished. Ahad Ha'am did not deny the persecution of the Jews, but he pointed out that within the situation of life in exile there is an ongoing absorption of the influences from the non-Jewish world. The first component of the situation cannot be negated, but an attempt should be made to confront the second component aiming at strengthening the creativity of the Jewish people that is so crucial for resisting external forces.

Ahad Ha'am pointed out that not only was Jewish creativity diminishing, but also the impact of the Jewish tradition on the Jews was becoming more and more limited. Hence, Ahad Ha'am represents the trend to withdraw from the circle of the influencing environment, not in order to gain release from the pressure, but in order to reinforce the standing of the Jewish people on its own and within its own boundaries.

Retrospectively, we can say that the two trends briefly described, despite the clash between them, prompted the conception of the independence of the Jewish people, regardless of the interpretation of independence. The central issue in this context is that the different formulations emerged within the settings of Central and Eastern European Jewry. These formulations were attempts to analyze the situation of the Jews in Europe before World War I and of course, World War II. With the establishment of the State of Israel there emerged a new context for the question of the Jews as well as the question of Judaism. The center of gravity of the Jewish people shifted from Europe to the United States.

The catastrophe that befell European Jewry was not the cause of the shift but historically the two events have to be seen in one context. The question facing Zionist ideology today is: Are the two orientations of the classical ideology valid for the Jews in the United States? As a matter of fact, Zionism as an ideology and as a movement directed by that ideology is dependent on this issue. To put it negatively: Is there room for a new approach to Jewish reality which is not a repetition of the classical views? We refer mainly to the Jews in North America, though obviously we cannot be oblivious to the obvious differences between their position and that of the Jews in South America, or the Soviet Union.

The characteristic nature of the present day Jewish reality, is mainly that the tension caused by persecution which was a constant feature of the situation of Jews in Europe and which found its expression in Zionist analysis, no longer exists. Jews attained human rights expressed not only in political and legal equality, but also in equality in social mobility. Jews became emancipated but not through their own struggle for their position within society and the state. Emancipation was granted them as a consequence of the processes of the society, the legal system, and the structure of the state. The Jews *got* emancipation; they did not *achieve* it.

Hence, within the self-consciousness of the Jews, we find not even a vestige of their struggle for themselves. This enhances the absence of tension between the Jews and their environment. Hence, the characteristic features of the classical Jewish question do not exist anymore. In any case, we cannot point to the Jewish predicament as it has been conceived in its classical analysis. The Jewish question, in the classical sense of that term, found its solution without taking steps to withdraw from the environment; on the contrary, it was solved by striking roots in the environment.

As a matter of fact, there is no longer any difference between the Jews and their environment. In the major day-to-day activities of the Jews, we cannot point to any barrier between them and their environment. This is so even though here and there, people refer to a latent anti-Semitism in the United States. The reference is to *latent* anti-Semitism. If such anti-Semitism exists, it is not a feature of the regime. In this sense, the phenomenon of assimilation has changed; Jews do not assimilate *to* the environment because they are part of it. In any case, an attempt to revitalize Zionist ideology cannot be based on "the Jewish question" because there is no such question.

How do things stand from the perspective of the question of Judaism? Here too, for different reasons, we have to conclude that that question does not exist either. This is so, since as we have seen, that question has been put forward against the background of the creativity of the Jewish people as a collective entity. In addition, for this question to be central we must assume that the Jewish people wants to maintain its cultural creativity within its own boundaries, that is to say, that it does not consciously and deliberately identify itself with the environment, that it does not want to absorb the environment, even when exposed to its impact.

But when the Jews are an essential part of the environment, they do not look for the breadth and the depth of the Jewish creativity, even when this or that Jewish author can be interpreted as being prompted by Jewish motives. The first, social, aspect of involvement in the environment leads to the second aspect, namely the assimilation of intellectual trends. This is so to a large extent because of the major change in the broad reality of the contemporary world. The encounter is no longer historical or religious traditions, as was the case in Europe, with the tension being largely a religious one. The contemporary encounter is with a universal culture or with a universal civilization which is scientific and technological. As such it puts aside historical and religious conceptions. As long as religious conceptions were present, universal civilization could not be the dominant factor. In the change that occurred the religious component becomes less than secondary and the scientific and technological climate of opinion becomes central.

Previously, Jews and Judaism faced traditional societies and cultures grounded in religion as a sum total of articles of faith and modes of behavior. Hence Jews were continuously aware of their unwavering adherence to their own tradition even without being reminded. The situation in the contemporary period is essentially different, since the surrounding culture and the society it guides, being scientific and technological, is no longer shaped by traditional components. For that society tradition is at most a reservoir of vestiges of the past. This applies both to the society and to Jewish existence. Though Jews may want to maintain their loyalty to refer to their history they are bound to place it at the margin of their existence, since they adhere to the society at large and are not at all willing to forego that adherence. Hence they demonstrate their Jewish loyalty not in faith and ways of life but in sentiments and organizations which are mainly of a ceremonial character.

This is a new situation which classical Zionism could not forsee. Hence, the concern with the situation of the Jewish people in our generation, even against the background of the existence of the State of Israel, is bound to refer to a different, essentially new reality. Therefore, we must ask: Is there still a Jewish question, or is it a question of Judaism, or is there a new combination of the two classical approaches to the situation of the Jewish people?

We can say that the major characteristic feature of the Jewish situation in the open contemporary society is that there is no public Jewish realm or Jewish comonwealth. The interaction between Jews is mundane and is based not on common ground, but again on some vestiges of the past which are marginal to the involvement in the surrounding society. To be sure, European Jewry did not and could not maintain a public Jewish realm, because of its situation in exile (*golah*). Still, there existed a community or communality based on common modes of daily behavior and this comprehensive Jewish way of life brought Jews to one another. In a situation where there is no infrastructure of such a communality, those components of reality which are not part of the surrounding society become scattered vestiges of an adherence to that which existed before. Then communality is not a comprehensive background for Jewish existence, but is relegated to the margins of the society at large.

If there could be, and should be, an attempt to anchor a new conception of Zionism in the reality as it is, it is essential to emphasize that component of a common Jewish reality. The conclusion is bound to be that such a common framework of reality is impossible in the situation of an open society. That which was characteristic of the classical aspiration to achieve Jewish independence — the search for a resolution of the problem of persecutions — must become the search for a new mode of Jewish existence. Independence becomes coterminous with a Jewish common reality.

This is the issue before us and it has to be said that Zionism, after the emergence of the State of Israel, did not address itself to this issue. On the contrary, we witness the disappearance of an ideological approach to the Jewish situation. An ideological approach founded in self-examination has been replaced by a continuous attempt to safeguard support for the State of Israel. That support is appealing mainly to the Jewish feeling of solidarity and that solidarity leads to continuous attempts to find a focus for Jewish comprehensive existence. Since that focus cannot be present in the day-to-day existence of the Jews in the diaspora, it is shifted outside it, beyond it, that is to say, to the State of Israel, as exemplifying the unity of the Jewish people.

At this juncture, we ask a theoretical question which is not confined to the Jewish situation: What is the significance of a public realm in human existence? The public realm is not only the meeting individuals or groups. That realm not only enables the meeting between people, it also shapes a certain mode of existence which by definition is beyond the activity of any individual person, however creative he may be. One of the basic manifestations of the public realm is the common language that serves as a background against which individual activity takes shape. The public realm is not only a ground for encounters, but also for communalities which become manifest in institutions and in the law.

Sometimes that common sphere is not defined, but in any case there is a continuous interaction between the individual existence and that which is beyond the individuals. In this sense, the public realm is one expression of the trans-personal component of human reality. The normative aspect of the public realm is but the other side of that trans-personal component. The trans-personal component is manifest even in the compulsion inherent in the public realm. Compulsion is a kind of equivalent or surrogate ensuring that individuals will go beyond themselves even when their intentions do not lead them in that direction.

In any case, the significance of the public realm as the communality of the Jews is a major issue for Jewish life today. That issue should be the point of departure for a new Zionist conception — a conception which does not yet exist. We must observe that not only does such a conception not exist but also that many of the analyses by Jews in the United States are rather self-satisfied and do not address the problem. The undeniable achievements of American Jewry do not indicate that the present situation contains the possibilities of common Jewish existence. The analysis must look to the future and not merely compare what the Jews have achieved today with what they had in previous generations. To apply the analytic approach, one has to adhere to certain presuppositions about the normative character of Jewish existence and recognize its inherent contradictions, as does classic Zionist literature.

One major sphere which exhibits the Jewish situation is Jewish education. It is well-known that Jewish education does not meet the needs and the problems. This is so because there is a built-in split in Jewish education. The majority of Jewish children are educated in non-Jewish schools. The preparation of the Jewish young person for self-sufficient existence in the future occurs outside the Jewish realm. The Jewish education does not meet the task of forming characters, of shaping personalities and beliefs. In addition, there is no educational personnel to meet the demands of the system.

This, in itself, underscores one of the basic differences between the Jewish educational system in Europe, for instance, in Poland, and that in the United States. In Poland, quite a number of the Jews who graduated from universities found no employment either in the universities or even in the secondary schools. They went to the Jewish schools and provided highly qualified personnel. But when all the gates are open, there is nothing prompting Jews to choose Jewish education over other opportunities. Where there is no commonwealth, there are no manifestations of a commonwealth.

The contemporary situation of the Jews or the Jewish situation is that the diaspora cannot contain a Jewish public realm and therefore cannot prompt an interaction between individuals and the Jewish community. The situation of the Jews in the open society displays the essence of the diaspora even while such historical features of the diaspora as discrimination have been overcome. Within that context there exists, or rather, may exist, a problem of the Jews or a problem of Judaism only for those Jews who believe there is a problem inherent in the existence in two spheres: the comprehensive sphere of the society at large and the limited sphere of the Jewish realm. The response to pressure cannot be what prompts Jewish activity but rather the acceptance of the norm of interaction between individuals and society. Choice becomes the major factor of a possible change in the Jewish situation and a choice is bound to be influenced by conceptual awareness and analysis. In order to reach that synthesis of will and concept one needs an initial decision linked to a conceptual awareness. Thus we have here a circular situation.

The existence of the State of Israel is by definition a structure of the activities of individuals taking place within the frameworks of a collective existence. Even — and this is an illustration of that structure — economic activity occurs within a common framework and even though the topic of the relation there is no possibility of a distinction between that which is human and that which is Jewish. The Jewish tradition and the Jewish religion is a constant issue in the Israeli society. In spite of the common structure, Israeli society faces the problem of willing involvement in the public sphere, taking for granted the existence of that sphere and its necessary features. Will the individuals in Israel rely only on the compulsion inherent in the framework or will they be directed by their choice to enrich the public sphere by their willful actions? Will Israeli society be just a consumer society?

The difficulty in sustaining an affirmative attitude to the public sphere is not solely a function of the words of individuals. It is also a function of the structure of the sphere as incorporating ultra-Orthodox components. The ultra-Orthodox Jews live within the State and are necessarily involved in the activities of it and society. They live in it *de facto* but do not recognize the State *de jure*. Indeed, this is not merely an ideological reservation since it has concrete implications for institutions. The most prominent example is the status of the Rabbinical Courts. They or their supporters pretend to give the Rabbinical Courts a status parallel or even superior to that of the courts of the State, in spite of the obvious fact that the status of the Rabbinical Courts in the areas of marital jurisdiction is under the authority of the Knesset. The ultra-Orthodox describe the courts, including the Supreme Court, as secular; this is obviously false. The courts have comprehensive authority since they are one of the embodiments of the common sphere of the State.

The strange position of this sector of the population is exemplified in the political life of the State. In spite of their refusal to recognize it *de jure* they participate in the government. The society did not develop a distinction between the right to vote for the Knesset, which is a right of citizens, and the right to shape the character of the State inherent in the activities of the government. This latter right must be limited only to those who affirm the status of the State.

The diaspora faces the problem of the choice to begin. Israel faces the problem of voluntary affirmation of a given reality and hence of the consequences grounded in having made the choice. It is possible that the voluntary decisions of Israeli society may have an impact on the decisions of Jews in the diaspora. But a possible influx of Jews from affluent countries to Israel may influence behavior of the Jews in Israel since the *olim* will show a preference for interaction between individuals and society rather than the cult of consumption. In any case, initially the shift to the new orientation will consist of a sum total of actions of individuals who could be described in today's vernacular as *engages*. Even those exposed to the pressure of the surrounding world were, in their decision, a minority. Masses did not follow the line. It is plausible to assume that that type of response is even more valid today. ∎

midstream
A MONTHLY JEWISH REVIEW

Israel and American Youth

By RONALD SANDERS

DURING THE MIDDLE EAST crisis of June, 1967, there was a sudden widespread outburst of enthusiasm in favor of embattled Israel on the part of young American Jews—and even some non-Jews as well—that took many observers by surprise. Here were young people, mainly of college age, hitherto indifferent to Israel or to the Zionist cause, who now were rushing to volunteer for the fight or to work in kibbutzim as replacements for Israelis who had gone to the front. When the crisis ended, so naturally did the fulness of that enthusiasm; but many friends of Israel and Zionism did not consider the matter to have ended there. Surely, they felt, those flames of enthusiasm could be fanned again, surely their sources could be tapped. A generation of young American Jews whose principal attitude towards Israel seemed to have been unconcern had now shown in the excitement of an instant that this was not so. Could the feelings they had shown in that instant not be awakened on a more permanent basis? Could a new generation of Zionists be molded out of them, perhaps even a new *aliyah*?

Such reactions were natural in those who had given their hearts to Israel's cause after witnessing in their own lifetimes the immense sufferings and struggles that had led to the founding of the Jewish state twenty years ago. To those who remember that era it is still difficult to believe that a generation of American Jews has now reached the brink of maturity with no recollection of it. Only that short time ago, the Jewish people and its agonies were the embodiment of the struggle against injustice in the world; to young Jews today in schools and colleges, raised in the midst of a Jewish life that has become in many ways an outward symbol of comfort for them, and engaged in the passions of Vietnam and the cause of Negro rights, their Jewishness seems irrelevant to the whole problem of justice in the world; those previous sufferings are ancient history.

I can recall my own feelings and those of my contemporaries when Israel became an independent state twenty years ago. I was then a student in a Brooklyn high school whose enrollment was overwhelmingly Jewish. There was of course great jubilation among us at the event, and like young people at any time caught up with such a passion, we looked with envy upon those we knew a few years older than ourselves who were over there taking part in the fight. We had all

3

been only children during the Second World War—and only American children at that—but none of us had been so small or so remote from the conflict as not to realize quite viscerally what Israel meant in terms of recent history, what an act of historic justice Jewish statehood represented in the wake of the immense disaster that had struck the Jewish people only a few years before. Beside an event of this magnitude we and our feelings were very small indeed and of little use to Israel; but we knew at least that we had been enlarged as well as humbled by it, and many of us who have been eager to affirm our Jewish identity vigorously ever since can trace our affirmation to this event. In this small way, at least, we belonged to history, and to the suffering.

In terms of American Jewish life, it is important to realize how decisive these events were in shaping the Jewish commitment of at least part of a generation; for many of us were quite marginally Jewish in our upbringing, and might otherwise have abandoned the Jewish fold altogether. Speaking for a large if rather special group, I can say that our historical passions, but for the Holocaust and the struggle for Jewish statehood, would not have been overtly Jewish at all. Even our sense of those events was based upon a conception of things we had inherited from the anti-Fascist cause of the thirties and early forties. We thought we found our spiritual identities somewhere along the spectrum of the political Left as it was then constituted in America. Ranging all the way from New Deal Liberalism to hard-nosed Stalinism in our attitudes, we were emotionally united, whatever the differences between us, in the common cause against Fascist evil in the world, and we passionately endorsed all acts righting the injustices it had wrought. It was primarily in this spirit that we welcomed the creation of Israel; but if we also felt within ourselves a special rejoicing at this because we were Jews, we did not have to consider this additional factor to be merely incidental. Rather it seemed to us at that moment that being Jewish was somehow a felicitous and organic fulfillment of our ideals, that we had been gifted with an identity which made us outwardly as well as inwardly living representatives of the cause against injustice in the world as we understood it in 1948.

I THINK THIS HISTORY is relevant to the problems of a large portion of American Jews of school and college age today, because it is a history of marginal Jewish identity resolved through an actual and vivid sense of Jewish suffering and struggle in the world around us. Today, the marginal group is surely much larger than it was then, and its marginality is more problematic, for the generations of Jews in America have moved still further away from the atmosphere of natural Jewishness provided by their immigrant forbears, and the ways of life in this country have stripped away many parts of the social and cultural wall that had, for better or for worse, shored up Judaism in Europe. In the open society, Judaism must argue its values to its young more than had been necessary for many centuries, and this at a moment when many of those values are themselves in transition. Indeed, it is a poor presentation of the argument and a frequent inability to pinpoint Jewish values on the part of many of the older-generation spokesmen that is leading many of the young to wonder why they should be Jewish at all.

This kind of questioning on the part of the young, it should be pointed out, is increasingly a symptom, not of the kind of craven assimilationism that was often its source in previous generations, but of a high degree of moral vigor. Today unfortunately, more and more of the young people who make their choice to stay within the framework of a more or less concretely defined Jewish communal life, do so on the basis of some ill-defined ethnic inertia rather than on the strength of clear convictions; while many of the morally vigorous look upon precisely this sort of blandness as reason to wonder why they should be Jewish at all. For Jewish history has come to an ironic turn in America today. This country, which was the great refuge of the Jewish people after more than a millennium of suffering on European soil, is now the scene of the most widespread comfort and prosperity that Jews have ever known. Today the suffering are around us but rarely include us, and in some cases—such as those of Jewish slum landlords—we are even among the oppressors. The former victims of pogroms, we now sit in the comfort of our living rooms watching images of Vietnam on the television screen. How different the relationship between Jewishness and suffering seems in 1968 from that of 1948! Here is the haunting irony: where were those television screens in the days of Auschwitz and Treblinka?

It is perhaps a sad reflection on our times that television has more power than history books, but the fact remains that a whole generation has now come to maturity in America for whom Jewish suffering is only an abstraction, while the sufferings of non-Jews in the ghettoes and in Vietnam are the reality. Many spokesmen criticize these young people for their lack of historical perspective, but whose fault is this? In what spirit can a young person absorb Jewish values that are filtered to him through a comfortable and often smug atmosphere of suburban teas, socials, entertainments and fund-raising programs? What if, in the midst of this, he should even take seriously what he is taught from the Hebrew prophets? The plush atmosphere of suburban synagogues has done so much to alienate those young people who are morally serious, that there are those who even are inclined to react to pleas to the congregation about the plight of Soviet Jewry as a "cold war" ploy.

This, then, is the atmosphere within which Israel's case is presented to them —for Zionism, like almost anything else in the Jewish heritage, today reaches most American Jews through the medium of the synagogue or community center. This situation presents problems, which are not taken seriously enough by many of those who come to the United States from Israel to speak their country's cause to American Jews. For an Israeli, the persecutions that gave rise to the Zionist idea and continue to justify it, the hard work that created his country and still dominates its life, the constant state of danger in which he and his countrymen are living, are the imperatives governing his history and determining his sense of himself. But for many American Jews these elements, no longer imperatives at all by the time a sense of them has filtered to this side of the ocean, are simply part of a proprietary image. Israeli valor and struggle are here often transformed into the mere vicarious projections of middle-class self-satisfaction, entitlement to which is bought by an annual contribution to the Jewish National Fund and a trip to Israel itself once every three years or so. It is natural for emissaries from Israel to be delighted by the warm reception they receive here from people whose attitude is of this nature. But the price they pay for that warmth is a renunciation of precisely the climate of feeling that can produce what they have come here for, since comfortable middle-class self-satisfaction does not give rise to *aliyah* from its midst, while those young spirits who might be prone to the kind of dedication and self-sacrifice that *aliyah* requires are alienated from the discussion at the very outset. The impassioned young Jews of the American campuses today are more likely to be carrying pickets against the war in Vietnam than attending Zionist meetings.

INDEED, the discussion of Israel's cause in America today, by both Israeli visitors and American Zionists, suffers greatly from not taking sufficiently into consideration the preoccupations of morally concerned American youth. The language used by these spokesmen is often still the language of another era, when Jewish suffering was a reality to Jews everywhere, and Jewish group self-interest was a cause sufficient unto itself to those deeply concerned with social justice. But it will hardly do to tell idealistic young Americans today that they should go to Israel in order to fulfill themselves as Jews or—most ineffectual of all as a plea in America at this time—to avoid the effects of anti-Semitism. What can this mean to a boy or a girl who scarcely knows anti-Semitism at all, but who feels deeply the scars of the Detroit ghetto or of Vietnam?

Both these latter problems have, in fact, given rise to subtle difficulties in the presentation of the image of Israel here. Events since the beginning of last June have done much to reinforce a tendency on the part of many peoples in the world to identify Israel with America. This tendency is especially strong in countries where both Israel and America are hated, where the little nation is viewed as a dire surrogate of the enormous one. One manifestation of this outlook is the way in which Arab propagandists will attempt to liken the treatment of the Oriental Jewish and Arab minorities in Israel to the treatment of Negroes in the United States. Another manifestation is a slander that is especially pernicious because there are some elements in American public life who take comfort in its existence and even seem to want to encourage it—this is the equation some make between Israel and South Vietnam. Indeed, there are even some prominent American-Jewish spokesmen who take this equation seriously, and think it to be in the best interest of Jews here to support the government's present policy in Vietnam. Fortunately for the moral health of the American Jewish community, such spokesmen are relatively few.

But these problems are nevertheless clouding somewhat the atmosphere of the discussion of Israel among American youth. If the most powerful progressive ideology in the world when I was in school revolved around the whole "popular-front" syndrome, today it is based on the conception of an emergent "Third-world". The present "Third-world" ideology is bound to have a powerful grip on the minds of idealistic American youth, because it binds together into a single world-view both the struggles of American Negroes and of Vietnamese. With these two peoples as its principle poles of concern, this ideology naturally makes the American white establishment the main focus of its hostility at the present time. This situation has therefore created moral problems for American Jews to the extent that they have become, after two thousand years of suffering persecutions, identified with that American white establishment, at the same time that they continue, by and large, to be sympathetic with progressive currents in the world. These problems, in particular, revolve around Israel; for Israel, at the moment, seems to have found some hard-earned favor in the eyes of the American establishment. Premier Eshkol's recent talks with President Johnson in Texas have even raised the question whether Israeli support for our government's Vietnam policy is to be part of the price of that favor. It certainly would be out of place here to hold Israel's problems of *Realpolitik* up to question; my point is simply that the atmosphere surrounding that *Realpolitik* will not always be reconcilable with the appeal to high idealism that the proponents of *aliyah* would wish to make in America.

THERE HAS THUS ARISEN, in the eyes of many young Americans, an unfortunate polarity between the pull of Israel and the claims that the "Third-world" ideology makes upon them. Like any world-encompassing ideology, vast and polymorphous, this one has its myths as well as its bases in fact; and many anti-Israel myths have made their way into it. I have already alluded to myths concerning Israeli "racism" and purported resemblances to South Vietnam; there is also, in general, the whole myth of Israeli "colonialism," of which these other two are by-products. What is especially remarkable about these accusations is that a genuine knowledge of the facts about Israel prove their exact opposite. Israel a "racist" society? It is rather, to anyone who knows it well, the most advanced experiment one can find in the juxtaposition and integration of European and non-European peoples. Israel like South Vietnam? Israel, the most vigorous parliamentary democracy on the Asian continent, capable of total mobilization to defend itself *without the help of foreign troops* even when hopelessly outnumbered? Or is it among some of Israel's neighbors that one finds dictatorships and top-heavy military establishments that vanish from the battle the moment the going gets rough? And as for the "colonialism" charge, can this really be leveled so easily against a people—settlers from Europe to be sure—but who did their own manual labor from the outset, and, far from claiming imperialist Britain as their mother country, were the first to throw off its overlordship in the Middle East? Obviously, it would be totally disingenuous to claim that the Jews of Israel (except for a tiny percentage of them) were an indigenous population in the same sense that the Arabs were; but it is equally false to claim, as some have, that they were *colons* in the same sense as the Frenchmen of Algeria. Here, quite simply, the truth is more complex than any myth.

But why is it then, that the myths are scarcely dealt with or challenged at all by spokesmen for Israel in the United States? Why is a genuine handling of these problems of Israel's "image"—especially of its image in the eyes of the idealistic young—dispensed with in favor of a familiar and superannuated Zionist litany? This is an especially distressing situation because, while tired slogans from the past are of no interest whatsoever to an energetic younger genertaion, the kind of discussion that would really excite these young people is also the one that would especially be true to the realities of Israel today. For example, if Israel is no longer primarily a nation of sturdy agrarian pioneers bent on a mission of "self-realization" and self-help, neither are idealistic young Americans any longer attracted to such a conception. They are more interested in finding ways of helping others than in helping their comfortable selves, and, as adherents to the "Third-world" ideology, they would above all be interested in ways of expiating their white American middle-class sense of guilt by helping non-European, non-white people to improve the conditions of their lives. Now, what aspiration could be more in keeping with the needs of Israel today, with its large Oriental Jewish and Arab populations? Why don't the *shlihim* from Israel talk more about this aspect of their country's problems? Why don't they talk about Israel and the "Third-world"—about, for example, what it has done in Africa and what it could do in the Middle East? Far from being the thorn in the side of "Third-world" aspirations that some myth-makers try to depict it as being, Israel represents one of the great possibilities in the world today for an experiment in cultural bridge-building between the West and the Middle East. Why are these possibilities—and the difficulties standing in the way of their realization—so rarely discussed at Zionist student gatherings in America?

IT would seem that one of the reasons for avoiding these crucial questions is a desire not to take up matters that might sully the image of Israel that has been bequeathed to American suburban Jewish communities by such phenomena as *Exodus*, in both its book and film versions. To talk honestly about relations between European and non-European Jews in Israel, for example, would be to discuss a record that is far from perfect and includes many painful aspects. But is it the task of propagandists to focus a light upon the unflattering parts of their case? The answer is: yes, they must do so, unless they really wish to attract to their cause only those people who make a habit of avoiding confrontations with difficult problems. Israel is a country that was created by young people who were not satisfied with the cliches about Jewish destiny that had governed the lives of their fathers, and who were willing to face great difficulties in order to find a new conception of Jewish life for themselves. In America today, Jewish communal life stands in danger of becoming governed by cliches again, only this time the situation is such that a rebellious younger generation threatens to leave Jewish life altogether, and not merely reformulate it. Israel, to the extent that the representation of it in America functions through the institutions of the organized Jewish community, has become entangled in many of these cliches.

Indeed, there is no question but that the whole problem of continuing Jewish identity in America is bound up with whatever the American-Jewish sense of Israel is to be. But in order for a sense of Israel to be worked out among a new generation in America, new questions must be answered, new preoccupations must be dealt with. The slogans of yesteryear have not only become dull cliches to many of the imaginative young; they seem to be a cover for any of the real problems that might otherwise be faced. The discussion of Israel must catch up not only with the vast changes that have taken place in the world in twenty years; it must catch up with the rapid changes of the past year as well. For the young people who rushed to volunteer for Israel as an underdog last June now see her resplendent in victory. That brief awakening of a youthful spirit of self-sacrifice for Israel in danger was not the same passion that produces lifelong commitments through quieter and more complex times. In times of danger, Israel can still count on widespread outbursts of support among American youth, on the spontaneous feelings that can still arise out of a general sense of her history; but to win their hearts in normal times, she must deal, in all its complexity, with the question: where is she going now?

Israel, Galut and Zionism: The Changed Scene

EFRAIM SHMUELI

AN EXTRAORDINARY EVENT OF SUCH DIMENSIONS as the Yom Kippur War, with the crisis which followed in its wake, calls for a critical reorientation of the whole philosophy of Zionism. Basic assumptions must be reconsidered calmly but definitely, beyond the euphoric state of mind produced by the Six-Day War and the melancholy of the recent experience. What follows is an attempt to re-evaluate the Jewish reality as it presents itself in the changed scene.

I. *Galut, Diaspora, and the Zionist Ideology*

For a period of more than a hundred years, before the establishment of Israel, Jews lived in a dual dimension: as continuing their participation in the collective self-realization of the Jewish entity (however it was defined), on the one hand, and as looking for individual self-realization (essentially, but not necessarily, outside the collective Jewish entity), on the other hand. The first, the traditional dimension, may be termed the Galut (Exile) dimension. The second, the secular—Diaspora (Dispersion), dimension.

The difference between Galut and Diaspora is the following: Galut is charged with a high voltage of religious and historical evaluation. It means a sojourn in a strange land, a sojourn which, someday, in the Messianic era, will come to an end. Between the fall—the destruction of the Commonwealth—and the eschatological rise, the Jew is a foreigner dwelling in the lands of the Gentiles, and he organizes his economic, socio-political and spiritual life accordingly. He builds his own institutions and strives, as far as possible, to be autonomous, if not sovereign, in legal and administrative matters, in language, and in all religious and cultural affairs relevant to his life and education. This is the positive aspect of the Galut dimension—the continuity of traditional collective endeavors of self-realization. Many historians, sociologists, poets and novelists have described the patterns of this autonomous collective self-realization. Some found in the "ghetto," or the *shtetl*, the highest moral and religious qualities.

That the Jew encounters rejection is understood and expected in these abnormal conditions, and is accepted by him as a destiny ordained by Providence. In Galut he lives with the expectation that his plans

EFRAIM SHMUELI *is currently professor of philosophy at the Cleveland State University.*

for collective self-realization will be continuously frustrated by the hostile forces of his host nations. This is the negative aspect of the Galut dimension, whose most horrifying manifestation was the Holocaust. Although hope is never abandoned that redemption will follow the tribulations, Galut ultimately means the possibility of a Holocaust. True, just as some nights are illuminated by the moon, Galut is not always sheer darkness (as Chaim Greenberg argued so eloquently). However, basically, the inherent quality of the Galut experience is habitual anxiety, a non-specified expectancy of grave events. Although the gloomiest prophets had hardly imagined the scope of the Nazi Holocaust, credit must be given to the Zionist theory for having foreseen it. Zionism's robust realism has stood out in times when the prevailing theory was evolutionary, liberal, progressivistic, and essentially, by its very character, did not take into account the possibility of catastrophic disruptions.

Reasons for both mild and catastrophic outbursts of anti-Semitism are manifold, and Zionist leaders were not the first who analyzed the causes of anti-Semitism, but they made this analysis the pivotal point of a broad politico-historical outlook. They realized that the positive aspect of the Galut dimension of Jewish life, namely the possibility for collective self-realization, could be almost annihilated in a modern, secular civilization, particularly in those countries where Jews enjoyed civil and political emancipation. They warned that an explosion might come, although nobody could foresee its ferocity. We shall return to this most ominous manifestation of Galut, but, first, let us see what Diaspora means.

The Diaspora dimension of Jewish life is devoid of the emotionally intense charge of a host of religious-historical meanings; it denotes, prosaically, the notion of a geographical dispersion, like the migration of any other nationals, witness the British or the Italians, without a specific providential destiny or mission. It is ideologically and emotionally indifferent, if not opposed, to the collective self-realization of the Galut dimension. The Diaspora dimension is mainly one of individual self-realization. In it the individual Jew attempts to adjust his ideas and behavior to the non-Jewish environment in a variety of degrees of "assimilation."

The positive aspect of this Diaspora dimension is manifested in the astonishing achievements of Jewish talent in all fields of human endeavors. In a relatively very short time emancipated Jews have not only absorbed, with great enthusiasm, the accumulation of ideas and techniques of Western civilization, they have also become pioneers of thought and skills in the techno-scientific mastery of nature. As individuals they have succeeded in gaining comforts which were inaccessible to their forefathers.

The negative aspect of the Diaspora dimension has been the loss of involvement on the part of the creative individual in the collective enterprise of the Jewish people. The Jewish community has not shared the gains of the successful individuals, yet has always been blamed for the errors or mideeds of those who failed the larger society, or who appeared to fail. In personal life, the negative aspect of the Diaspora dimension has been most visible in the emotional and intellectual tensions of the so-called "marginal" Jew.

Beyond any relationship to both the Galut and the Diaspora dimensions stands the totally assimilated Jew. Zionism believes that assimilation is an actual solution for individual Jews, but it can never solve the "Jewish problem" on a mass scale. Kissingers are admired, suspected, feared or lamented, but they can never become an example for the solution of the problem presented by the Galut dimension, and not merely for the very fact that such outstanding personalities are so very few.

More basically, Zionists, even today, after the emergence of a relatively prosperous and influential American Jewry, which exemplifies perhaps the highest possible achievements in the Diaspora, are not convinced that the negative aspect of the Galut dimension has, indeed, been eliminated from Diaspora life. Against the liberal and progressivistic modes of thought which are deeply ingrained in the minds of Western Jews, Zionism voices a conservative warning. It deplores the loss of adhesiveness offered by the collective self-realization, that is, the loss of the only positive aspect of the Galut dimension, and cautions that its negative aspects might still be present.

II. *Zionism and the Freedom of Self-Determination*

Zionist ideology, in its Western form, was born out of the dilemma of the Diaspora dimension. The Diaspora Jew, that secular or semi-secular individualist looking for the enjoyment of his newly-acquired rights and benefitting from a more-or-less liberal legislation and tolerance of opinions, felt deeply wounded by the outbursts of anti-Semitism in the last quarter of the 19th century. He could not lightly dismiss the new and old forms of hostility as residuals of the Dark Ages, destined soon to pass. Anti-Semitism was too potent a force in contemporary life, and was particularly painful to emancipated Jews. Pinsker, Herzl and Nordau saw anti-Semitism as a post-emancipation and post-Enlightenment conflict destroying the basis of the Diaspora dimension in its positive aspect, and not permitting the adjustment of Jews to their changed environment. These leaders maintained that civil and liberal emancipation was not sufficient to guarantee a peaceful existence to the Jews in the countries of the Diaspora. The aspiration of individual self-realization, within the framework of the non-Jewish collective as a main reference group, could not be fulfilled as long as Jews bore the stigmatized status of an unwelcome, homeless minority. Pinsker stated this idea in a classical paragraph in his *Autoemancipation:*

> The essence of the problem, as we see it, lies in the fact that, in the midst of the nations among whom the Jews reside, they form a distinctive element which cannot be assimilated, which cannot be readily digested by any nation. Hence, the problem is to find means of so adjusting the relations of this exclusive element to the whole body of the nations that there shall never be any further basis for the Jewish question.

Assimilation, then, was no solution. Besides, Jewish history has proven that even individual Jews do not assimilate easily.

Herzl proclaimed the purpose of Zionism, in the so-called Basel program, as the securing for the Jewish people of a "publicly recognized, legally secured, home in Palestine." The program deliberately exhibited a low profile with its ambiguous term of a "home," and the tortuous terms of "legal security" and "public recognition." The idea, however, was always clear: a third dimension, namely, the State dimension, would be the synthesis of all positive aspects of Jewish individual and collective life, as briefly described above.

Anti-Semitism, Herzl argued, has many sources and faces—religious and emotional, socio-economic and ethnic. In a word, most irrational and most rational causes and motives intermingle to produce the impossibility of Jewish survival, both in the Galut dimension, as well as in the Diaspora dimension. With all their belief in the rational progress of humanity, the Zionist founding fathers were liberals deeply wounded by the events of their time (the Dreyfus trial, the pogroms) and unhappily convinced that the advancement of tolerance would take many generations. Individual self-realization had to be sought within the realm of collective self-realization. The positive Galut aspect must merge with the positive Diaspora aspect within a third dimension, namely, that of a Jewish State, the dimension of freedom of self-determination.

This freedom of self-determination comprises the positive elements of both individual and collective self-realization. Individual self-realization, adjusted to the needs of the group, it was widely believed, would enrich the whole community. Within the legitimate collective framework, personal fulfillment could be complementary, and not antagonistic, to group fulfillment. There had often been complaints that talented Jews could not find an outlet for their creativity in the ghetto. The State of Israel would certainly provide a more fertile ground for the growth and cultivation of Jewish talent.

III. *The Mythological Distortion*

The negative aspect of the Galut dimension included discrimination, persecution and sporadic outbreaks of violent hostility. A typical pogrom was characterized by the ferociousness of an incited population and the helplessness of the victims, with the safeguards of law and order appearing only after the disaster, or when the Jews defended themselves. Very often the police took away the weapons of the victims and blamed them for provocation or aggresion.

The epitome of this disastrous situation was, as we know, the Holocaust of our time. Psychologically, it was made possible by a deliberate revival of the old myth of the eternal struggle between the "Children of Darkness" and the "Children of Light." All the evils of nature and of society were concentrated and personified in this Manichean myth of the demonic Jewish power of destruction. The Jew became the personification of perniciousness itself, the incarnation of all that plagues mankind. Therefore, he had to be destroyed.

It is of interest to note that Pinsker's explanation of anti-Semitism already emphasized the irrational source of hatred of the Jews. He called it "Judaeophobia," and described it as a disease, a form of suffering from fear of demons, "a psychic abberation" which, he believed, was hereditary. Since this particular disease had been transmitted for 2,000 years, he also believed it to be incurable. The Jews, he argued, lost their political entity and yet were not destroyed. They continue to live in the frightening form "of one of the dead walking among the living." However, Pinsker prescribed a remedy in rational terms, namely, the resettlement of the Jewish people on a land which they could call their own.

Later analysts, who also emphasized the irrational source of the problem of anti-Semitism, although on a more subtle level of theory and detailed clinical research, neglected to point to a political solution of this problem of the Jewish people. Sartre, in his *Portrait of the Anti-Semite,* and the authors of *The Authoritarian Personality,* blamed the anti-Semite who was using his passionate hatred as a defense mechanism in the economy of his inner disturbances and compensations, or they blamed repressive socio-economic, political conditions, particularly authoritarian family structures, which produced totalitarian views on the inevitable apocalyptic battle between the principle of good and the principle of evil, a battle which would continue until the destruction of the representatives of evil. With all their subtle observations on the character of this anti-Semitic Manicheanism, these scholars did not discuss the premise that the restoration of Jews to their homeland might resolve, or at least allevate, the conflict. Only after the publication of their work did Horkheimer, Adorno and some other coauthors of *The Authoritarian Personality* admit the significance of the Zionist solution for the alleviation of the anti-Semitic prejudices. So did Sartre.

After World War II there began the process of de-mythologizing in the Western world as well as in Russia. But this process was interrupted simultaneously in Russia and the Arab countries at about the end of the '50's.

In the recent struggle between Soviet Russia, the Arab nations, Israel, and its "patron," the U.S.A., the irrational Manichean myth was again fostered and intensified. The Soviet and Arab propaganda machines are now piling new distortions on the wild caricature of the *Elders of Zion* in torrents of verbal violence, mostly demagogery for "internal consumption," which is tolerated by many as the legitimate rule of the game.

The hatred of the Arabs toward the Jewish State cannot be conventionalized as a national conflict like any other. It is very different, for example, from the conflict between Iraq and the Kurds, Iraq and Iran, the Algerians and France, or the classical conflict between Germany and France. The rejection of Israel has an obsessive depth and intensity and it extends to the hatred of all Jewish qualities and to the very existence of the Jewish people as the incarnation of the spirit of evil. It is no wonder that the *Protocols of the Elders of Zion*, that fictional anti-Semitic tract produced at the beginning of this century and full of gross falsifications, became so widespread in the Arab propaganda machine, and that King Faisal of Saudi Arabia recently distributed the *Protocols* to French journalists who visited him when they accompanied the French Foreign Minister. Earlier, on December 30, 1973, in a speech delivered in Mecca before an audience of Moslem pilgrims and diplomats, King Faisal said, "We must unite against Zionism and Communism, which are both the most dangerous enemies of Allah and the faith of Islam."

This is the main idea of the Palestinian Liberation Movement. In its Palestinian National Convenant, this Movement has declared that Israel is a "constant threat to peace in the Middle East and the entire world." Only those Jews who lived in Palestine before 1917 are to be recognized as citizens. Only Palestinian Arabs possess the right of self-determination, and the entire country belongs to them; warfare against Israel is legal; any solution that does not involve total liberation of the country is rejected; and Israel's self-defense is illegal.

The Arabs' conception of the conflict between them and Israel is strongly colored by mythological distortions, produced by a concentrated intensity of "autistic hostility," as some psychologists term this kind of antagonism. The Arabs deny the right of existence of the State of

Israel, of the very identity of the Jewish nation. (The Jews are allegedly not descendants of the people who lived in Palestine in ancient times.) Israel has become the symbol of all the demoniac evils which plague Arab ambitions on both the personal and political level.

Detailed psychological analyses have explained some grounds for the propensity of the Arabs to accept mythological images and to reject rational avenues for resolving their acute socio-economic and emotional problems at this stage of their transition from a semi-feudal, traditional society to an urban, secularized, oil-rich, and large, influential bloc of sovereign nations. The autistic denial of reality has been made easier by the use of totalitarian slogans, which suggest the apocalyptic nature of the struggle between the apostles of freedom and equality on the one side, and Zionism, Imperialism and Colonialism on the other.

The mythological character of the Arab conception of the conflict has been explained, by Yehoshafat Harkabi, as a defense mechanism which substitutes for achievement, as a compensation for failure, and as a help both to inspire faith in the change desired by the leading elite and to mobilize support for it. An ideology elevated into myth cannot be disregarded as a mere jumble of rhetoric. It is influential. It works, because it fulfills significant functions in the economy of emotions and reflects both pressures and ambitions. That such an ideology commits to action cherished by the whole community has been shown to be quite obvious. The discrepancies between action and ideology do not decrease the "realistic" value even of the most unrealistic mythology.

The myth of the Arab ideology justifies the aim of liquidating Israel, as Harkabi and many others have sufficiently documented. In the eyes of the Arabs, the liquidation of Israel rectifies an historic injustice on the part of the Jews, who robbed the Arabs of their country. The obligation to respect the sovereignty of a state, even if acknowledged by the United Nations, cannot apply to Israel. The State of Israel is aggressively expansionistic. It aspires to occupy Arab countries and, ultimately, to dominate the whole world, as the *Protocols of the Elders of Zion* have described. The conflict with Israel is a "fateful struggle" which cannot be avoided, an "absolute war for life and death," or, as Haykal, the editor of *al-Ahram*, put it, in his journal of June 12, 1964:

> The dispute between the Russians and the Americans . . . is an ideological dispute, over a way of life. On the other hand, in our case, here with Israel, the dispute is life itself; to be or not to be.

The aim of the Arabs must be, therefore, the disappearance of Israel. The very existence of Israel poses the greatest danger to the whole reality of Arab nationalism and Arabism in general. The conflict becomes an absolute metaphysical clash which transcends all boundaries of rationally controllable forces.

Even if one does not accept all the tenets of Harkabi's analysis, one cannot disregard the documents which corroborate his arguments. No other voices of the Arab leadership or press have clearly expressed a different opinion on the nature of the conflict, although it is true that Sadat attempts to avoid the radical mythological phrases used so lavishly by his "charismatic" predecessor.

IV. *The Post-Yom-Kippur War Predicament*

It is safe to say that the recognition of Israel by Egypt is a result of Israel's capacity to assert its presence in the Middle East. But, because of a discrepancy between Israel's military power and her political influence, the Israeli army was stopped in the midst of the momentum of a great victory. It was mainly the Russians, but it was also Kissinger and the U.S. State Department, who insisted that Israel should not totally defeat the Egyptian army. A victory, Kissinger argued, would endanger a peaceful settlement. Thus, recognition of Israel by the Arabs was promised.

However, negotiations about the disengagement of armies and the settlement of territorial disputes, and even the acceptance of Israel as a state, as proclaimed by Egypt, are not compatible with the demand to restore "the rights of the Palestinians," or, as the other popular code words put it, "equitable solution," "the restoration of natural rights," or "the restoration of Palestine's Arab character." Adjustments of relations between two states is of a different origin and character than the claim of the Palestinians which threatens the very existence of the state. If the problem were merely the adjustment of territorial disputes, it could have been solved without too many difficulties. It is the Galut aspect which creeps into the political situation and distorts reality by its mythological character.

Israel was precisely dedicated to the demythologizing of the negative Galut aspect by the ingathering of the Jewish people and, thus, removing the causes of anti-Semitism. Zionism intended to turn the mystery of Jewish Galut life into a problem which could be rationally solved by return to the homeland. But this last war, endangering the very existence of the State, shattering all confidence in the invincibility of the Jewish State under all conditions, and showing how the nations, those safeguards of law and order, kept help from the defending army, has cast a shadow of Galut on Israeli existence.

Could it be, then, that the many peaceful and military efforts of the Zionist settlers and their descendants, of the refugees from the Holocaust and from the Arab countries, that all their achievements of turning desert and swamps into highly developed agricultural areas and techno-scientific urban centers, were only destined to reproduce the Galut dimension in the very core of the radical attempt to overcome it? Horrifying as this possibility is, it cannot be easily dismissed in the light of the Yom Kippur War and its aftermath. The outcome of the war clearly indicates the vast superiority of Israel's army, although outnumbered in manpower and sophisticated, deadly weaponry. Yet, the traumatic experience of the Arabs' attack and the strength and intensity of their fighting power in the large battles thereafter cannot be easily eradicated by the Israeli victories, especially since they could not be brought to a triumphant end because of the imposed ceasefire. The political conditions in the struggle of the world powers and their "clients" in the Middle East shatter any excessive confidence that the Galut dimension of Jewish life has, indeed, been de-mythologized and the situation of the Jewish people has become "normalized." Both on the ideological and the practical level, the mythological aspect of the Galut dimension lurks in the background of the very existence of Israel. It is interesting to note that those Jews in Israel who had gone through the experience of the Holocaust were less shaken than were the others. Galut anxiety prepared them for the worst. The lesson they had learned so well is that Galut is always, and everywhere, a possibility, but they also realized that Israel has provided possibilities for efficient defense.

Indeed, the following difference between Galut existence and Israel can be immediately observed. In defending their sovereign State, the Jews in Israel are not helpless. Even when many previous friends and supporters have become neutral bystanders, or even open antagonists, believing that their antagonism may be repaid by the money and oil of the Arab potentates, Israel is hopeful that it will be able to defend itself. This is not a pogrom situation with the policemen looking by, or disarming the defenders. This is not even a Munich situation. In a most decisive sense, the Israeli will to survive as a sovereign State is quite different from that of Czechoslovakia. Ultimately, Jerusalem, and not even Washington, decides, although the views and actions of foes and friends, particularly the supply of hardware, carry much weight in the decision-making of a self-determining Israel. The détente cannot be bought by endangering the survival of Israel in a Munich-type settlement. The elements of the conflict are very different, primarily because the Israelis are determined to stand their ground against any appeasement policy by the super-powers at Israel's cost.

The dual formula for the acknowledgment of the Jewish State, namely, the withdrawal from all occupied territory, and the restoration of the national rights of the Palestinian people, is a contradiction of claims. The second demand implies a dismantling of the State, the restoration of the negative aspect of the Galut dimension. Every time this claim is mentioned, a basic insecurity is introduced, which touches the very core of the conflict. The redemption from the Galut dimension lies in the acceptance of the truth that this land belongs to the Jews by right, as testified by history and as proclaimed by the League of Nations and the United Nations, and not by chance, usurpation or conquest. This land was never a state before Israel came into being. A peaceful solution must acknowledge three basic facts:

(1) historically, this land never belonged to "the Palestinian Arabs,"
(2) there was an exchange of refugees between Israel and the Arab countries, one of the many which our times has envisaged, and
(3) Jordan and the so-called "occupied" parts of Israel are inhabited by Palestinians and are the natural basis for their own sovereign state.

The Galut dimension of Jewish history can become the cause of a world catastrophe. On the other hand, the elimination of its negative aspects could be a blessing for the world, as the founders of Zionism long ago foresaw.

The highly dialectical process of the interpenetration of Galut, Diaspora and Israel into each other's domain is of great theoretical and practical significance. The Israelization of the Diaspora, wide-spread after the Six Day War, has deepened and broadened in this war, through an identification with the destiny of the Jewish State in its struggle for survival. The will for collective self-realization, which characterizes Galut, has been strengthened in the old and new centers of Diaspora. But, also, the threatening aspect of Galut has influenced Diaspora thinking about individual self-realization.

The most shaking experience, however, is the Galutization of Israel, that is, the increased anxiety that the very survival of the State and its population is at stake through the basically genocidal character of the Arab mythology which its proponents aspire to put into action. In a world climate of cynical self-interest and brute force, and forsaken by allies and quasi-friends who no longer acknowledge their obligation to undo their own atrocities of scarcely a generation ago, Israel's position might, indeed, invoke forebodings of a pogrom. The post-World War II emotional and intellectual climate, which helped to establish the State, seems to have changed in a threatening manner. The task of Zionism, therefore, is not complete as long as the negative aspects of the Galut dimension endanger not only some countries of the Diaspora, but primarily Israel itself.

V. *Implications and Conclusions*

This article has purposely not discussed a variety of salient points in the Arab-Israel conflict; it has only hinted at some. Its main topic is the reassessment of the unique character of this conflict: the denial to Israel of the very right of existence. But in order to make the conclusions more understandable, certain views which have not been mentioned must be explicated, at least briefly, even if they are not fully clarified.

The threat to the very existence of the State, which I termed above the negative aspect of the Galut dimension, has accompanied the history of the State from its very establishment and even preceded it. Thus, it is nothing new. But it was never so close to reality as at the beginning of the Yom Kippur War. The full realization of this threat is now agitating Israel and the Jewish world and is causing a state of anxiety, not to say depression.

Whether the undecided outcome of the war has, for the first time, provided a chance for a peaceful settlement, as so many experienced academic observers and active political leaders maintain, is still to be seen. We would like to believe in the statement of Sana Hassan (in *The New York Times Magazine,* February 10, 1974):

> There can be no doubt that the Arabs now accept the reality of Israel's existence and that the war was aimed not at the destruction of Israel but at breaking the stalemate, regaining some of the conquered territory and achieving a stronger bargaining position.

Unfortunately, Miss Hassan does not bolster her assumption with open statements by Arab leaders. (She quotes only anonymous "moderates" for this opinion.) Those who hope that a new atmosphere of peaceful arrangements has emerged are wishing for a great, great deal now. It would be a dangerous fallacy not to work for the fulfillment of this wish and, simultaneously, not to realize the difficulties on the path to its fulfillment.

The soul-searching which is going on now in Israel, insofar as it touches not only actual military or political negligence or misbehavior, but, rather, the moral stance, is certainly in good, old Jewish tradition. I mentioned above the merging of collective and individual self-realization in the freedom offered by a self-determining state. By this freedom, I meant not merely the idea of national self-determination in the ordinary political discourse, but, also, the effective power to determine the *self* of a nation by whatever decisions or plans the nation makes concerning what it shall do or what it shall become. The decisions to change are made by the majority of the people through a due democratic process. The presupposition of such freedom is the idea that the *self* of a people is determinable by a deliberate policy. Such a policy, however, does not necessarily always harmonize with individual self-realization or even with traditional collective self-realization. The self-determining state has its own momentum of demands which often clash with the desires of the individual. The tensions between individual and collective self-realization in the Galut dimension or in the self-determination of Israel are hard to overcome. Self-realization must be bounded by legal and moral norms.

The three premises of a peaceful settlement for the Arab-Israel conflict certainly need more clarification. They are the core of both the problem and its solution. A vast literature has been published on each of the premises.

The problem of the Arab refugees seems to reproduce, in a way, the Galut situation which Zionism intended to dispose of for the Jews, and thus, ironically, to introduce the negative aspect of Galut into the Arab-Israel conflict. A discussion of the different nature of the problem of Arab refugees and their claim to the land of Israel must be reserved for another occasion.

Finally, since this conflict is more than a regional one, Israel's anxiety cannot be relieved without an easing of the tensions between the superpowers on a global scale. Because of its oil resources and its strategic position, the Middle East is the "soft underbelly" of Europe. It adjoins both Europe and Soviet Russia. The Soviets have relentlessly advanced their ambitious plans toward the acquisition of direct access to vital points and to the vast material resources. They act as "friend and ally" of the Arabs. The not-too-optimistic view of the near-future, expressed in this article, is due to this situation. Not all depends upon an Arab-Israel détente.

The opportunity for a negotiated, real peace, provided probably for the first time by recent moves in the Middle East, is not unambiguously free of dangers. The dangers are of two kinds: (1) that the Arabs will consider the ceasefire merely as a tactical and temporary phase in their effort to annihilate Israel, and (2) that the Soviets will totally dominate the whole area. The genuine hope for a *Sulh* (genuine peace) lies in a strong and always alert Israel which seizes the opportunity without disregarding the dangers. The second danger, paradoxically, could induce a new, definite sobriety into the Arab states. Instead of wasting their resources and energies in a continuous struggle with Israel, which would certainly keep them for a long time in the embrace of their "friend and strategic ally," this sobriety could call the Arab states to invest in the improvement of their rapidly growing populations. The clear grasp of the second danger, then, might contribute to an actual oportunity for Israel to overcome the fear of being annihilated and for the Arabs to abandon their fear of "Zionist Imperialism." This opportunity is worthy of the most genuine efforts on both sides.

WHITHER DIASPORA JUDAISM?

Phillip Sigal

I

In Quest of Definitions

At times we become so immersed in old problems and embroiled in previously conceived ideas which have received the stamp of urgency from history that we tend to neglect new directions. Thus, in Jewish life, for some years now, Jewry has been overwhelmingly preoccupied with the struggle for Zionist objectives. Now that the State of Israel exists we still have a tendency to allow Jewish interest to be largely activated by philanthropic and political considerations aimed at the essentially worthwhile goal of achieving political and economic security for that state. Rabbis, lecturers, writers, and teachers still appear to make "loyalty to the Jewish people" the center of their Jewish dialogue.

Yet, we must reckon with the time when Jews will inevitably become accustomed to taking Israel for granted. As the third and fourth generations of Jewish Americans grow up, they will increasingly shed the "rich uncle" psychology toward Israel and will lack what is presently a ready-made Jewish identification in fund-raising. There already exists evidence that younger Jews are groping for a Jewish affiliation which is not necessarily related to the State of Israel. Unfortunately, these people are not helped by ideologies that stress what is a modern form of social and cultural ghettoization in intensive Jewish community organization. They desire an identification which is neither one of the many varieties of Zionism nor some *quasi* ethnic-cultural "community" that will provide them with "Jewish" art, music and drama. They are not pursuing a proposal to migrate to Israel, despite the fact that *aliyah* is suggested by some to be the highest rung on the ladder of Jewish identification. As laudable as some of these aspects of Jewish life may be, what the young Jewish American really requires, and what the future of Judaism demands, is a rich and vibrant spiritual tradition to claim as his own.

Perhaps confusion over definitions is one of the foremost stumbling blocks preventing us from attaining a clear and enriching picture of Judaism in the Diaspora. We are told Jews are a nation and are destined forever to constitute an ethnic minority outside of Israel. Hence we are offered cultural pluralism as the democratic solution to our problem. Usually the chief external factor in motivating us to remain Jews is diagnosed as anti-Semitism. As a consequence, we are told, we have no alternative but to be "ourselves," and that

Rabbi Sigal is the spiritual leader of Congregation Beth Abraham in Bridgeton, New Jersey.

being ourselves implies that we unite in community councils and return to a modern version of the medieval "community within a community."

Undoubtedly, the proponents of these ideas are well-meaning, but there are underlying fallacies to contend with. The key to understanding lies in definitions. For one thing, we must recognize that Jews are not a "nation" in the same sense as, for instance, Frenchmen are. A Frenchman, born in France, grows up in the midst of a total French culture and owes allegiance to the French flag. In his religion he might be either Catholic, Protestant or Jewish. If he is Jewish, he certainly does not imbibe the same culture as one who professes Judaism in the United States. They speak different languages, wear different clothing, and have varied tastes in food and entertainment. Yet both are Jews though they do not share a common national origin or the other elements that make up a nation such as contiguous territory, a common language or an identical political loyalty. They are Jews because both profess to believe in and participate in a specific religious tradition, even if only in the breach. They do not necessarily share a common hope and similar aspirations for international problems. Whatever the bonds between a Frenchman and a citizen of the United States professing Judaism as their religion, these bonds are neither ethnic nor national-political. They are neither socio-cultural nor biological. The bonds are elusive, transcendent and spiritual. Since this is the case, and since into the foreseeable future Jews of western, democratic lands will be of similar status, it follows that the logical designation of Jewish Americans is that of a "religious community." It is true that Judaism concerns itself with more than mere creed, observance and salvation. But so does Catholicism. Both are denominations that include an interest in extra-American shrines and sovereignties and both are engaged in international associations for charitable and religious purposes. Protestant groups are no less inclined to international associations as the ecumenical movement clearly indicates.

The best evidence that Jews are not an ethnic group *per se* is the great conglomeration of ethnic groups that today constitute Israel, all of which are collectively known as Jews. People of Israel will be known as "Israelis" for residing in contiguous territory, owing allegiance to the state of that name, speaking Hebrew and participating in Hebrew or Israeli culture. But only certain Israelis will be Jews, for there are Israelis who profess other religions. The bond that unites Israelis is nationalism. The bond that unites Jews, on the other hand, is religion. It is a transcendent bond, a force that binds together the Jewish Israeli, Jewish Frenchman and Jewish American, even when these people are not living their religion in accordance with its highest demands.

There is another point to consider. In Europe Jews were always "alien." Dr. Agus has referred to this view of the Jew as the "meta-myth" and has shown how Jews have contributed to it by regarding non-Jews as "the enemy camp" as the title of a recent novel describes this psychology. Non-Jews, living in environments of mystic-biological nationalism, did actually regard

Jews as "other." In North America, however, they tend to be integrated more and more into the general population. German Jewry, considered more highly assimilated than East European Jewry, was never really integrated in this manner. German Jews were either compelled to pay taxes to the *kultus gemeinde* or did not identify themselves as Jews. They could not freely regard themselves as Germans. If they did not want to be part of the "community" which was as much ethnic as religious, they were simply resigning from the Jewish People. They could not simply live as Germans and be affiliated with a Synagogue of their choice and hence truly "Germans of the Jewish Faith." No Central or Eastern European Jew, from whom the greatest bulk of American Jewry is descended, ever thought of himself quite in the terms of a North American Jew.

It should be borne in mind that even the so-called physical characteristics of some elements among Jews will disappear on these shores as a consequence of the very high rate of intermarriage and conversion to Judaism. Names too will become more "Americanized" as generations pass. What will remain will be either the will to disappear or persevere. To persevere one will require a theology. He will need a system of belief and a הלכה that will in some way integrate his creed and his environment. God must be brought back to the centre and peoplehood removed to the periphery. We must recapture the sense of being a "holy people" or a "nation of priests," in short, a "religious community," if we wish to ennoble an otherwise tragic history.

By concentrating on the fact that Jews once constituted a sovereign nation with a national culture, whether in Palestine or in Diaspora enclaves, Zionism and the community patterns of Reconstructionism become essentially reversions to the pre-modern societal conception of Jewish life. At best Reconstructionists hope to restore the religious element. But they are a minority among like-minded advocates of the centrality of peoplehood and nationalism who are largely secular and areligious. They would, therefore, fail in their primary ambition. Moses Mendelssohn preached a creditable philosophy of Jewish life for the eighteenth century but his one overriding error — his dogma that Judaism has no dogmas — undid whatever benefits he may have been able to achieve for Judaism. Reconstructionism, similarly, although on an entirely different level, would fail in its religious program even if it finally achieved its societal aspirations.

History cannot be reversed. No more than we would seek to restore religious patterns of Eastern Europe or ancient Judea, should we be concerned with reviving medieval or ancient concepts of society. The process of Jewish history has seen us move from a nation dedicated to religion, to a Synagogue-centered community, to a religious denomination. The difference in the two last terms resides mainly in function and quantity. The former served as the substitute for national life throughout the pre-emancipation period and included Jewish civil and criminal law in its orbit. The latter term better identifies the post-emancipation Western community which includes only the theological aspect of culture, in the case of Judaism, creed and הלכה. To continue to speak of Jews as a nation or as an ethnic-cultural "people" is to play havoc with Jewish destiny.

The Napoleonic Sanhedrin and the Classical Reform movement propagated this view of Jews constituting a religious denomination. But their error was in their failure to grasp the fact that the status of Jews has never really changed. They were *always* a religious association, some forming a sovereign state, others living in a variety of states. In North America Jews form a religious community and are Jews by virtue of that fact. Biology might make a Jew Anglo-Saxon in appearance. Culture might produce a pragmatic, materialist American. Politics creates a Republican or Democrat. Sovereignty demands his allegiance to the flag of the United States. What is it that determines he is Jewish? Only the fact that he participates in a religious tradition, even if this be a disinterested participation. And it has never been otherwise throughout Jewish history.

Once we grasp this essential historical truth concerning Jewish status, we must acquiesce in many possible revisions in our thinking. One of the most central problem that concerns all rabbis, educators and parents, the bulk of our Jewish citizenry, is that of Jewish education. Our methods and our goals, our curricula and our emphasis will have to be geared to the concept we advocate. If we preach that Jews are a "people" and that from that hub radiates all else, we will have one concept of Jewish education, perhaps best signified in the terms "Hebrew education" and "Hebrew school." But if we believe that Jews form a religious community, that Torah is the hub and all else radiates from there, we will inevitably evolve a different pattern of Jewish education, perhaps best identified in the terms "religious education" and "religious school." The emphasis and goal in the two types of schools would naturally vary. The methods employed and the content of the curricula would consequently differ as well. The future of Jewish education, the very future of Torah in America, the rôle of the Synagogue as a Bet Midrash, and the type of community organization we work for are involved in our concepts of the Jewish status.

Another significant problem that requires revision in our thinking is the type of community organization we should strive toward in North America. This is an ideological question of extreme importance, for upon it will depend whether we perpetuate a cultural ghetto on these shores or evolve a Synagogue-centered religious group. Intimately bound up with this naturally is the problem of the indigenous American phenomenon known as "Community Center." Also involved in this area is the relationship of the religious or irreligious Jew to the religious community. In all these areas we must begin evaluating our endeavors and clarifying our direction. It is modestly hoped that this paper will begin at least to adumbrate the direction we ought to take if we are to remain loyal to the dictates of Torah and the destiny entrusted to us at Sinai.

II

A Pattern for Jewish Education

In the foregoing I have proposed that we seriously consider the designation of "religious community" for Jews of North America, a term used by many writers today, among them, Will Herberg. The term is both feasible and probably inevitable, for religion alone should serve as a true cementing factor among Jews. This would give rise to considerable revisions in Jewish life. The implicated consequences for Jewish education, for instance, are far-reaching.

If Jews constitute a religious group it implies that other than in the realm of religious music, art or architecture we should not be concerned with "Jewish culture" to the extent that we are presently occupied with it. For instance, a painting of a bouquet of flowers should not be regarded as "Jewish art" simply because it was painted by Marc Chagall.

Art, music or literature depicting themes which include Jews, folk-lore involving Jews, or music of the Israeli countryside, is not necessarily "Jewish" anymore than "From The Terrace" is "Christian" literature. The Jewish community is spending vast sums of money on "culture" which only turns the clock back, further inducing an "ethnic" psychology in our ranks. To have the flag of modern Israel in our synagogues is also questionable procedure. Jewish education must take on a primarily religious objective. Hebrew must be taught as a *functional* language — functional in regard to one's ability to use and understand the prayerbook and Bible in sacred services and study. The definition and concept of "Jewish culture" must undergo drastic revision. Only that which is related to *Judaism*, as religion, should legitimately be considered "Jewish."

Certainly language never has been, cannot be and should not be a criterion of Jewish fellow-feeling. When Moslem Israelis and Christian Israelis speak Hebrew, they do not thereby become Jews. It is the ideals and values of Judaism which must be transmitted to our youth, not necessarily a conversational ability in Modern Hebrew. We must pass on to them a warm feeling for commitments to the הלכה, a religious sense of "before Whom they stand," a reverence for Jewish religious thought and action.

While it is psychologically true that the earliest years of a child's life are often the determining ones, we should not overlook the fact that our children unfortunately do *not* acquire a sense of personal commitment through example in their early years because our religious schools are unable to compete with the home and general environment. Consequently, the values we must transmit to them are best taught in the maturer adolescent years after Bar-Mitzvah. Our educational efforts must therefore be geared to the high school level rather than overwhelmingly in the direction of the pre-adolescent child. The age of Bar-Mitzvah might wisely be set at eighteen.

The chief task confronting us in the childhood years is to teach, through action-symbols, the religious faith we later teach in more abstract theory. Thus, our religious schools must be primarily involved in a religious program including and stressing such elements as daily prayer, Sabbath and Festival observances with all the music and drama that can convey this. The סידור must become the centre and the backbone of the whole curriculum. It must acquire the status of the basic and major text. A child should be familiar with everything in it, with the entire cycle of worship. And, following that, a child should be introduced to the חומש and be taught the content and arrangement of the Pentateuch, be given to understand the תורה־הפטרה relationship and be initiated into the original Hebrew text with its תרגום and Rashi accompaniments.

This may seem like a reversion to the old *ḥeder* method. But let us not confuse content and method, substance and form. We all know our present-day curricula are unrealistic and insubstantial. Our "graduates" — and why should a Jewish child feel he has ever "graduated"? — know extremely little about the prayerbook or חומש, often read very haltingly, can conduct very little other than a "junior" service, and are largely devoid of familiarity with the כלי ראשון, the primary vessel of our religion, the Pentateuch.

The Mishnah and Talmud are, of course, closed books to the overwhelming proportion of our children today. These too must somehow be brought into our curriculum, even if only in a descriptive course in the vernacular. But we must move mountains to reach out beyond the banner of ignorance in Jewish life. We must return the Jewish classics to the focal point of our curriculum and must reintroduce הלכה and religious commitment to the centre of our interest. Indeed our religious schools, at least those connected with congregations, must become centres of indoctrination to teach and nurture loyal Jews. Jewish education cannot be neutral. It must be "education to be a Jew" and that means *religious* education. Our children must be taught to recite blessings which are essentially formulas of thanks for benefits received. They must be taught to pray daily and to pray with warmth and feeling. They must be shown that the ritual, which are action symbols, are the signal lights which illuminate our way for us on the ethical road, that they are markers preventing us from driving off the highway of faith into the ditches of darkness.

Undoubtedly the implementation of such a drastic revision in our present system and objectives would involve a long period of orientation and adaptation. But that should not deter us. As Rabbi Abraham Karp has pointed out in the Summer 1957 issue of *Conservative Judaism*, the Conservative movement has attempted to balance the triunity of God, Torah and Israel. It has done this by emphasizing Israel while at the turn of the century both other movements laid deep stress upon God alone or Torah alone. He cautions us lest we overemphasize Israel and thereby again disturb the balance.

It is fashionable in many quarters to pose the interesting proposition that the Torah exists for the Jewish people, that the latter is the centre and the former is the instrument. What I am suggesting when I advocate the reversal of this proposition is not original. It is authentic Judaism. The Jews were chosen to be the instrument of Torah. Torah has centrality and priority. The Jew is the vessel through which Torah is conveyed. The Jew is the conduit through which Torah radiates among men. The religious education of our children must be predicated upon this premise.

III

Jewish Community Organization

Once the philosophy of Jewish life is oriented to the "religious community" idea, Jewish community organization, no less than education, must undergo considerable revision. We must intensify congregationalism. The congregation is the strongest unit of North American Jewry, for it best expresses the differentiation of religious faiths in a liberal democracy. Community councils which are primarily fund-raising agencies can continue their operations as Welfare Funds but must cease demanding a role as a co-ordinating executive in Jewish life.

There are various institutions in Jewish life such as orphanages and old folks' homes that must continue to be "Jewish" in name and form, not because of ethnic reasons but especially because of the religious factor. There is the problem of dietary laws and other ritual observances. Welfare Funds remain a necessity in some communities to help maintain some of these established social welfare institutions. But education should not necessarily be the obligation of the whole community, nor is it proper to claim that a Jewish school does, or should, serve the entire community. It is particularly in this area where congregationalism must assert itself, for Jewish education is "religious education," and as such cannot be neutral. It must be intimately connected with the Synagogue, and the spiritual guidance of a Rabbi, so that Synagogue, School and Home represent a modern triad analogous to the traditional trinity of God, Torah and Israel.

Jewish hospitals are not a necessity. They are a burden upon Jewish money which could be better expended upon Torah. Most hospitals today are willing and co-operative in arranging for Jewish religious matters and so the need for "Jewish" hospitals is wholly eliminated. "Defense" agencies should not constitute as heavy a drain upon our financial resources either. Jews could maintain the ever-decreasing need for vigilance in matters of civil rights through the existing general organizations. There is no real need for three or more Jewish defense agencies. Social Action committees in synagogues, like Israel committees, would be adequate to deal with both so-called "defense" matters and problems affecting our relationship with Israel.

Jews cannot afford to revert to pre-modern societal organization. We should allow the normal development of North American life to affect us, for it means only greater integration of the Jew in North America and subsequently a happier generation of Jews. If we labor at providing Jews with a religion that gives them purpose in being Jews, we need not fear assimilation. If we cannot give meaningfulness and vitality to the Jew in his religion, what is the real object in *not* assimilating?

IV

THE JEWISH COMMUNITY CENTER

Linked closely to the problem of community organization is the "Community Center," that strange creature of the free American environment. Here, in a land where for the first time Judaism can thrive in an open market and Jews are free to integrate into the world around them, well-meaning but muddleheaded social workers, secularists and fellow-travelers have evolved an institution which can be Frankenstinian in effect. Paradoxically, as the ghetto walls crashed to the ground, the so-called libertarian Jews who "liberated" themselves from East European Judaism and sought the Americanization of immigrants, gave rise to a new ghetto.

There is little connection between the YMCA and the Jewish Center organization (or YMHA). The former is predicated upon Christianity. The latter is at best informed by and infused with some peculiar thing we have come to call "Jewishness." This is a bizarre blend of ethnic culture with "folk" psychology, a twentieth century reversion to medievalism. In theory the Centers will philosophize about assimilation and integration or adjustment. But in practice, the ghettoization of our youth does not make for adjustment, but for maladjustment. Making it *kosher* for a Jew to be a Jew without religion does not "adjust" him. It fosters confusion. Once and for all a distinction must be made between "Jewishness" and "Judaism." The term "Yiddishkeit" as used by our forefathers was not "Jewishness" as used by us. It was religion. It meant one's degree of Judaism. This contrast was admirably confessed by Dore Schary in a recent article in Torch Magazine where he wrote concerning his background, "Jewishness was in my bones, my heart, my soul — but alas — I cannot say as much for Judaism." Happily, Schary found his way out of Jewishness back to Judaism. But our million-dollar centers, some even generously non-sectarian, are not necessarily conducive to this repentance.

Any "program of Jewish culture" not religious in essence is fraught with danger. The centers compete well with the Synagogue, often victoriously. But the "Jewish Center" Jews who are behind the movement, who spearhead the drives and promote the institution and its sterile philosophy, are gaining Pyrrhic victories wherever they outmaneuver a Synagogue. Jewish boys and girls are being duped into believing that one is a good Jew virtually without really being a Jew at all.

V

WHAT OF THE IRRELIGIOUS?

An objection to much of what has been said may be posed in the proposition that many North American Jews are not religious, do not wish to affiliate with a religious community, and regard the writings of Peretz as significant as the compositions of Schechter. Some might indicate that Hebrew ditties are as important as learning to sing Adon Olam and much easier for a child in primary school. They maintain the Hebrew ditties will give this child a sense of fun and the child will learn to love his "Jewish" school and thereby come to love his "heritage." No less a significant figure than Ben Gurion insists that Spinoza belongs with Maimonides. And in future anthologies of Hebrew literature the Psalmist sweetsinger of Israel may receive no higher ranking than the Hebrew poet laureate of Apollo.

Many people identified as Jews will protest they are unbelievers and reserve the right to be "racial Jews" like those of South Africa. Others will insist that humanistic ethics is all that matters and theology is puerile. They want their children to learn history and thereby receive a deep rooting in the past of their ethnic forebears. The reason is presumably so that when Hitlerism strikes them they will not be too overwhelmed. They will realize that Jews have always been "aliens" and sooner or later must face the enemy.

Any number of non-religious, anti-religious, and areligious arguments may be offered against stressing that Jews are a religious group. Each proponent of an objection is naturally entitled to his view in a free society. *But Judaism must take a stand for its authentic tradition.* Even if the ranks of Jews in the United States were halved by such a stand, it would be of immeasurable spiritual benefit. There is a great mass of American Jewry which is entangled in an ethnic network which is the dubious achievement of our many nationalist and cultural organizations. Those masses of Jews may not be observant of the הלכה and may not be believers in the traditional theology, but they do consider themselves primarily as members of a faith — even if in the breach. They are really wearied by discussion of what a Jew is. They take for granted he is a member of a religious group, even if in the breach. Rabbis, Synagogue, and the "remnant" of authentic Jews, must finally come to the fore and take a stand. They must combat the theories propagated by ethnic-cultural, secular-humanist and Zionist proponents. And those who truly deny their roots in religion, those who honestly and conscientiously disclaim their interest in and connection with *Judaism*, should be permitted to disappear. I have not read anywhere of a mitzvah merely "to survive." In the one place where the Torah does command us וחי בהם, it is only בהם — "through the מצוות."

205

VI

A Summation

What I have written is an outline of some of the revisions I believe our thinking must undergo. Undoubtedly, many a hiatus exists to be bridged. The problems of Jewish education and of community organization will not be easily solved. This is especially so in the mid-twentieth century after a host of great and daring thinkers and educators, Zionists and others, have erected a rather formidable structure of Jewish life in this country based upon a pattern from which I find I must dissent. Undoubtebly, however, these very architects and builders of twentieth-century Jewish life, who dissented from the pattern into which they were born, would be the first to recognize the right of a present-day reformation.

If Judaism is a religious civilization, as has been propounded by Rabbi Mordecai M. Kaplan, the mentor of most writers and thinkers in the vineyard of Judaism, then within Judaism there reside multifarious aspects and possibilities. We may take the liberty to redefine his concept and draw new conclusions. A civilization is pluralistic and so can express itself one way in one era in a given geographic locality, and another way elsewhere in some other period. If Judaism is understood to be a "civilization-like religion," the word "religion" rather than "civilization" being the substantive, then it is not bound by time and space, and is in no way subject to a static definition. The nearest analogy would perhaps be the Catholic Church although we happily lack its hierarchical forms. But it too is a "civilization-like religion" in that it embraces variegated ethnic groups and cultural backgrounds within one faith. There are Catholic "states" and Catholic "denominations" depending upon geography and history.

Judaism then perhaps becomes, what Rabbi Jacob Agus calls it in another connection, "function." Judaism is the "function" whereby an individual Jew realizes his personal salvation. In Israel it might be through a religious civilization grounded in national mores, Hebraic culture and Middle Eastern orientation. In North America, the greatest area of Jewish life, the most significant in numbers and presently, in this writer's opinion, the richest in inner quality, the Jew must be a Jew by virtue of religion alone.

Jews can constitute no other type of grouping in a healthy democracy. Confronted with the ever-expanding horizons of democracy, we are denizens of a country where it is natural to integrate. We should reject any patterns which suggest cultural autonomy. We are here free to become the first truly emancipated Jewry in our history. This is not "assimilation" in its discredited sense: the desire to flee Judaism. It is "integration" in the best American tradition and implies devotion to Judaism. We must, therefore, occupy ourselves with the ideological dynamics of a new understanding of Judaism. We must rethink the implications of emancipation and democracy.

REFORM AND CONSERVATIVE JUDAISM IN ISRAEL TODAY AND TOMORROW

Reform and Conservative Judaism in Israel: Aims and Platforms

EPHRAIM TABORY

REFORM AND CONSERVATIVE JUDAISM HAVE had an institutional presence in Israel for over ten years. As the denominations with which millions of Jews outside of Israel are affiliated, their establishment in Israel marks a milestone in their development as religious denominations. This is especially so because the religious establishment in Israel is clearly not receptive to what it perceives as "deviant" and religiously "inauthentic" movements. Actually, only a few thousand families have affiliated with the approximately forty Conservative and ten Reform congregations in the country, and many of the families are of Anglo-Saxon background.[1] Nevertheless, the foothold that these movements have established in Israel carries with it a religious alternative for native Israelis in the future, if not the present; the possibilities of the movements' developments in the future warrant an understanding of their developments at the present time.

The Reform Movement

The Israel Movement for Progressive Judaism, herein referred to as the Reform movement, according to its platform,

> aspires to strengthen the commitment and loyalty of our people to their Jewish heritage, and to shape life in the State of Israel in light of the moral principles for individual and collective behavior prescribed by Judaism. The movement strives to cultivate among Jews in Israel and elsewhere a Jewish way of life that is imbued with love for their people and with a creativeness that draws from the wellspring of Judaism.[2]

---

1. Ephraim Tabory, "A Sociological Study of the Reform and Conservative Movements in Israel" (unpublished doctoral dissertation, Bar-Ilan University, Ramat-Gan, 1980).
2. *Platform of the Israel Movement for Progressive Judaism.* Adopted 1977.

EPHRAIM TABORY *is a lecturer in sociology and anthropology at Bar-Ilan University.*

The way in which these aims will be fulfilled, the platform continues, is by stressing that Judaism should not be confined to matters of ritual and personal status, and that the obligations of the *miẓvot* should impinge on the relationship of man to his fellow man, as well as of man to God. The method of determining which *miẓvot* to follow is based on the following principles:
1. the purpose of a *miẓvah* and its historical development;
2. the possibility of sanctifying life with its observance;
3. the feasibility of fulfilling it in contemporary conditions;
4. the impact of the *miẓvah* on *Klal Yisrael*; and
5. there being no conflict between the *miẓvah* and the dictates of conscience.

The emphasis on the commandments between man and his fellow man is in keeping with the prophetic view of Judaism, an emphasis broached by Reform Judaism in the past. The platform further indicates those social problems in Israel which require the application of these precepts as commandments. They are: the social gap; the integration of the various ethnic groups; the absorption of immigrants; and the existence of a large, non-Jewish minority in the state.

In the context of the present study, two questions are asked with regard to the Reform platform. First, why did the Reform movement feel the need to issue a formal platform? The fact that the Conservative movement has not issued a movement platform serves as a backdrop, or framework, in which this question is asked. Second, how is the specific content of the platform affected by the situation of the Reform movement in Israel?

The answer to the first question relates to the place of Reform Judaism in Israel. The argument raised here is that it is the relative failure of Reform Judaism to make a greater impact in Israel that has led it to undergo introspection to determine for what it stands. Evidence for this comes from the statement of the past Coordinator of the movement, Rabbi Ady Assabi, at a conference of the World Union of Progressive Judaism.[3] Rabbi Assabi argued that Reform Judaism has not had a greater impact in Israel because its description of itself is less a positive statement of what it is than a negative description of Orthodoxy. As one leader of the Reform movement wrote in the Israel Reform movement's periodical, *Telem*:

> Go out to the members of the movement and ask them what Progressive Judaism is. Most of the respondents, veteran members as well as the new ones, will stand on the importance of the shortening of the prayers, abolition of the separation of men and women, musical accompaniment in some of the congregations and their negative attitude toward *Halacha*. This is a symbol of poverty, not for our members, but for us, the formers of the movement, the leaders and rabbis.[4]

---

3. Jerusalem, 21 November, 1976. Recorded at the conference.
4. *Telem* (10, 1976):2. In the past, the Reform movement in Israel published two Hebrew publications. *Telem* was a newsletter-magazine, while *Shalhevet* was a journal devoted to less

The feeling of some members in the Reform movement is that "before we correct the world and become a 'light unto the *goyim*' (in this case our brothers in the streets of Israel) let us ask if we have 'shown ourselves' to ourselves enough."[5] This is to be accomplished, the writer continues, by discussing an ideological platform and delineating what are the borders with regard to *miẓvot* and religious ritual. As the movement Coordinator said at the conference of the World Union of Progressive Judaism, only after the Reform movement defines *itself*, can it put forth its "calling card" and place claims before the Israeli public.

The manner in which the movement defines itself in Israel is influenced both by the social environment, as well as by the personalities of the members. In stating that *miẓvot* are to be kept, and that they are binding on all individuals, the movement is adopting a more traditional approach to Judaism than has generally characterized Reform Judaism in the past. The justification for the observance of *miẓvot* (according to one of the members who feels that they should be observed) is that "as religious Jews we surely do not want a life style that dictates that 'every person may do as he sees fit'."[6] A guiding principle adopted by the movement in determining which *miẓvot* are to be followed is that of *Klal Yisrael*.

> If remaining alive as Jews is the central worry of the Jewish enterprise, all matters dealing with personal affairs are of central importance. If we accept converts in order to "save" assimilating families, it is important that this be done in accordance with the accepted *halachik* criteria of all world Jews ... we have to provide documents that will be accepted, at least in principle, by all Jewish denominations ... in other words, everything having to do with religious attitudes, concerning *Klal Yisrael* should be done *halachikally*.[7]

Such a position has implications for the role of the rabbi. In the past, the rabbi in Reform Judaism has been considered to be a teacher of Jewish values, but not an authoritative prescriber of personal behavior. Now, however, some movement members want their rabbis to prescribe behavior, much as Orthodox rabbis are empowered to instruct their followers. The legitimacy of the authority of the rabbis would have to be founded on a rationalistic-legalistic basis. As one of the leading members of the movement points out, charismatic personalities cannot be "ordered up," and legitimacy based on traditional authority can evolve only after a tradition has evolved.[8] It is for these reasons that, in the final analysis, the principles of the *miẓvot* to be observed are those which can be found acceptable by those persons who are to be bound by them. In other words, members will accept as commandments only those items which they are

---

time-oriented issues. The frequency of publication of both publications has decreased in recent years, and in 1980 they were merged into one publication, *Shalhevet*. All citations from these periodicals are translated from the Hebrew.

5. *Telem*, (10, 1976): 2.
6. *Telem*, (5, 1976): 2.
7. *Telem*, (21, 1978): 2-3.
8. *Shalhevet*, (19, 1978): 3-5.

willing to be bound by. The rabbi can then be a "determining authority" as long as he does not breach these bounds.

The issue of the *miẓvot* provoked much controversy during the formulation of the Reform platform. Opposition to viewing the *miẓvot* as obligatory was expressed by two of the more ideologically committed members, who preferred that all requirements concerning religious practices be left to the absolute discretion of the individual. As one of the movement's leaders wrote (in reference to an earlier article endorsing the observance of *miẓvot*):

> Most of our members... negate the *Halacha* as a principle in their lives and actions — and their will is to be honored. We are willing to accept parts of it, as long as this is carried out on a logical basis of moral content or historical significance, and not on the basis of authoritative-rabbinic determination.[9]

The more liberal position in the Reform movement is also revealed in the opposition expressed to the inclusion of a passage inviting all Jews who identify with the movement's aims and methods to join its ranks. At the movement's annual meeting one member expressed the opinion that a more open invitation should be offered, not dependent upon "anyone's agreeing with what I think."

Despite the limitations on the *miẓvot*, the platform, as adopted, was felt by many members to be a significant step forward. As one of the Israeli rabbinical students said, "This platform shows that we are not merely Orthodox Judaism minus."

As mentioned, the platform reflects both the influence of the social environment and the members' personalities. First, the principle of observing those commandments which make larger societal participation possible demonstrated an openness to the larger environment. An example is *kashrut* in the synagogue. It is a principle of the Reform movement that all synagogue and movement functions are to be *kasher* so that no person be prevented from attending because of his desire to keep *kasher*. (One of the movement's leaders also mentioned this principle as a reason for his keeping *kasher* in his own home.) By way of contrast, the *halakhah* concerning *kashrut* in American Reform life may be quoted from *A Guide for Reform Jews*: "although Reform Judaism does not adhere to the traditional dietary laws, many Jews abstain from eating the meat of the pig."[10] (There are other religious practices performed by the movement that are indicative of this consideration, such as the observance of two days of *Rosh Hashanah*. Both days are national holidays in Israel.)

The personalities of the members also affect the Reform movement. On the one hand, there are those who feel that the movement should not obligate members to perform ritualistic rites. These members seem to be more interested in the prophetic aspects of religion, with emphasis on

---

9. *Telem*, (19, 1978):2.
10. Frederic A. Doppelt and David Polish, *A Guide for Reform Jews*. Revised edition (New York: Ktav Publishing House, 1973), p. 93.

elevating moral principles to a religious level.[11] On the other hand, there are those who do want a list of commandments which they can follow in an orderly manner.[12] Quite significant in this regard was the request by the representatives from the Reform Kibbuz, Yahel, at the February 1977 annual meeting of the Reform movement, for a set of *halakhik* regulations to guide their communal life. Observance of *mizvot*, as ascertained in interviews with the Reform leaders in Israel, also seems to be supported by most of the young Israeli rabbinical students. The binding character of the *mizvot* may become, in the future, an area of severe conflict as one side takes a more radical position (i.e., accepting or refuting the principle of *mizvot* as obligatory) than can be tolerated by the other side. Furthermore, this raises the question of just what are the members' *religious* needs.

An additional problem which may be mentioned is the implication of a more traditional identity of the movement. If Reform increasingly accepts the spirit of *halakhah*, in what way is it different from the Conservative movement? Is there justification for the existence of two separate movements? Indeed, some Reform leaders do feel that the Reform and Conservative movements should be combined into one liberal religious movement.[13]

The Conservative Movement

The movement of M'sorati Judaism in Israel, hereafter called the Conservative movement, does not have an official platform, thus indicating that it has not felt the need to issue a "calling card," as Reform has done. The argument presented here is that the Conservative movement feels that it is meeting an existing need in Israeli society. Its continued growth makes theological deliberations (or justifications) unnecessary. It might even be advantageous for the movement to refrain from discussing sensitive theological issues that would only complicate its relationships with the established rabbinical State authorities, with Orthodox persons, and perhaps even with its own members and clergy.

The Conservative movement became incorporated as an Ottoman Association in February, 1979. As is requisite under the procedures of incorporation, the objectives of the new organization are listed in its charter statement. As they have been reprinted in the movement's English news bulletin, these are:

1. To advance Jewish values in Israel and to safeguard and develop Jewish tradition in its historical context.
2. To encourage devotion to the Torah in accordance with its developing historical interpretation.

---

11. See, for instance, *Telem*, (15, 1977): 4.
12. For a summary of the positions on this in the United States, see Sylvia Lawrence Wolf, "Reform Judaism as Process: A Study of the Central Conference of American Rabbis, 1960-1975" (unpublished doctoral dissertation, St. Louis University, 1978).
13. I have discussed this in Ephraim Tabory, "The Conservative and Reform Movements in Israel: Questions of Legitimacy," *Midstream* (forthcoming).

3. To deepen the sense of identity with Eretz Israel as the homeland of the Jewish People and in the Jewish People's effort to build and strengthen the State of Israel and to work for Israel's well being and for the encouragement of Aliyah.
4. To integrate Jewish values and ways of life with those of our times; to nurture Jewish values as they are expressed in traditional mitzvot and in accordance with the needs of the State.
5. To encourage and nurture scientific research into our spiritual and cultural heritage.
6. To strengthen our ties with all the people of Israel by encouraging Jewish brotherhood in Israel and by the maintaining of close ties with Jewish communities throughout the world.
7. To aid our brothers in distress, wherever they may be, as an expression of the unity of the Jewish people.[14]

The objectives of the Conservative movement are *not* to challenge Orthodoxy. In fact, a modern Orthodox movement could possibly subscribe to these very same aims, with their emphasis on the inculcation of Jewish values in Israel, and on the importance of the relationship between Israeli Jewry and world Jewry. This characterization of the goals of the movement is perhaps more for the benefit of American Jewry than for Israeli Conservative Jews. The objectives, as listed, appeared only in the English language edition of the bulletin (which is to be "published quarterly for overseas distribution"). The Hebrew language version did not list the objectives, despite the fact that this was the first issue of both bulletins.

The literature issued by the Conservative movement in Hebrew (much of which has also been issued in English — an indication of a large English-speaking population in that movement) shows that the movement emphasizes educational and congregational activities more than theological and ideological deliberations. This is exemplified by an information pamphlet, issued by the United Synagogue of Israel in 1975, which answers the question of "why the need for Conservative congregations?"

> These congregations were created in Israel in response to the search for a viable alternative for religious self-expression. There are those who find a spirit of reverence and dignity in our prayers and are attracted by the active participation of the children and young people, congregational readings and meaningful Bar and Bat Mitzvah ceremonies; others seek a creative religious framework and an educational program for their children. Many members identify with our progressive approach to tradition which emphasizes historical and evolutionary development.
>
> The congregational-communal nature of our congregations as well as the concerned efforts of our rabbis to be personally involved in the lives of their members, appeals to our adherents.

What characterizes the Conservative movement, with regard to its purpose in Israel, is the perceived response to the needs of the local population. The movement claims that it is providing services which are very much in demand. In a fund-raising letter sent abroad under the

---
14. News Bulletin, *The Movement of Masorati Judaism in Israel*, Vol. 1, No. 1. (Summer, 1979).

auspices of the united movement in Israel, the Director of the Conservative movement wrote, in 1978, that the creation of new congregations in Israel has been brought about by a "new and more profound awareness by the population of Israel of the fact that they have deep spiritual needs which have not been fulfilled by any of the Jewish institutions active in the country up until now" (emphasis deleted). It should be pointed out that the significance of such statements for the present discussion is not whether they are accurate reflections of the religious situation in Israel; what is more important is that the movement does not wish to see itself, or be regarded, as a closed "sect," withdrawn from the mainstream of Jewish life in Israel. It wishes, rather, to be considered an integral part of the religious scene there.

Essentially, the present aim of the Conservative movement is to establish more congregations, whose attractive features, aside from family seating, are decorous services and their more general, communal nature. Little thought is given to the underlying ideological considerations. In this sense, the movement in Israel is not much different from the American one, where such questions are also not often discussed. The "large" number of Conservative congregations (at least relative to the number in the Reform movement) provides them with a sense of purpose and accomplishment. This is absent in the Reform movement, whose slow growth makes it necessary for its leaders to justify their existence as a *religious* grouping. This is to prevent the movement's being branded a mere *landsmannschaft*. That is not to say that the Conservative movement is not an ethnic grouping, but the continued establishment of new congregations does make the leaders feel that it is serving a legitimate purpose.

Interview Data

Responses by congregation leaders in interviews about the goals of the movement and what the movements are trying to do in Israel support the findings already reported. General replies by almost all of the respondents referred to the ability of their movement to offer an option for non-Orthodox Jews. Eight of the seventeen Reform respondents, and four of the twenty Conservative leaders specified that an active attempt should be made to attract non-Orthodox persons. The other respondents were content for their movement to provide an option for those persons seeking a liberal religious synagogue. Characteristic of the former attitude is the statement by one Conservative rabbi who said that the movement should "reach out to the majority of the population that, at the moment, is not involved Jewishly-religiously, and make them think about areas in terms of their Jewish identities." The latter is represented by a Reform leader who said that "we are attempting to fill a gap between the observant and non-observant Jew. We are not a missionary society . . . it is the law of supply and demand. We are supplying a demand."

A "prophetic" approach to religion is mentioned by a few Reform leaders, as is the desire to provide children with a richer Jewish education. On the whole, though, Reform leaders do not have many concrete things to say about the goals of their movement. Younger Israeli rabbinical students feel that the purpose of the movement is to provide an ideological basis for Jewish society in Israel. While the number of persons mentioning this point is small, the strength with which such statements are expressed is great. Representative of this feeling is the statement that "Israel lives as a result of catastrophe . . . but there is no ideological basis. . . . If there is no stronger feeling of what it is to be a Jew, I am fearful for the future." Likewise, writes another young Israeli rabbinical student in the movement's journal, Israel is "on the verge of ideological bankruptcy. Zionism and *chalutziyut* (pioneering) have achieved their major goals and there is now a vacuum in the ideological sphere."[15] The persons holding these positions may be the key to the future path taken by the Reform movement. Their interest stems from the larger social implications that they feel the movement has, beyond their own personal, religious needs. It is not a religious awakening which seems to be guiding a few of these persons as much as a rationalistic cognitive awareness that the principles of a socialistic-Zionistic state which, in the past, had been instrumental in forging a dynamic and cohesive society, are losing their relevance. The search for a functional alternative, that is, a different mechanism for the integration of society, has drawn them to the Reform movement.[16] It is also significant that the proponents of this position appear to be found primarily (and almost solely) among native-born Israelis.

Another theme that emerges from the interviews relates to the importance of the local congregations in the lives of the members in the Conservative movement, to the exclusion of interest in the "national movement."[17] This "local" versus "cosmopolitan" orientation[18] is evident from the comments made by the head of one of the larger Conservative congregations. Asked what are the goals of the movement, he replied that "the movement has no definite plans or goals or program. . . . Our own local goals are just to pray together and build up our own congregation." Similarly, another Conservative congregational leader said that "I don't know what the movement is trying to do; I just know what we are trying to do here." And "what we are trying to do," explained the chairman, is "to assist our own members." The "ethnic" function of the congregations is

---

15. *Shalhevet*, (9, 1972): 10-11.
16. See Simon N. Herman, *Israelis and Jews: The Continuity of an Identity* (Philadelphia: The Jewish Publication Society of America, 1971), p. 202 and Simon N. Herman, *Jewish Identity: A Social Psychological Perspective* (Beverly Hills: Sage Publications, 1977), p. 191, for a discussion of the increasing "privatization" of Israeli identity from Jewish identity, and its separation from a collectivist approach toward fellow Jews.
17. One of the reasons why the Conservative movement in Israel has not held a formal founding assembly since its incorporation is the fear that hardly anyone would come.
18. See Wade Clark Roof, "Traditional Religion in Contemporary Society: A Theory of Local, Cosmopolitan Plausibility," *American Sociological Review*, 41, 2 (1976): 195-208, for the application of these concepts to religious groupings.

well expressed by the leader of yet another Conservative congregation, who said that "We are rather egocentric — we are concerned about our own synagogue. Many of us came with our families but left behind family, and the congregation is like one extended family."

The preoccupation with the local congregation has, also, in some instances, affected the relationship with the rabbis. One chairman complained that there was some friction with the rabbi because he spent too much time on national affairs and, consequently, devoted less time to congregational affairs. This complaint was made in a Conservative congregation, and it is to be noted that it is the Conservative rabbis who are very much active and powerful on the national scene. The limited time that is available for congregational rabbis to devote to national affairs because of the demands of their local congregations has implications for the forging of a "national movement."

The "local" congregational orientation, as stated, seems to characterize the Conservative movement more than it does Reform. The observation presented here is that the Conservative movement has no formally thought out movement goals. It is catering to the requirements of its local members, many of whom have similar needs, scattered though the members are throughout the country. The theological considerations of the members are secondary. As one Conservative chairman stated:

> The only people who know what the Conservative movement is here are those who know it from the United States or those few who take the time to sit down and read the theory of what the movement is. To the rest of the people it is mostly a question of the acceptability and compatibility of (their local congregation) rather than a question of the principles behind it.

Finally, an ethnic function concerning the absorption of immigrants was mentioned by several interviewees, all from the Conservative movement. The Conservative movement has, in fact, a national "absorption desk," and has sought to establish projects for the absorption of immigrants. While national projects have not been successful, local congregations also undertake absorption activities, which encompass attempts to make the members "feel at home." In effect, this function complements the previous finding concerning the "local" orientation of the congregations. By serving as an "extended family" they are helping to ease the burdens involved in migration.

Discussion

An attempt will now be made to explain the differences between the two movements by suggesting what might be considered a "model" for their development. It is argued that social movements become increasingly aware of themselves as movements to the extent that they are not fulfilling their potential.[19] The Reform movement in Israel is aware that

---

19. See Albert O. Hirschman, *Exit, Voice, and Loyalty: Responses to Decline in Firms, Organizations and States* (Cambridge: Harvard University Press, 1970), p. 11 ff.

its growth is slow. New congregations are not being formed. The failure in this regard is all the more striking when viewed against the backdrop of the Conservative movement's relative expansion in the past few years. How can Reform become more dynamic? One way is to establish itself as a *religious* movement to counteract its stigmatization as a mere "ethnic" grouping and as an "irreligious" phenomenon. What the Reform movement has done, in this regard, is to formulate a platform which emphasizes what it is, rather than what it is not. Inasmuch as the values of the general society seem to be more receptive to Orthodoxy rather than to non-Orthodoxy, the values encompassed in the platform will have to reflect this situation. This is because the movement's aim is to gain acceptance in the larger society. Of necessity, then, it will appear more religiously traditional as it reflects on what it represents as a religious denomination. The degree to which the Reform movement in Israel is more "open" to the larger society is particularly demonstrated by its adoption of the principle of *Klal Yisrael* in determining which *mizvot* are to be kept. Conformity with the religious precepts accepted by the majority of Israel's Jews (at least in principle, if not in practice) would constitute a first step in gaining legitimacy.

The platform formulated by the Reform movement may eventually help it to attract new members and achieve further growth. At the same time, it may serve as a dividing force. Persons less interested in new religious demands may be alienated if such demands are, in fact, incorporated into religious practice. A further question that is raised is whether a more religious Reform movement will strike a responsive chord in Israeli society. Although the number of persons involved is too small to produce an answer, the question must be raised: Is it a religious need which is attracting the young Israeli leaders or, as has been indicated, might some persons see the movement as a replacement for a Zionist-socialist credo?

The situation in the Conservative movement is somewhat more complex. It might be argued that, objectively, the number of congregations founded is insignificant within the framework of Israeli Judaism. (Estimates place the number of Orthodox congregations at over seven thousand.) On the other hand, Conservative leaders do perceive the movement to be successful, especially when comparing it with the Reform. What the Conservatives are trying to achieve is to consolidate their gains and to build a national movement. The problem which they face is that local congregational members may not feel as much of a need for a "national movement" as for adequate, autonomous congregations. To some degree, local leaders who also fill national positions in the movement face a role conflict. On the one hand, their members expect them to be loyal to the congregation, and to dedicate their resources to its development. On the other hand, there is some demand on the national level for uniformity throughout the congregations and for a national viewpoint.

It may be surmised that, on the local level, members are not anxious to be placed in a situation in which there is much tension with their neighbors, and there is some pressure on them to refrain from activities which might lead to friction in local religious and municipal councils. As a result, religious behavior in the local synagogue becomes more traditional. (An example of this is the willingness of several of the Conservative congregations to have separate seating, so as not to antagonize the local religious council.) National leaders (who are, in most cases, also local officials) must then consider the needs of their local congregations.

Thus, the platforms and the leaders' statements reflect the situation of the movements in Israel at this time. Both are still struggling to ensure their continued growth in the future in light of their development to date. A question of interest for the future is how the movements, as they evolve in Israel, will interact with, and have implications for, the world movements of Conservative and Reform Judaism as religious denominations. More basically, there is the question whether the organizational transformation of the movements in Israel will be successful in attracting large numbers of native Israelis to their midst in the future.

Acknowledgements

Adam, Yehudi. "Zionism and Judaism." *JUDAISM* 29 (1980): 279–85. Reprinted with the permission of *JUDAISM*. Courtesy of Yale University Sterling Memorial Library.

Alexander, Edward. "Seeking Ease in Exile." *JUDAISM* 32 (1983): 267–70. Reprinted with the permission of *JUDAISM*. Courtesy of Yale University Sterling Memorial Library.

Alexander, Edward. "Where is Zion?" *Commentary* 86 (1988): 47–50. Reprinted from *Commentary* (1988, September) by permission. All rights reserved. Courtesy of Yale University Sterling Memorial Library.

Alexander, Edward. "Liberalism and Zionism." *Commentary* 81 (1986): 28–33. Reprinted from *Commentary* (1986, February) by permission. All rights reserved. Courtesy of Yale University Sterling Memorial Library.

Auerbach, Jerold S. "Zionism as Americanism." *Midstream* 31 (1985): 35–38. Reprinted with the permission of the Theodor Herzl Foundation, Inc. Courtesy of Yale University Sterling Memorial Library.

Eisenberg, Judah M. "American Jews and Israel: Two Views II." *Midstream* 18 (1972): 62–67. Reprinted with the permission of the Theodor Herzl Foundation, Inc. Courtesy of Yale University Sterling Memorial Library.

Fishman, Hertzel. "An Agenda for Conservative Judaism in Israel." *JUDAISM* 31 (1982): 410–13. Reprinted with the permission of *JUDAISM*. Courtesy of Yale University Sterling Memorial Library. Author of a forthcoming book, *The Challenge to Jewish Survival*.

Gittelsohn, Roland B. "American Jews and Israel: Two Views I." *Midstream* 18 (1972): 58–61. Reprinted with the permission of the Theodor Herzl Foundation, Inc. Courtesy of Yale University Sterling Memorial Library.

Gottschalk, Alfred. "A Strategy for Non-Orthodox Judaism in Israel." *JUDAISM* 31 (1982): 421–24. Reprinted with the permission of *JUDAISM*. Courtesy of Yale University Sterling Memorial Library.

Hertzberg, Arthur. "Judaism and the Land of Israel." *JUDAISM* 19 (1970): 423–34. Reprinted with the permission of *JUDAISM*. Courtesy of Yale University Sterling Memorial Library.

Horowitz, Irving Louis and Maurice Zeitlin. "Israeli Imperatives and Jewish Agonies." *JUDAISM* 16 (1967): 387–410. Reprinted with the permission of *JUDAISM*. Courtesy of Yale University Sterling Memorial Library.

Lang, Berel. "Zionism the Ideal and an Idea of Religion." *JUDAISM* 7 (1958): 235–41. Reprinted with the permission of *JUDAISM*. Courtesy of Yale University Sterling Memorial Library.

Neusner, Jacob. "Judaism and the Zionist Problem." *JUDAISM* 19 (1970): 311–23. Reprinted with the permission of *JUDAISM*. Courtesy of Yale University Sterling Memorial Library.

Neusner, Jacob. "A Stranger at Home: An American Jew Visits in Israel." *JUDAISM* 11 (1962): 27–31. Reprinted with the permission of *JUDAISM*. Courtesy of Yale University Sterling Memorial Library.

Neusner, Jacob. "Zionism and 'The Jewish Problem.'" *Midstream* 15 (1969): 34–45. Reprinted with the permission of the Theodor Herzl Foundation, Inc. Courtesy of Yale University Sterling Memorial Library.

Petuchowski, Jakob J. "Diaspora Judaism—An Abnormality? The Testimony of History" *JUDAISM* 9 (1960): 17–28. Reprinted with the permission of *JUDAISM*. Courtesy of Yale University Sterling Memorial Library.

Petuchowski, Jakob J. "Zionist Polemics in a Post-Zionist Age." *JUDAISM* 17 (1968): 92–99. Reprinted with the permission of *JUDAISM*. Courtesy of Yale University Sterling Memorial Library.

Polish, David. "The Tasks of Israel and Galut." *JUDAISM* 18 (1969): 3–16. Reprinted with the permission of *JUDAISM*. Courtesy of Yale University Sterling Memorial Library.

Rawidowicz, Simon. "Israel: The Ever-Dying People." *JUDAISM* 16 (1967): 423–33. Reprinted with the permission of *JUDAISM*. Courtesy of Yale University Sterling Memorial Library.

Acknowledgements

Rotenstreich, Nathan. "Can There be a Revival of Zionist Ideology?" *Midstream* 36 (1990): 7–10. Reprinted with the permission of the Theodor Herzl Foundation, Inc. Courtesy of Yale University Sterling Memorial Library.

Sanders, Ronald. "Israel and American Youth." *Midstream* 14 (1968): 3–8. Reprinted with the permission of the Theodor Herzl Foundation, Inc. Courtesy of Yale University Sterling Memorial Library.

Shmueli, Efraim. "Israel, Galut and Zionism: The Changed Scene." *JUDAISM* 23 (1974): 264–75. Reprinted with the permission of *JUDAISM*. Courtesy of Yale University Sterling Memorial Library.

Sigal, Phillip. "Whither Diaspora Judaism?" *Conservative Judaism* 14 (1960): 35–44. Reprinted with the permission of the Rabbinical Assembly. Courtesy of Yale University Divinity Library.

Tabory, Ephraim. "Reform and Conservative Judaism in Israel: Aims and Platforms." *JUDAISM* 31 (1982): 390–400. Reprinted with the permission of *JUDAISM*. Courtesy of Yale University Sterling Memorial Library.

For Product Safety Concerns and Information please contact our EU
representative GPSR@taylorandfrancis.com
Taylor & Francis Verlag GmbH, Kaufingerstraße 24, 80331 München, Germany

www.ingramcontent.com/pod-product-compliance
Lightning Source LLC
Chambersburg PA
CBHW061712300426
44115CB00014B/2653